GOD
CHRIST
CHURCH

GOD
CHRIST
CHURCH

A Practical Guide to Process Theology

New Revised Edition

Marjorie Hewitt Suchocki

CROSSROAD · NEW YORK

1989

The Crossroad Publishing Company
370 Lexington Avenue, New York, N.Y. 10017

Copyright © 1982 by Marjorie Hewitt Suchocki
Revised edition © 1989 by Marjorie Hewitt Suchocki

Printed in the United States of America

Library of Congress Cataloging-in-Publication Data

Suchocki, Marjorie.
    God, Christ, Church : a practical guide to process theology /
Marjorie Hewitt Suchocki. — New rev. ed.
        p.   cm.
    Includes index.
    ISBN 0-8245-0970-6
    1. Process theology.   2. Theology, Doctrinal.   I. Title.
BT83.6.S93   1989
230'.046—dc20   89-34532
                                                        CIP

In Memoriam
Faith Hewitt Downs

CONTENTS

CONTENTS

Part IV Wisdom
CHRIST IN GOD: A PROCESS ECCLESIOLOGY

Part V POWER
THE REIGN OF GOD: A PROCESS ESCHATOLOGY

CONCLUSION

Part One

THE PROCESS MODEL

Theology in a Relational World

1

A RELATIONAL THEOLOGY

EACH Christian generation expresses anew the assurance that God is for us. The immediate catalyst for these expressions may well be the profound conviction that God is a force for love, trust, and hope in a world of diverse cultural communities. The conviction carries with it a drive for expression, and the expression itself becomes a call to the ever-new creation of communities of love, trust, and hope. God is *for* us! Therefore, we speak, creating a tradition that is continuously appropriated and transformed within our cultural diversities, so that we might live as a complex community called the church.

Expressions of faith must partake of more than traditional categories if they are to be creative of community in the world. Communication is necessary to community, and communication depends upon using thought patterns that constitute the "common sense" of a time. If ordinary perceptions of the world deal in categories of subjects and objects, such that persons are subjects and all other forms of existence are objects, then expressions of faith will also use that language. Otherwise, the "God for us" message will not address the reality of the subject/object world of one's interpreted experience, and how then will the message be heard? Likewise, if the world is understood in terms of unchanging substances with accidental changing surface qualities, faith must also incorporate those categories or find itself addressing a world unrelated to the "real" world of everydayness. And if the dominant understanding of the world is through categories of interrelationship, process, and relativity, then this sensitivity must be picked up by the language of faith. Theology, as the way we interpret existence in a world where God is for us, will then be expressed in relational language, and the church that embodies the theology will likewise deepen its relational sensitivity in mission and structure.

The importance of expressing theology through the thought patterns of an age is hardly new. Augustine, for instance, gave an enduring formulation of faith by drawing heavily upon the understanding of the world that had been fashioned by the third-century philosopher, Plotinus. Plotinus, working from his own unique study of Plato, had powerfully defined the structure of existence. His thought provided a popular framework within which people could understand themselves in relation to the whole of reality. Augustine used Plotinian thought as a vehicle through which to express the faith that was his through his study of Christian scriptures and tradition and through his personal redemptive experience. In the process, of course, the vehicle became intermeshed with the message, powerfully and profoundly shaping the structure and mission of the community.

Centuries later Thomas Aquinas utilized the newly discovered teachings of Aristotle to express the dynamics of faith. Christian experience, scriptures, and tradition were interwoven with the philosophy. "Philosophy is the handmaiden of theology," was the watchword of the day, meaning that philosophy did not dictate the content of faith, but was merely the tool through which faith was explicated systematically. But in explicating faith, the philosophy also shaped faith, as it does in every age, thus providing a unified vision of reality. The understanding of the natural world and the understanding of faith were compatible. The paralysis of a compartmentalized religion was avoided, and there was vigor to Christian thought and life in the continuously developing community of faith.

Augustine and Aquinas represent critical moments in Christian history, when shifting philosophical worldviews became intermingled with Christian faith. But they are only two of the more outstanding examples of this dynamic. Implicitly or explicitly, positively or negatively, for two thousand years Christians have expressed their faith in ways that have been generally compatible with the dominant worldviews of their time.

Our own age is one that has seen profound and rapid changes. Darwin, Freud, Marx, and Einstein are familiar names to us. Each one has contributed to a shift in the fundamental way we view the social/physical world, moving us in the direction of a very relational view. It is not simply a matter of understanding the details of what each man said, nor is it even necessary to have a particular familiarity with the school of thought each man represents. Nor is agreement with the theories propounded by them the issue. Rather, they have changed the intellectual climate within which we all think.

The social climate of thought has also changed radically in our times. The social changes are not at all unrelated to the intellectual changes named above, for if the scientists have highlighted the relativity of experience, African-American, feminist, and third world proponents have insisted upon the social consequences of relativity. Their radical questioning of one's normative assumptions has changed the ground of certainty. Each shows that positions of power and place fundamentally shape the assumptions one makes and how one thinks, often at unconscious levels. Further, the implications for social reality are awesome, for thought forms growing out of places of privilege then function to legitimate those very places of privilege. Insofar as such thought forms are named Christian, they are distortions of the gospel that calls us to communities of'radical love, trust, and hope.

Finally, technological changes in communication and travel have brought the pluralism of the world's cultures and religions into contemporary consciousness. No longer can one so easily assume a universality to one's own worldview. The relativism first introduced into our understanding by thinkers such as Einstein, and then radicalized by the social critiques of liberation movements, has been further radicalized by a crowded world where cultures and religions different from one's own are no longer across the world, but across the street.

In such a context, even when we strive to repeat the thought patterns of a previous age, we must do so against the counterforce of the contemporary milieu. It is as if we view the world as a kaleidoscope, filled with shapes and colors that can be described in terms of a particular pattern. But then someone turns the kaleidoscope, and not only do all of the pieces shift, but it even seems that some new ones have been added. There is familiarity and some continuity, for the colors are still there—but their tones seem somehow different in the altered positions, and while at first we try to see them in their familiar form, we nevertheless find ourselves struggling to express the difference in the way of seeing. Finally we must recognize the newness of the pattern, and we reach toward a familiarity with the new that can be as assuring as that which we remember—or project—as belonging to the old. But the kaleidoscope will never repeat exactly the same pattern. Darwin, Marx, Freud, Einstein, social movements, and technological changes have all turned the kaleidoscope of our world, changing the configurations of what we call reality.

Christians remaining true to their tradition will take the kaleidoscopic shift of our time seriously, and engage in the task of expressing again the redemptive realities of Christian faith with a critical openness to the changes entailed. They will inquire into a biblical understanding of the nature of God, of Christ, of the church, and of the reign of God, and seek to give these faithful expression in thought forms appropriate to our own day. The proclamation of faith in terms that speak to the whole of reality depends upon the church's self-critical and creative responsiveness to this task.

The most pervasive factor of the contemporary configuration is the heightened importance of relationality and therefore change, and indeed, most theology written in the mid- to late twentieth century gives far more positive importance to relational categories than was so in previous centuries. But the most explicitly relational theology is that known as process theology. The philosophical vehicle through which this mode of thought is expressed is that of Alfred North Whitehead, who formulated his particular understanding of reality as a result of his work in physics and mathematics in the early part of the twentieth century. Not content to confine his data to these fields, he drew as well from areas such as history, sociology, and philosophy. He gave particular priority to the data of religious experience. Therefore, even though his model of reality reflects his highly technical background, it ultimately rests upon a broad understanding of experience in a relativity-conscious age. By using this model to express Christian faith, we push toward the rewards of communicating Christian faith in thought forms that reflect a contemporary understanding of reality.

When one strives to express Christianity in new thought patterns, however, many critical issues emerge. What is the substratum with which one works? We speak of "Christian faith" as if it were indeed one thing, enduring throughout the ages, albeit expressed in different thought forms! Many scholars have devoted much effort to uncovering an "essence" of Christianity that pervades whatever thought form might be utilized. The difficulty, of course, is that the thought forms are inextricably woven into Christian faith. There is no abstract "Christian faith" apart from the living reality of people who are Christians, and who give expression to their faith. The thought forms they use not only define their faith, but their very lives. Thought forms are not so easily abstracted from living faith, leaving some "essence" to be discovered! Even the biblical witness, in its own time, is a contemporary expression of the living faith that God acts for us through Jesus Christ. Each new generation inherits the expressed witness of the previous generations, with a double transformation occurring. On the one hand, the new generation is shaped by the faith it inherits, but on the other hand, it transforms that faith through its own living witness. The "essence" of the Christian faith may well be that it is a malleable witness, depending upon transformations again and yet again of an inherited word that God is for us.

The expression of Christian faith is further compounded by the deep human needs that find their way into all expressions of faith. For example, consider the way in which the doctrine of God is related to our experience of need. God is considered as creator, redeemer, provider, sustainer, judge, king. Do we require a grounding to our existence that is more than ourselves? Why not simply accept the mystery of existence as given; why must we find a ground to existence in the understanding of God? Our need pushes us beyond ourselves, to an ultimacy that can be known both intellectually and emotionally as our source and destiny, and we name God the creator. Through sin does existence seem somehow awry, distorted? Rather than rest content with that as a tragic or absurd given, we dare to say that God is the great redeemer, forgiving and restoring us in order that we might achieve a destiny beyond our failure. Are we dependent, and does our dependency extend beyond our daily needs for physical existence? Do we know a spiritual need for an ultimate sustenance of our deepest being? We name God as that provider and sustainer. Further, we ask that in the encompassing governance of our universe there be just that—governance, some ultimate power of rightness addressing the evil and wrongs—

and God is judge. Shouldn't this ultimate rightness be unchallengea-
ble? If it is "right," should it not also be eternal? God must rule in a
realm that is stronger than our evil, enduring everlastingly in an
established, unshakable order of justice. God: creator, redeemer,
provider, sustainer, judge, ruler—the theological assertions concerning God are so intensely tied in with human need that theology
faces the challenge in this post-Feuerbachian, post-Freudian age
that our doctrines are no more than wish-fulfillment, supplementing
our finite sense of poverty with an infinite realization of what we
know or imagine to be good.

   In such a situation, the church's responsibility to give a reason for
its hope is fulfilled in part through attention to the philosophical
context of theology as well as to the biblical and historical tradition
of Christianity. This does not mean that philosophy becomes the
arbiter of faith, and it certainly does not mean that philosophy
supplants what we know of God through the biblical witness. It
simply means that faith dares to express itself within the widest
possible understanding of existence. Whitehead provides this by
developing a model of God that is rationally consistent with an
understanding of relational existence. The experience of God in
relation to human need may then indeed fill in the content of what
we know as the nature of God, but the resulting doctrine of God will
not be reducible to human need. Through the process model, we
have the basic philosophical outlines of a doctrine of God. Faith
utilizes these outlines to express anew the Christian conviction that
God addresses our needs in order to lead us toward the richness of
relational existence in community.

   What is the process model? We can illustrate its understanding of
existence through "Catherine." Imagine that Catherine is a stran-
ger whom you have just met. When asked to tell you something
about herself, she replies first of all with her name. She lives in
Pittsburgh, is a historian, and teaches at the university. She is
married, has two grown children, and is a member of a Presbyterian
church. She loves hiking, listens to music often, and plays the
piano. Somewhere in her busy schedule she finds time for some
political activity, and always she seems to have time for her friends.
In this brief introduction Catherine has described herself. Notice,
however, that every element in her description involves a primary

reference to that which is not herself. In order to describe herself, she must have reference to others.

Her name, Catherine, was chosen for her before her birth because of her parents' feelings about the name. Perhaps it was the name of a loved relative or friend, and feelings for that person were associated with hopes for the child. A name like Catherine could have been chosen because of its association with saints in the Christian tradition, in which case certain attitudes toward holiness could have been involved in the choice. Even if the name was chosen at random, the very lack of anticipation through association is significant. A name, given at the beginning of existence, is full of meaning: that meaning enters into the shape of personal existence. We begin life with borrowed meaning.

To define oneself through a locality such as Pittsburgh is also to be defined through that which is not oneself. Localities bear their own characteristic stamp: a river town, pushing the edges of the east toward the midwest, steel and smoke, parks, hills and bridges, and inevitably, given western Pennsylvanian weather, potholes in all the streets. The last is not at all insignificant for the illustration, for common frustrations turned to wry humor become binding qualities among inhabitants of a locality, marking them as "insiders," as those who share a place. To live in a town or city is to discover its own peculiar character, and in a sense to bear that character. The locality, while certainly more than oneself, enters into the reality of one's identity.

A historian is defined by a long tradition that precedes individual history. Association with that discipline is defining in that it marks specific interests, shaping them still further. To teach in the field also indicates perseverance in following these interests into professional competence. Catherine's self-definition as a historian goes deeply into who she is, but it does so primarily by reference to that which is more than herself.

To define oneself in terms of marriage and motherhood most assuredly requires reference beyond oneself; husband and children are necessary if one is to be wife and mother. Further, the particularities of that husband and those children influence the particular way Catherine is a wife and mother. Those whom we deeply love deeply shape our identity.

One could go through each element Catherine names, and see that who she is takes shape through her relation to that which is external to her. Her internal reality is understood through external reality. Relationships beyond herself are necessarily involved in her self-constitution and her self-understanding. External reality becomes internal through relation.

Does this mean that Catherine's life is evidence of a determinism, as if she were the passive puppet of forces that are beyond her? Not at all, for she is not reducible to any one of those forces. In fact, just as they shape her, she shapes them. Look again at the reality of her name, that definition of who she is that was given to her at birth. In every moment of her life she makes the name her own, so that for those who love her, "Catherine" becomes a name associated with the warmth of her person and their personal relationship. The initial meaning of the name was simply given to her, but in her process of living she has invested the name with a meaning of her own making. Even if she actualized the intimations of the name, she has still filled the name with new meaning. She has made the name her own.

Likewise, her association with Pittsburgh will be either a positive or negative response to the city that affects the totality of what the city is. She will represent the quality of that city to those who know her. In her political activities, she actively works to influence the government of the city, stamping it with her own individuality, even as it influences her with its corporate character.

As a historian, Catherine contributes to her discipline through her own scholarly work in research and teaching. Her students form their opinion of what history is partly through their experience with Catherine. The discipline of history, affecting Catherine, is not a finality but a continually moving process, having its own history. That ongoing history is shaped by the selectors and interpreters of history, the Catherines who study and write history, as well as by the ongoing activities of the world.

Through Catherine's influence on her family, her grown daughter, becoming a mother in turn, will pattern much of her own motherhood by the model given her through Catherine. The external realities used to understand Catherine must themselves be understood through her. Identity is more than the external influences affecting one; identity is also one's influence on that which is beyond oneself. Relationships, received and given, are integral to who we are.

Thus far we see one person, Catherine, with many relationships—family, profession, locale. Given the multiplicity of influences upon her, how do we account for Catherine's unity? The question is important, for this unity constitutes the power of her own influence upon the world. How can she have such unity? Why is she not simply a will-of-the-wisp, now this, now that, blown hither and yon by the bombarding power of external forces? What must be the case to account for the unity of her being that results in her own forceful influence on the many?

In order to account for relational existence, the one and the many must be complemented by a third term, creativity. How else can we understand the reality that many influences are unified, producing one individual? Unification must be a process of feeling many influences, evaluating them, and selectively integrating them according to one's own purposes. This is creativity. This creative process is the emergence of one from many. "One," "many," and "creativity" are all essential terms for understanding relational existence.

How all the influences affecting one shall be welded together finally depends upon the person. Imagine Catherine studying history at the library. No matter how much importance her immediate studies have for her, this importance must be balanced by her sense of her students' needs in her next lecture. This sense of student needs, however, does not obliterate Catherine's family situation. Feelings of family are also present as she sits in the library. Furthermore, the environment has an importance—air conditioning, contrasting with her immediate memory of the walk to the library through the sultry day with its summer heat, smog level, and traffic noise; this, too, affects Catherine's studying. Which influence will dominate? Does it not depend finally on Catherine's own determination of the relative importance of each influence, based upon her choice of immediate goals? This weighing of importance, this comparing of influences, this decisive movement toward one response rather than another may finally take place at subliminal levels of consciousness, but the process nevertheless takes place, allowing Catherine to achieve her immediate goals. The process is a creative unification of reality according to a single purpose. This entirety constitutes Catherine at that particular moment. She *is* that purposeful, creative unification of the many into one.

Notice, however, that the very dynamics of relational existence require that Catherine be understood not as a single process of unification spanning many years, but as many different single processes succeeding one another serially. The reason for this is simply that no sooner does Catherine respond to relationships in one way than she has changed them all to some extent. Further, her own immediate past response constitutes new data for her present. She must then respond again to the changes, in a new process of creative unification.

Reconsider Catherine's situation in the library. Should she decide to daydream instead of focusing upon the studies immediately before her, she has lessened the relative importance of the other influences. Studies, students, family, environment: all are distanced in the daydreaming, their importance relatively diminished, perhaps even levelled for the moment. Catherine then suddenly decides to respond to her studies; she renews her attention, and begins to read. The Catherine-who-is-reading is not precisely the same as the Catherine-who-is-daydreaming, for the reader succeeds the daydreamer, and must renew her studies against the ennui set into force through her daydreaming. A new fact has been added to her world, and it constitutes the most influential relationship of all for Catherine: her own immediate past. She relates not only to studies, students, family, environment, but also to her own successive responses to all of them. How she has responded to each in the past is part of the data influencing her response in the present. If, however, her own past also constitutes an influential relationship for her present becoming, then her existence is continually in a state of flux. Identity is constantly being created through a series of becomings. The continuity of the self must be provided through the successiveness of instances in particular relationship, and not through some unchanging endurance through time.

Thus far, we have considered existence as a series of instances of becoming. This becoming is through and through relational. Relativity is therefore constitutive of existence, and not simply accidental to it. Becoming takes place in the creative response to the past;

in this becoming, something new comes into existence. This new instance of reality is itself a force, demanding a future to succeed it, to incorporate it along with many other influences that are also instances of existence into a new unification of reality. Relation pushes existence into being; once having become, that new being likewise demands relation to a future. Relationships are the beginning and ending of each unit of existence.

Notice the implications that have arisen with regard to time. Catherine's present is made up of her own decisive response to the past, but once that response is made, it too becomes past, demanding its own future. The present holds the past and future together in a dynamism that determines the importance of the past. This dynamism also sets boundaries for what the future might become.

The issue of the future requires attention since, in this philosophical model, the future becomes the key to a notion of the universe that can only be coherent if it includes the existence of God. Power is located in the energy that comes relationally, in molding the many relations into one and in thrusting the force of that unification into the immediate future. But the future is more than the past. How do we account for the power of that "more than," if power must be rooted in a unification of relationships? The implications of this issue clarify the philosophical outlines of the doctrine of God, allowing formulation of a theological notion of God that can illumine our contemporary experience and the witness to the nature of God contained in biblical and church history.

This consideration of Catherine introduces the relational model of existence utilized by process theology. The process of integrating relationships produces reality. This process is dynamic, ever giving rise to new relations, new integrations, new realities. The terms "one," "many," and "creativity" become key terms for understanding this process. But relational reality is hardly exhausted by human existence. Process is not simply the prerogative of the human condition, but is fundamental to all reality. Change pervades existence and change is a function of relationality. If relationality is the key to change in human existence, and if human existence is not foreign to the world and the wider universe but is itself simply part of the larger realm, why should not relationality be the key to all change?

Consider the pervasiveness of change. The mountains that appear so enduring are in constant response to pressures within themselves and their environment, and they change: lifting higher into the sky, flowing down with the water into the sea. The ordinary solid things of our daily lives, like tables and chairs, are just as surely in motion, composed of atoms of energy bombarding each other, reacting, moving. Only the connectedness of their activity creates the solidity that we utilize so happily as the enduring realities of tables and chairs. The sky above us changes more obviously to our perception, with droplets of moisture condensing, dispersing, falling, yielding to currents of wind, motion. Our own bodies are in a continual process of change, with a total replacement of the cells of our skin every twenty-eight days! And yet within all this flux of movement there is also continuity, bringing with it whispers of permanence. What is the nature of this reality? How is it to be understood? Given such overwhelming change, what is the basis of continuity? What must be the way of things, for such existence to be?

Whitehead posits that all existence, from the level of so-called "empty space" to the most solid ton of iron, from the wispiness of a puff of smoke to the highest mode of existence in God, is essentially relational. He developed a model that builds on the knowledge that to exist is to have an effect. Each element of existence draws from the transmitted energies of its past, combining these energies in a creative movement toward its own actuality. Thus feelings from the past are incorporated into the present; the relationship to the past is internal.

The creative response to the energies of the past is a selective response, combining what can be combined, negating incompatibilities. The norm for selection is some grasp of what might be, some immediate (or, in the case of highly complex and novel entities, more distant) sense of the future, or what might be. For most of reality, this sense is by no means conscious; it is a simple force for unification. But whether we speak of a conscious or a nonconscious reality, the very act of combining the energies of the past with intimations of a future involves a measure of freedom. In nonconscious entities, this freedom is at the level of indeterminism, but as one moves along the scale of complex existence, indeterminism becomes freedom. What one deals with is simply given by a past, but how one deals with it depends upon one's capacity to envision and incorporate a future. The selective response to the past depends upon this measure of freedom/indeterminism, as does one's responsibility to the future.

From the perspective of the present reality, the relations to the future, unlike those to the past, are purely external. This is because the present can only incorporate the future into itself in the mode of possibility. What actually happens in the future is finally to be decided by the realities succeeding the present, in a new generation of actualities. The relation of the present reality to those future successors is therefore external.

In the movement from past to future, one sees change and continuity. The change rests in the reality that there is ever a new past to be incorporated into an ever newly arising present, but the continuity rests in the fact that the present internally incorporates the influences of the past within itself. There is an essential connectedness to all existence, a togetherness in a relationality that continuously moves beyond itself.

A more detailed description of this process model is given in the Appendix at the close of this volume, along with a glossary of the technical vocabulary common to process thought. Those wishing to understand more fully the dynamics of the model that informs this theology might turn next to the Appendix, but others might choose to move directly into the next chapter. Each chapter will, in addition to discussing a particular facet of Christian faith, also build as non-technically as possible on the discussion of the model that we have begun in this chapter.

The model thus far denotes a reality full of relation, where all of existence is a giving and a receiving, like a dance whose rhythms unite the universe. But this is an incomplete picture of existence indeed! We live in a real world where there is not simply the goodness and beauty of relationship, but also ambiguity, sin, and evil. How is it that destruction and sin should interrupt the relational dance with tragedy? How does this process way of doing theology explain such things as sin in the world? The question is crucial, since the power of a theology is the extent to which it can address the human predicament of existence gone awry through an understanding of the God who is for us.

2

SIN IN A RELATIONAL WORLD

IT should be a wonderful universe, then, shouldn't it? If the process model we have sketched is so, and all the world's a dance, then the many contribute to the one and the one, enriched, gives back to the many. The old intuition that justice and harmony are the foundations of the universe would be right, and the world should be idyllic. Sometimes, when we hear descriptions like that, we wince. We look around us, and, if we dare to admit it, within us, and it seems the dance has gone awry. Perhaps some invisible violinist is out of tune, or the drummer does not hear, giving an off-beat. Or perhaps we simply haven't learned the steps of the dance too well.

How is it, in a world so good, that we do not enrich each other? How is there room for sin in the process model? Because the model describes relational existence, it offers a peculiar clarity with regard to the dynamics of sin. The interrelatedness of existence provides the structure whereby enrichment occurs. The many are for the one, and the one for the many. But this is also precisely the structure whereby sin occurs. The inescapability of relationships means that the avenues of enrichment may become avenues of destruction. The effects of relationships are internal, and therefore, we are peculiarly vulnerable to each other. The world as described by process thought may indeed be beautiful, but it is also dangerous.

The traditional Christian understanding of sin has had a dual focus, the one personal and the other impersonal. Sin as personal indicates a violation of relationships, resulting in a state of alienation from God, nature, one another, and the self. The condition of alienation, however, is one into which we have been born. If there is a sense in which sin precedes us, then obviously there is an impersonal element in sin. This has been described as original sin and the demonic. Frequently Christians have personalized these powers and projected them away from ourselves as a nonhuman being, a devil, whose temptation of humanity in its very beginnings resulted in transgression and original sin. Process theology suggests a more tragic view, naming the cumulative acts of human beings in society as the source of the demonic. We are ourselves corporately responsible for the societies we create and the ill effects they engender. The demonic element is that we are each individually born into a society we did not create; insofar as it contains powers of destruction, these originate prior to our being. These powers can and do overwhelm us, involving us in the condition of alienation that is manifested in personal sin. In the grip of these powers, we continue to perpetuate them. Thus in a process world, the past can be understood as the conveyer of original sin and the demonic.

This can be illustrated through the story of a high-schooler whose family has always lived in one of the poorest sections of the city. The high crime rate of the area is evidenced by the condition of the school. Windows, once clear, are now either boarded up or barred to prevent breakage. Lockers are useless for storage, since they are always forced open for theft. "Rest rooms" are a macabre misnomer, since they are dangerous places inviting attack. Teaching is poor, for few teachers survive the unruly classroom atmosphere— faculty turnover is high. Students have organized themselves into ethnic power groups, each of which gains in prestige as it wields power to terrorize nonmembers.

The school is not this student's only reality. Unlike some of his friends, he has a close-knit family life. There is humor at the evening meal, and a sense of solidarity as he and his family spend evenings before the television set. Two modes of life are frequently communicated through the stories. There is a portrayal of the rough reality already known, albeit in an adult fashion. The tough investigator/policeman/lawyer enters into a world as harsh as the school, tracking and punishing the enemy. The tactics of the hunter are as violent as those of the hunted, and the scenes bear too much resemblance to the hunters and hunted of the school experience to present any alternative mode of life. The alternative is seen on the situation comedies that portray a saccharine reality so far removed from experience that there is no means of differentiating the television fantasy from fantasies of life as it might be in better neighborhoods.

When the boy first began high school, he was frightened by the power groups, and attempted through passivity to avoid the terror they presented. If he could only be invisible! In fact, of course, he discovered that he could be. Conformity was a way of becoming invisible. If he was just like everyone else, then he would not endure any special notice or violence, or at least no more than average. Conformity, however, carried the strong pressure to take the drugs he had already encountered but resisted in junior high school. Conformity also offered a still more powerful way to cope with the problem. Why not conform to the hunters? If one joins the powers of destruction, surely one is safe from the powers of destruction. So by sixteen, the boy had become a leader in one of the terrorizing power groups, exercising his power over the frightened incoming youngsters of the freshman class.

Has this youngster escaped destruction? His life has become as split as the two worlds of television. His harsh "real" world is the world where violence and violation dictate the nature of relationships. By contrast, his family life is a less affluent and less consistent version of the fantasy world, exercising an increasingly limited power of influence over his life outside the home. His ability to develop a richness of humanity wherein his relationships are avenues of well-being is stunted: poverty of spirit is his deepest poverty.

If original sin and the power of the demonic refer to that which precedes the individual and is greater than the individual, have we not given names to the reality just described? The boy was not responsible for the violence of the school when he first entered it, nor for the poverty and crime in his section of the city. Long before he was born, the conditions were forming. These conditions are transpersonal in that they are not the result of any single person or influence. Rather, they are a confluence of many powers, some remote and some near, all of which create an environment that will pressure toward destruction.

The great cry against the oppressive "isms" of history—racism, sexism, classism, handicappism—is precisely a cry against the demonic. The persons and groups targeted in these oppressions are born into a situation oriented against their well-being. They are pressured toward conformity with the negative images imposed upon them, with the harsh irony that such conformity then serves to justify the continuing projection of the image. The deepest tragedy is when the persons within these disadvantaged groups themselves internalize the image as that which is appropriate to them. The negative images, of course, likewise reinforce the systemic exclusion from access to financial and social resources leading to personal or group power, for how could persons "like that" be trusted with responsibility in society? The corollary is that the group as a whole most often tends toward poverty. And the tragic reality of this demonism is that its effectiveness begins not with a strongly formed adult, but with a tiny child, not only at birth, but often in prenatal existence through drugs, disease, or insufficient nourishment. ´

As the society most immediately affecting one becomes increasingly incorporated into the personal past, it is woven into the continuing formation of the self. The past, which was originally an objective reality into which one was thrown without one's consent, enters into one's subjective reality. When that past works against positive relationships that enrich the person, then that past is indeed demonic. The incorporation of that past into the self can be named an instance of demonic possession. The person so affected becomes a bearer of the demonic toward others, perpetuating demonic power.

Sin is involved in assent to the demonic. True, the power is greater than the individual, since it comes with all the weight of a past that cannot be avoided. But in the process model there is always a wedge of novelty that entails a degree of freedom and responsibility. The degree may be great or small, and the very reason for naming the powers we have described as demonic is because they leave but small room for freedom. But they cannot annihilate it completely. Therefore, to the degree that there is free assent to the past, there is responsibility for perpetuating that past. The sin is toward the self and toward others: toward the self, since every future moment of existence must reckon not simply with a societal structure of evil, but with a personal history of assent to that evil. In the assent, the evil is made subjective, woven into one's life. With each instant of assent, the evil is strengthened to the level of habit, becoming more difficult to resist.

Sin toward others takes place in two ways. In a process universe, that which one is in oneself becomes an effect upon others. To assent to evil in the self is to become an influence toward evil for others, thus increasing the power of the demonic. As the oppressive power of evil in the immediate environment is increased, resistance to that power is made much more difficult for others as well as for the self. In addition to this inward effect of one's choices for evil on others, there is also the external effect that accrues when one's destructive actions bring about physical or psychic harm to others. Regardless of whether the sin toward others is internal, external, or both, it is obvious in a process universe that sin with regard to oneself can never be limited to the self alone. Always, that which one is in the self has an effect upon others. Sin toward the self has a rebounding effect on those in relation to the self.

Sin imprisons. The sin of the demonic imprisons one in a particular form of the past. By choosing to become a bearer of the demonic, one allows that past, which was originally felt as oppressive, to become the determiner of one's reality. For example, in the illustration of the high-schooler, we began with two major influences: home and school. The demonic power of the social environment, which was at first only one structure from a past that still allowed other alternatives, was granted the power to overwhelm the alternatives. The demonic consumes the past and denies any future but its own perpetuation, under the illusion that the future must be only more of the same. The lie in the demonic is in the fact that the family influence was also real, and in the fact that no past can be simply repeated. By denying the multiplicity of past influences and the novelty in the immediate future, one becomes imprisoned in the particularity of a past that is allowed to swallow up all other forms of existence.

The power of the demonic can be seen in any situation in which the cumulative weight of the past denies a richness of well-being to anyone. Structures of society that contribute to racism, sexism, poverty, or oppression of any type can be experienced as demonic, shaping one's present toward an impoverishment of spirit held in bondage to the past. The structure of the demonic power is overwhelming, making the individual feel helpless, to the point that the only "reasonable" alternative would seem to be to join that power. Does the society say that blacks are servile? Perhaps the best way for a black to survive in such a society is to be servile, and the demonic power is reinforced. Does society say women are inferior to men, not capable of bearing the "burdens" of full equality? Then perhaps a woman will find that her best mode of survival is to develop modes of dependence that capitalize upon her supposed helplessness. The demonic power will be reinforced.

The process model stresses the fact that relationships are internal. Through relationships we become what we are. We, in turn, affect the becoming of others, who must internalize our effects. In Whiteheadian terms, there is a transmission of feelings from the entire past. Obviously, in such a model, the strength of the past is enormous. How one deals with the past is open, but that one must deal with the past is not. Since the dealings are through transmission of feeling, there is an inheritance in the present of that which each element in the past was in itself. Was an element of the past destructive? Then the present will inherit the feelings of that destructiveness. That which was there is now here. Conformal feelings bring about a transference, so that the past lives in the present.

The whole Christian doctrine of original sin attempts to describe just such a situation. That which was done in the past has an internal effect upon the present, adding a determining power to the present. That power is a call for repetition. It is not as if the temptation to sin were simply an external matter; the situation is far more dire. The temptation is internal, brought about by the inevitability of conformal feelings transmitting the reality of one occasion to another. The process model indicates that this basic sense of original sin is the foundation for the further power of the demonic. We must internalize the past. Obviously there is strength in numbers in such a situation. This is why societal evil is so powerful: a particular form of behavior is reinforced by innumerable instances of its repetition. When all of these instances must be felt, then the influence toward conformity will be particularly strong. The situation of original sin is then given a specific societal shape, with a strength so invidious and awesome that it calls for an opposing social force to address it.

Our experience of sin takes more forms than that of the demonic.

There is also the imprisoning power of sin that comes, not from being overly bound by the past, but through fear of the future as death. Death itself is not sin, any more than the past is sin. But just as the past, when experienced as a threatening and overwhelming power, can become the occasion of sin, even so the future as the death of the present can be experienced as a threatening and overwhelming power, leading to sin.

Death is as complex as life. We find our physical life through bodily stability, which in turn is sustained through the surrounding environment. Our emotional life comes about through the rich food of love in relationships. There is a deep interdependence between these two facets of our living: our physical condition affects our ability to participate in emotional relationships, and these in turn affect the health of the body. To add to the complexity, there is what we might call spiritual existence, or the sense in which we integrate our total living in terms of purposes and meanings that go beyond ourselves. Death can come to us through all three facets of our lives: physical death, of course, threatens our total existence. But emotional death and the death of meaning are also severe threats to our well-being. Part of the pain of the latter two forms of death is the paradox that while we are experiencing those deaths, we continue to live; our bodies are still sustained by the environment. Hence against the living death of emotional/spiritual loss, we sometimes see the finality of physical death as preferable.

Death does not wait for the future: it invades the present. Most obviously, it becomes part of present experience through anxiety. The knowledge or fear of death can be a foreboding that colors the present, so that the present is no longer experienced in its modes of richness. Instead, these are dwarfed by that which is yet to come— and yet is already present through anxiety.

For example, consider the case of a particular woman as she faces her own imminent death. She has been accustomed to walk in the park each noon after lunch. The enjoyment takes on a keenness throughout the seasons, and she particularly enjoys the changing modes of play seen in the children who come to the park. But on the day when she confirms her growing fear that the discomforting symptoms are indeed the first stages of an illness that will soon end her life, her perceptions of the world around her change radically. The trees are lightly tinged with green, preparing for their burst into springtime splendor; children run and play tag. How can the world be so oblivious to her pain and fear? How dare the trees bloom against her death, or the children ignore their wealth of time? Yesterday she saw similar sights with pleasure; the difference between yesterday and today is death. Knowledge brings the death of the future into the present, annihilating the beauty of the present with the fear of that which is not yet. No wonder persons fearful that they may be carrying a dread disease resist the official diagnosis and confirmation; they are attempting to keep death from beginning too soon, robbing the days of their delight. The paradox, of course, is that to keep death at bay through maintaining uncertainty is already to have admitted death into one's life.

Death also enters the present through loss of relationships in the process of our living. Sometimes death parts us long before death happens—there is a death that can come to emotional relationships apart from the death of our bodies. Nourishment comes to us through relationships. When important relationships fade or are broken, then that nourishment ceases, and we ourselves experience a form of death. Here the problem is frequently compounded by self-recrimination: had I done thus and so, had I been thus and so, would this have happened? Would not love and life as it was have continued? The bewildering continuity of physical life against the reality of an emotional death only intensifies the pain. With the loss of a relationship, there is a loss of ourselves, for we are formed in the mutuality of relation.

We also experience forms of death in the present through threats to the meaning of our existence. Is there a crisis of faith? Then there is a crisis in which we are threatened by a form of death, for when we have so constituted ourselves that a way of seeing God and the world is essential to our self-identity, loss of that way of seeing is like a loss of ourselves. Our world can appear to be in shambles, crumbled around the shaken foundations of faith, and where are we in the rubble? Death comes in many forms, invading the present.

Yet none of these forms of death is sinful. It belongs to the nature of finite existence that we know a "perpetual perishing." As we saw through looking at Catherine, we are continuously moving beyond a past and into a future, and therefore we are continuously in a process of change. It is possible in such a universe to move beyond past forms of relationships, and we shall surely move toward death. And since our perspectives are so limited, we must expect that our viewpoints can hardly be mirrors of absolute meaning, whereupon, of course, our private constructions of the world will be challenged. All three forms of death belong naturally to our condition, and while each can be experienced as evil, none of the three is evil in and of itself. But because the forms of death are a threat to our existence, death can be an occasion of sin just as invidious as that which we found in the structure of the past experienced as demonic.

Neither fear nor anxiety with regard to death is sin. These are appropriate responses, and are in fact expressive of the vitality of life. Through fear and anxiety, we can take measures for the protection of life. Sin enters the picture when our response to death is to close ourselves off against a future that is still possible for us. Perhaps this can be seen most clearly in a response to the death of relationships. The paradox that physical life continues despite the demolition of the emotional life occasions a strange form of imprisonment, for we can take refuge in physical life as if it were in fact the only form of existence. One is thereby locked away from the danger of death entailed in the emotional life. The trauma of divorce can illustrate the principle. A relationship is over, and the reality of existence is the throbbing ache of the loss of one's self. The depth of the pain is searing, but physical existence continues, and the sharpness of the emotional pain turns to an ache and finally a numbness. Meanwhile, one continues to live in a world where there are relationships. But how can one dare to risk such pain again? What if there is a deep undesireableness about the self that is hidden in the superficial dailiness of contacts, but that would be dreadfully revealed in a relationship that moved beyond the surface of life? How could one risk exposure of such an awful truth—isn't it better to hide it? And so one can draw deeply inside, allowing only the "safe" forms of relationship to continue. While this behavior might be appropriate in the early stages of healing, there comes a time when the behavior turns to sin. The turning point is when the refusal to go beyond the surface is not for the sake of healing but for the sake of protecting the present against a future that is too threatening. Complications multiply, for of course the very healing process required is only completed through reaching beyond the surface of relations into the depth of giving and receiving from the places where one really dwells. Thus continuation in a place of hiding becomes a sin against the self.

Once the behavior turns to sin, the initially protective wall starts growing. Always, in sin, we build a prison for ourselves. The refusal to live toward others from the depths of who we are then acts as a way of filling those depths with stones, until finally they have been reduced to shallowness, and there are no longer any depths to give. We become imprisoned within the self against the risk of relationality. The future is denied because of its threat of death. But the chosen mode of life is a deeper form of death than that which would be experienced even in another failing relationship. Sometimes we escape death by choosing death, but the death we choose is worse than the death we think we escape. In such choices, there is sin.

We can also respond in sin to the threat of physical death. The natural process of living toward a known death involves stages, each of which allows us to integrate the approach of death. This integration involves strong negative emotions—anger, hostility, denial—but these are appropriate to the process, and in no sense are they sin. The movement into sin is at that point where one refuses to move into the integration process, so that one refuses death its appropriate form. A deeper mode of this sin is not in the exigencies of a known and relatively immediate death, but when we constitute our living almost entirely as a protection against death. What happens here is that one allows the death that is in the future to pervade that future so that the future is seen solely as a form of death. Protecting oneself against death then requires that one ward off the future. One then builds one's present into a prison, but of course death is not the prisoner; the self is.

There is also temptation to sin in the threat against our spiritual meaning. Sometimes a person can hold a form of Christian faith that is not only considered orthodox, but that seems to rule out any alternative mode of Christian belief, as if contemporary worldviews never entered into the expression of Christian faith, transforming it in every generation. One equates one's own contemporaneity with the whole of Christian history. Differences can be accounted for by granting that there have always been heretics, just as there are today, but of course this is only in accordance with scripture. Tares grow with the wheat, and there will always be unbelievers in order that the true believers may shine forth. What would happen if such a person began a study of Christian history? At first there might be no problem, given the ability to read all stories as reflections or repetitions of one's own. But if the study continued, gradually the reality of history's tales would impose itself, entering the crack of newness presented in every moment. Realization would follow that the Christian faith has taken many diverse forms. No single mode of faith—not even one's own—has been held unchangingly for two thousand years. Further, with eyes to see it, one could discover the sorrow of much evil in Christian history, often justified in the name of "right belief." The center of life's meaning could be challenged.

What are the options? There is the possibility of dismissing the histories as if written by heretics or cynics. If this happens, then the continued maintenance of faith will become impoverished, imprisoned against the past. The former security of faith will turn to that afforded by a maximum security prison. Alternatively, the former faith could be totally denounced as false. Perhaps all faith is but an illusion, deceiving one into meaning; perhaps a bitter cynicism is the best option. Again, however, one builds a prison, this time against one's own past, for in fact faith was experienced redemptively. Both responses are a denial of the past, imprisoning one in the present. Richness is relinquished in the death of meaning.

In a process universe, every moment inherits from the past, but it cannot simply repeat the past. The richness of the present is the degree to which it incorporates its past in a positive movement into the future. Each form of faith inherited from the past was in its own day a response to its contemporary conditions, for good or for ill. To remain true to that inheritance, one must be willing to receive faith creatively. The spirit of faith is in the dynamic movement whereby it can dare to incorporate all data, moving constantly into a creative future. That which appears to be death can, through faith, be a gateway to resurrection.

Sin cannot be considered only through the past and the future. There is also the mode of sin that affects experience of the present. This sin is the violation of relationships, whether those that contribute to us or those to which we contribute. Strictly speaking in a process universe, we are still referring to a past (the relationships that affect us) and a future (our effect upon others). But in the dailiness of our lives, the immediacy of this past and future flows into our sense of the present. And here, too, one can give way to sin.

In process terminology, the many become one and are increased by one. Existence is a movement, a dance, of mutual enrichment. The many contribute the wealth of their experience to the becoming one, who in turn contributes to all successors. As we saw through Catherine, if it were not for the value she received from many sources, she could not have achieved her objectives in terms of becoming a teaching historian. Suppose that Catherine recognizes this dependence but sees it not as an enriching process that calls forth her own responsibility, but simply as her due. Conceivably, she could assume that since she has been helped by others, she ought to be helped by others, and that her basic right in life is to receive such help. Her own ego would then be the determiner of the value of others. Insofar as they contribute to her well-being, they are valued; insofar as they do not directly impinge upon her welfare, they are inconsequential. There is little attempt to understand from another point of view, save as it becomes helpful to her own cause. She has become a receiver of the good, and gives to others only to foster the sense in which others will continue to give to her. In effect, others have become as objects to be valued in terms of usefulness.

This egotism is sin, for it is a distortion of existence. Catherine makes her own self the terminal point of all relationships, when in fact she is not. In a process universe, every actuality is a center, in which case no actuality can become an absolute center. We are in a universe of "centerless centering." Every actuality is a receiver and a giver. The giving is for the purpose of receiving, and the receiving is for the purpose of giving. When Catherine violates this reality in her life, she sins against herself and others. She attempts to imprison herself in the present by making her own well-being the end of existence. It is as if she builds a wall against her giving for the well-being of others. Their own well-being is of little concern to her, save as she perceives it affecting her own. In fact, since others are the source of her richness through relation, their full well-being should be of concern to her. Her failure to give back is a failure to enrich. To the extent that she in fact impoverishes others, she impoverishes herself.

In a reverse situation, Catherine's emphasis would not be on what she receives, but on what she gives. Her self-understanding is "it is more blessed to give than to receive" with a vengeance, for she sees herself totally at the disposal of others. She attempts to respond to all demands upon her, negating herself for the sake of others. When she is tired and weak she consoles herself by considering it the cross she deserves, and if someone attempts to compliment her or give to her in return, she becomes profusely embarrassed. "No, no," she says, and immediately attempts to deny the compliment or to turn it back. If she must receive the gift, she quickly gives it to someone else.

Her refusal to receive from others is a distortion of reality, for in fact she is as dependent upon others as she would like to think they are dependent upon her. If Catherine in the first instance absolutized herself by making herself the subject of all others, Catherine in the second instance absolutizes herself by making herself the object for all others. In neither case does Catherine enter into the full meaning of her own subjectivity, which is that of a receiver/giver. Her life is in both cases built upon a lie, denying the full richness of a self.

Absolutizing the self is the denial of relational existence. Extreme forms of this sin move by degrees to modes of degradation and/or violation of others or of self. Regardless of degree, the sin becomes once more an imprisonment against the true nature of reality. Habituation in the sin builds the walls of the prison stronger. Release must come by renewed strength in the weakened pole of reality—self or others. But in the imprisoning nature of sin, the other pole lies beyond the walls that have been built. How, then, is the other pole to be regained?

Throughout all the forms of sin considered there runs a single thread: sin is based upon and requires a distortion of the nature of existence. Assent to the demonic requires that the demonic be given a determinative power, as if the demonic conditions encountered are the only conditions possible. But to reduce the past to a single power is to deny the full complexity of that which really does precede us. To distort the past into a single influence is also to deny the inherent ability to transcend that influence.

Distortion takes place again when the power of the future as death becomes the occasion for sin in the present. To consign the future solely to death is to deny the reality of life. Even though the forms of death are inevitable in our finite condition, and even though perpetual perishing marks all existence, it is not so that only death pervades the future. Perpetual perishing is also perpetual birth, and every death allows the possibility of resurrection life. To see the future only in terms of death and to act accordingly is to distort the fullness of promise in the future.

Distortion is perhaps most obvious in absolutization of the self with its denial of interdependence between the one and the many. To live as if either the one or the many were a terminus point in existence is a distortion of the process world. Because distortion is fundamental to each form of sin, one might say that the most basic description of sin is "The Lie." Sin is the pretense that reality is what it is not. Action in accordance with this distortion then involves us in modes of existence that go against the grain of things. To maintain the distortion requires a continuous denial of the fullness of reality, and the energy required to maintain "The Lie" drains us of our vitality.

By distorting reality and living against the grain of relational existence, we cut ourselves off from the full resources of existence. We lock ourselves away from our true well-being through sin. The paradox is that while we ourselves built the prison, we built it with our own existence. Therefore, we do not have the strength to break the prison down, and we are trapped by and in sin. Release must come from beyond ourselves in a counterforce to sin. We require a force in the past strong enough to counter the demonic, a force in the future that is stronger than death, and a force in the present that can enable us to live in the full interchange of relational existence.

3

THE RELATIONAL GOD

THE discussion up to this point has dwelt primarily on an understanding of experience. The process dynamic suggests a multifaceted richness of experience that nonetheless contains a fundamental ambiguity of good and evil intermingled. If the power of sin is its imprisoning nature, then the experience of release from sin can lead to the sense of a power greater than ourselves, able to help. Does a relational understanding of the universe hold any implications for an understanding of God that can illumine the experience of release from sin?

The process model builds upon the notion that energy transmitted from past actualities[1] (called "actual occasions" by Whitehead) evokes a new instance of becoming, and that the unification of these energies is the creation of a present. This unification takes place through the power of the future. The newly becoming actuality unifies the past on the basis of what it itself may become. "What it may become" is the selective norm whereby the many influences of the past are sorted and settled into just this actual occasion. With its own completion, the entity is one of the many other entities in the universe, placing its own demands upon a new present to come into being.

What is the future? In terms of the model, the future must be understood in an immediate sense. It is that which an entity might become. The distant future is not lost to view, for given the rela-

---

1. I am using the words "actuality," "entity," "unit of existence," and "particle of reality" interchangeably in this chapter, although a more technical development of process thought could not do so. Technically, the phrase "actual occasion" refers to the basic element of finite existence, as does the phrase "actual entity." "Actual entity" (but not "actual occasion") is also used of God. Please refer to the Appendix for a more precise formulation of the process dynamics with reference to God and the world.

tionality of existence, every entity has some drive toward effectiveness beyond itself. Ordinarily, this drive is simply toward repetition, but in highly complex actualities, the drive may also include a push toward transformation. In any case, this drive beyond itself is incorporated into the entity as a simple or complex possibility for the future, guiding the formation of the entity in the present.

Consider the power of the future in relation to Catherine. She decided to become a professor of history, and therefore she chose to go to graduate school. This decision can be explained in part by her past—her successful completion of college, her resources, her interests, the encouragement of family and friends. However, the major factor in her decision and subsequent career was not the past at all, but the future. She desired to be that which she had not yet become. This desire toward the future powerfully affected her, causing her to order her world in such a way that the possibility of teaching and researching history might become an actuality.

Whitehead makes the claim that possibilities are not effective simply once or twice within a lifetime. To the contrary, an ordering principle representing a future, such as we see in Catherine, is in fact operative in every particle of reality, whether it is a unit in "empty space" or in the finely tuned complexity of personality. This means that every unit of existence is formed through the conjoining of past and future. Since the future presupposes a given past, the past is primary, so that Whitehead argues that all finite occasions of existence begin with their feelings of the past. The influences of the past and the possibilities of the future are combined by the becoming entity in its own creation, which is the creation of the present. The power of the past is fundamental, since the past sets down the parameters of becoming. But the power of the future is also critical, giving the entity the ability to transform these parameters in terms of a new thing.

The power of the past is located in the completed actualities transmitting their energy. What is the source of the power of the future? For the future, unlike the past, does not yet exist. How does that which does not exist emit energy, influencing the present? A fundamental notion of process thought is that all reality is relational, and that power comes from reality through relation. Power does not emerge out of nothingness. If there is power, there is a source in actuality. There is a power to possibility. What, then, is the source of this power?

There have been many attempts to locate the source of the power of possibility in the finite world. For one thing, the power of possibility is operative throughout the unification of an entity; it is the selective power that renders the chaos of competing influences into contrasts that yield order. Thus if we call a grasp of possibility a grasp of what might be, of the future, then this sense of the future is operative along with the energy from the past from the very beginning of the entity. Could it be that the sense of possibility is also rooted in the past? Could the competing nature of all those influences generate possibilities for how they might be combined? What if possibility is not simply from one source, but from many?

The difficulty with such a resolution is that it calls for many actualities to combine to create an actual possibility, which then generates an influence. The trouble with this, however, is incoherence. It accounts for possibility by turning it into an actuality. But then it would function like all other actualities, as past rather than future. Possibility must be rooted in actuality, in order to exert power, but at the same time it must transcend actuality, in order to exert power as *future*.

The dilemma is that all power of influence must be rooted in actuality; the future has power of influence; how can it be rooted in actuality, since by definition all actuality is past? Whitehead approached the conundrum by a radical reversal of the dynamics of actuality. Every particle of existence is evoked into becoming by the past. The particle comes into existence as it unifies this past according to some grasp of what it itself might yet become. The process of becoming is precisely this unification. Once complete, the unit of existence becomes a force, along with many others, evoking yet another present into a new mode of becoming. What if there could be an entity that begins not through the primacy of the past, but through the primacy of the future? What if there were an entity for whom feelings of a "future," or feelings of all possibilities whatsoever, were absolutely primordial? Could this entity account for the power of possibilities, grounding them in its own actuality?

At first such a thought seems wild, and totally outside the principles of process. And yet the dynamism of becoming depends upon a connection between possibilities and power that can only be medi-

ated by an actually existing entity. Ordinary entities cannot account
for that power—why not experiment with the notion of an extraordinary entity, and see if a reversal of the dynamics of existence
in that one entity might account for the power of possibility? If it
can, so that the only difference in the entity is the implications that
follow from the reversal of the dynamics, then it would be a coherent explanation for the phenomenon of possibilities.

And so Whitehead groped his way toward a notion of God. He
was reluctant at first, saying only that there had to be a principle of
limitation in the world. He associated this principle of limitation
with a hierarchy of possibilities that were sheer abstractions in all
manner of combinations. Eventually Whitehead revised his thinking, so that the principle of limitation became a primordial togetherness of all possibilities harmonized in a great vision, and released as
an influence upon the world. But of course this was not yet a full
application of the dynamics of existence to this extraordinary entity, in which case, how was it an entity at all? And how could it
exert power? Finally, toward the close of writing his monumental
Process and Reality, Whitehead dared to apply the full dynamics in
reversal to God, so that the actuality of God included not only
unification through possibility, but also the feeling of other actualities.

The result is a notion of an entity that "begins" with possibility.
But possibilities simply "are." They are not temporal, save in
relation to some actuality. Possibilities do not "begin" at all—in
which case the entity that grounds the possibilities does not begin,
either. This entity would be, like possibilities, atemporal, or eternal. But as the actual ground for those possibilities, the entity
would have to order them, holding them together not chaotically,
but in some vision of their harmonious togetherness. After all,
actuality is a unification, and possibilities are themselves principles
of unification. If all possibilities are grounded in an eternal actual
entity, they must themselves be unified by that entity.

If the possibilities are unified by the actuality we now can call
God, then this unification is the expressed character of God. An
entity beginning in the unification of all possibilities does not feel
the constraints of a delimiting past. That phenomenon we discussed
as original sin or the demonic, or the "thrownness" whereby finite
existence finds its freedom vastly limited by that which went before,

would simply not apply to God. Rather, "beginning" in the unification of possibility means that God defines Godself, out of an awesome freedom, unconstrained by any other existent reality.

But the self-definition of this God would be the togetherness of all possibilities. *All* possibility is almost unimaginable to us—what complexity, what infinity! For it is the very nature of possibility that one thing suggests another; it's impossible to come to an end of possibility. Each possibility opens up new avenues of adventure in still further reaches of possibility. Only actuality itself can hold possibility in leash, paradoxically putting a limit on infinity.

Consider possibilities from the point of view presented in a very ordinary day. Even when the things one does throughout the day are fairly well established through routine, precisely how and at what second of the day one does them is enormously variable. Even a trivial possibility, once actualized, can change the course of a life—a marriage can result from a chance encounter. And to choose one possibility can immediately open a whole new set of possibilities that would have remained forever irrelevant had that initial possibility not been chosen. Had the Catherine of our introduction chosen pharmacy rather than history, her circle of friends, her place of employment, her city, perhaps even her family would have been different. How many "alternative lives" have been closed off through the choice of one rather than another possibility?

Possibilities are infinite, often mutually suggestive, interlocked in tenuous ways in great complexity. If there is a God who is the togetherness of *all* possibility, then almost by definition this God's character will be toward harmonization, with a power of holding opposites together in a deep complexity of beauty. Possibilities would exist not in chaos, but in swirling combinations of value, and value yet again, in a depth of awesome harmony. The nature of the harmony would be determined by God, expressing God's own chosen reality.

But this reality of God must exhibit the dynamics of existence, if this God does indeed exist—the vision of all possibilities even in a mighty harmony is not sufficient to constitute God. To exist is to be internally related to that which is other than the self. But if possibilities are grounded in God, they are not other, and cannot constitute the depth of relation necessary for God's existence. Furthermore, if the dynamics of existence are reversed for God, then the movement from actuality to possibility, or past to future, in the unity of the present, must become the movement from possibility to actuality, or future to past, in the unity of an everlastingly present God. The relatedness to the actuality of the world would be essential to God, and this relatedness would be internal.

Just here, of course, is the rub. Traditionally, God has been understood to have only external relations to the world. Internal relations would mean that God is affected by the world, but traditionally, God is *not* affected by the world. Before we rule out this possibility too quickly, let's explore the dynamics, and see what it would mean for God to be affected by the world in the unity of "future" and "past."

The dynamics of process indicate that to be is to have an effect, that every actuality is a transmitter of energy to all its successors. But if God as the ground of possibility is eternal, then God is always in a finite entity's past, and always copresent with the finite entity, and always in the finite entity's future. God spans all time. Therefore, would it not be so that God has an effect on every finite entity whatsoever? And that God likewise feels the effects of all finite entities? Would not God be the Supremely Related One?

How, then, does God affect and be affected by the world? As the source of possibility, of course, God's effect upon the world is to provide the world with possibility. This would mean that before an actuality came into existence, God would know that which it could become. Further, as the knower of all possibilities, God would know that which it could best become, given its finite circumstances. Thus God would be not only the source of the entity's future, but the source of its best future. And yet, this future is only possible, and we have noted that all possibilities are by nature suggestive. For an entity to receive the future as possible is for the entity to receive an open future, for *this* possibility can suggest *that* possibility. What the finite entity becomes, then, depends finally upon that entity, given the parameters set down from its past and the possibilities relevant to its future. But its becoming is always the actualization of a possibility, whether that one optimally presented by God, or some suggested alternative actualized instead. Once the entity becomes, it is itself a force generating an effect. And God, as well as the world, receives that effect.

God, receiving the effect of the world, integrates it into the divine nature. We will argue later that God's reception of the effect of the world is in fact the resurrection of the world into God's own life.[2] For now, however, we will simply note that God, receiving the world, does so with a judgment born from God's knowledge of what that world could have become, compared to what in fact that world did become. Furthermore, God receives not simply one effect from the world, but all effects. Just as the finite entity receives influences from all the past, and unifies them in a comparative process in light of what might be, even so God would receive the elements of the world comparatively, feeling each influence in relation to all others in graded orders of judgment.

At this point we can speak of a twofold evaluative process in God. First and always, there is God's primordial valuation of all possibilities in a comparison of their possible interrelationships. Second, and consequent upon both this primordial vision and upon the actuality of the world, there is God's valuation of the world itself as received by God. Notice the work of the reversed dynamics, since what the world calls future (i.e., possibilities) is more akin to a past in God, and what the world calls past (i.e., completed actualities) is more akin to a future in God.

If God is actual, manifesting supremely the dynamics of existence,[3] then it is not sufficient simply for God to evaluate possibilities and actuality; God must unify these evaluations in the dynamic act of God's own existence. Furthermore, given the eternal nature of possibilities and the ongoing nature of the universe, this dynamic act must be everlasting.

Therefore, the primordial vision (constituting God's self-created character) is the norm by which God transforms the world, unifying it with that vision. The primordial vision of all possibilities held together in harmony everlastingly yields an actualization of that harmony through God's transformation of the world in its light. This means that the world is transformed according to the norm of God's own self, and thus made a partaker of God's nature in everlastingness.

2. I have developed a very technical Whiteheadian argument for resurrection in *The End of Evil: Process Eschatology in Historical Context* (New York: State University of New York Press, 1988).

3. Whitehead is famous for saying that God cannot be an exception to metaphysical principles, but must be their chief exemplification.

The model requires that God's integration of the actual world into God's own self be connected with the possibilities in God in two ways. First, as we have just indicated, the transformed world in God manifests the character of God, actualizing the great harmony of the primordial vision. Second, this process of transformation yields an influence upon the becoming finite world. Remember, to be is to have an effect, and that effect can be twofold: a drive toward repetition of the values embodied in the self, and, given sufficient complexity in the entity, a drive toward a particular mode of transformation. God, as the most complex entity of all, gives a drive toward transformation that reflects, to whatever degree the finite world can bear, the transformation occurring in God. Thus as a result of God's own unification of the world with the primordial vision of all possibilities, particular possibilities become relevant to the becoming finite world. These possibilities will reflect, to whatever degree the world can sustain, a transformation of its past in terms of harmony, akin to God's own nature.

We earlier raised the question concerning God and internal relations, asking if the positing of God's internal relatedness to the world was indeed a violation of a Christian understanding of God. From the above, it is apparent that while it may not be traditional to posit such a thing, it does in fact yield enormous possibilities for interpreting the deeply Christian insight concerning a resurrection and judgment of the world beyond history. These possibilities will be developed further in Part V. Theologically, then, the internal relatedness of God to the world is the ground of resurrection; philosophically, this same relatedness is the ground of the world's temporal movement into novelty. Possibilities and therefore the future are grounded in God.

One final step needs to be taken. In the process model, each becoming unit of existence receives the influence of the whole past actual world, and must unify this world in light of one possibility. That's an enormous task for one finite entity! But God, receiving all the world immediately upon its completion, is in God's own self already a unification of the world from as many perspectives as the world offers. God's possibilities, offered to the myriad world, already reflect the divine movement toward unification. Therefore, the possibilities given to the world are unifying possibilities for existence that are nonetheless transformative. They constitute the needed dimension whereby the chaos of many influences from the past may be rendered into the coherence of a new actuality.

A more technical discussion of this model for God, using some of the unique language of Whitehead, is included in the appendix. For the purposes of following the unfolding theology, one simply needs to keep in mind that God is eternally self-created through a valuative unification of all possibilities; and that this God of all possibilities is supremely open to the world. God receives each element of the world in every moment of its completion. This reception of the world is evaluative and transformative as God integrates the received world into God's own everlastingness.

Such a God is the future of the world in two senses. First, God offers the world its immediate future in history through every moment of its becoming. But second, God is the destiny of all the world beyond history, since God receives the world into God's own self. Such a God thus offers hope of release from sin's imprisonment—first, by providing the possibility of our transformation in history, and second, by providing the reality of our transformation in God.

Given this model, how do we develop the traditional categories of Christian faith? What does revelation mean in such a model, and how do we understand and even appropriate the power, the presence, and the wisdom of this God? How is this God related to Jesus Christ, and to the community called church? Process theology, like all Christian theology, is an attempt to express the wonder of the God who is with us and for us. The categories may be new, drawn from the relational sensitivities of our day. But the story is as old as the gospel.

Part Two

GOD FOR US

A Process Doctrine of God

4

GOD REVEALED

EVERY single unit of existence (or actual occasion) in the world begins with physical feelings, and the most important of these feelings is the one from God. This feeling received from God is directive, offering a possibility for the occasion's best future. It is as if every becoming occasion in the world begins with the touch of God, called by Whitehead the "initial aim." This aim received from God orients the occasion toward an optimum way of harmonizing the feelings of the past received from the world.

Every occasion is touched by God, but this touch necessarily comes at the earliest phase of an occasion's becoming. Since consciousness is a late phase of each occasion, the touch of God is necessarily in the preconscious stage of those occasions that develop consciousness. This means that when we wish to talk of theology and experience, we must recognize that the experience of God is not necessarily given to consciousness. There is an indirectness to knowledge of God drawn from experience. The relationship with God, while constant, is not necessarily apparent; it not only is at the beginning stages of each occasion, but it is then overlaid by the responsive activity of the occasion. The occasion receives its initial aim from God, but in its own free act of becoming it adapts this aim to its own subjective choice of that which it will actually become. What is finally apparent is not the aim as given by God, but the aim as adapted by the creature. The world becomes the veil of God, hiding the face of the divine presence. God is hidden in the world.

God is also hidden in that God's guidance to us is necessarily adapted to our circumstances. Were this not the case, then God's guidance would not *be* guidance at all, for it would be irrelevant to our situation! But if God speaks to our condition, then God speaks in terms applicable to our condition. This means that what we call knowledge of God is necessarily reflective of where and when we are; our own situation is interwoven with our knowledge. How do we abstract the "knowledge of God" from the conditions of our culture or our personal history? Even were God to speak to us in audible words of our own language, and in categories well-known to us, the resultant knowledge would be as much if not more reflective of ourselves as it would be of God. For example, the amazing reality of radio waves means that there are many "messages" being conducted through the atmosphere around us—but only if we have a receiver, with it turned to a proper station, can any of these waves be transformed into understandable sounds. Frequencies that are not included on our radio will simply be ignored or turned to static. If God meets our condition, then God must adapt to the particularities of ourselves as "receivers" in order to be known at all. But how much of God is communicable to us? What "frequencies" can never reach us, simply because of the limitations of our human condition? And how "distorted" must the knowledge of God become through culture or class or perspective in order to be named "knowledge of God" at all? Paradoxically, for God to be revealed to and through our condition is also for God to be hidden through the veil of our condition.

There is also the problem of sin. If sin is basically a distortion of existence, then sin is like another veil, obscuring still further the true reality of God's presence. In every instance of sin, there is an "as if" quality. One lives "as if" the past blocks all change in the present; one lives "as if" the future were only death; one lives "as if" the self were absolute. The influence of God in the initial aim, however, is always toward correction and transformation; this is the faithfulness (or grace) of God. God's aims lead us toward the wider past, toward the possibilities of the future, toward the mutuality of relationships. The denial of these is at the same time the denial of God; such deviation from God's presented aim for us is sin. How, then, can God be discerned through the veil of sin?

Against this, the whole tradition of Christianity affirms that God is self-revealed in the world. Usually Christian theology speaks of revelation in two senses, and each addresses at least in some respects the obstacles to knowledge of God, even though in a process world, one can never posit an unambiguous knowledge of

God. General revelation is the witness to the nature of God through the creative mark of God in the world, like footprints not yet erased from the sand. Special revelation is the unfolding of the character of God through the history of Israel and Jesus. This mode of revelation is redemptive, addressing the distortions of sin. Process theology sees the dynamics to be the same in both general and special revelation.

God's aims for the world flow from the primordial harmony of God. Each aim is God's adaptation of divine harmony to specific conditions in the world. Consider the situation through a metaphor of light. The primordial vision is like a beam of light, containing all color within it—but as potential, not actual. God's aim is then like a prism, reflecting the light to the world. However, the colors in the light do not become visible, thus truly revealing light, until they meet with the actuality of the world, be it a drop of moisture in the air or a flower upon the earth. When the light is finally reflected, it reveals not only its source, but that which it touches as well.

If we follow the metaphor, God's light is revealed through the actuality of the world. Just as light reveals the nature of the objects that hold it, even so the actualization of God's initial aim in the world reveals the shape of the world. This means that the revelation of God is never pure; it is always twofold. God and the world are seen through the same light.

We must go beyond the metaphor to speak of the further qualification that, as noted above, what is actually seen as we observe the world is not the initial aim of God, but what has been done with that aim in the world's own dealings with it. In the dynamics of process, the influence from God is directional, orienting the occasion toward its best mode of being in the world. The occasion deals with this influence in the privacy and freedom of its own becoming. The subject adopts or adapts the initial aim into its own subjective aim. Only upon completion of the process is the occasion itself capable of contributing to others or, in process terms, capable of being felt by its successors. The practical effect of this for revelation is that we can never see directly what God's aim is for another. We can only see what the other has become.

The stages that result in revelation are therefore reconstructed as follows. Each element in the world receives an aim that has been peculiarly fitted to it in light of its particular past. At this stage we refer simply to the initial aim, but it is already reflective of the world as well as God. It represents the real possibility that God can offer to the world, given all of its finite circumstances. Then the aim is adapted by the occasion itself. The world, in its solitariness, decides what it will do with all the data from its past, including the data received from God. True, the divine aim is the most influential, giving a way to deal with all the past. However, the aim is still but possibility, and as possibility it carries implications of alternatives. The occasion has the power of decision over all its available alternatives. Thus the completed occasion is the result of what it has done with the aim from God. Revelation through the world is two stages removed from the fullness of the divine harmony in which it originates. It is the harmony as adapted to the world by God, and the harmony as adapted by the world in the world's response to God. The revelation is therefore indirect.

A further complication occurs when we attempt to read nature as revelatory of God. We become interpreters of nature, which means we are removed by yet one more stage from the aim initially given by God to the world. Consider an illustration of this. The heavens present to our vision a remarkable drama of beauty. From our perspective, we see the sun moving across the sky, sometimes in a splendor nonetheless wonderful because we are accustomed to it— the sky, an incredible blue; the clouds, forever in motion, as if they dared the sun to catch them in their race toward the horizon; and then evening comes. It is as if the sky begins to feel itself as color, finally exploding into experiment, testing gold, tinged with pink, becoming rose, a touch of violet, and finally the deepening indigo that will give way to night. And the night sky! The moon appears to replace the sun, followed first by a single star, daring its dance beside the moon. One by one, others join in, and when the sky's dusk is fully turned to dark, the sparkling stars reveal their dance in stately silence across the universe. And we watch!

With equal sensitivity, the Palmist might cry out, "the heavens declare the glory of God," while one like Camus might muse in wonderment, giving quiet deference to the "benign, indifferent universe." Both watch, and see, and wonder, and interpret. Revelation, indirectly given through the medium of the world, is ambiguous, subject to varying interpretations, depending upon the total situation of the interpreter, the interpreter's particular circumstances, and the givenness of the observed world.

Consider a further ambiguity. Aims given to occasions in the natural world may mediate order and beauty, and nature may then display a serenity that we interpret as reflective of God. The ocean, sparkling in sunlight as if to recreate on its daytime surface a remembrance of the stars of night, may seem majestic, mysterious, serene, its waves gently lapping the shore. But what of those times when its depths churn angry gray, with waves crashing upon the earth in a fury that smashes pavement, floods homes, and wreaks awesome destruction? How do we read the one as reflective of God, and not the other? And does God indeed lead the ocean to crash the boundaries we hoped were so secure? What can we read that reflects divine harmony in the roar of an ocean gone wild? And suddenly, perhaps, it seems we can read what we wish into the world of nature, constructing as many notions of God—or of no God—as the variable world may afford. Dim comfort it is that the overall way of things works to the support and intensity of life, when the particularities of existence threaten to overwhelm us. A God of harmony and purpose and persuasive love might be revealed in nature, but ambiguously so, and in a way that can only be read if the other factors in our situation are conducive to such a reading. The immediate situation in the world is only ambiguously revelatory of God, although the makings of revelation are there.

Given the constancy of God, the cumulative witness of the world is more revelatory than the immediate witness of the world. Here we speak of the sense in which the world has inexorably moved to greater and greater complexity, greater and greater intensity, greater and greater order. It cannot be argued that the order is only in the eye of the beholder, for the beholders are themselves a part of the world perceived. Order within the observer is therefore order in the world as well.

Furthermore, order apparently gives rise to its very perception. Consider the perspective provided through a phenomenon such as the Grand Canyon, where to walk through it is to witness the progression of the world of nature toward life. According to the record of the fossils, once life is achieved, the progression moves steadily through eons of time into deeper modes of complexity. Each stage of development supports the next, but is transcended by the next, as if the world responds to a call always pulling it beyond one achievement to yet another of increasing complexity. In such records we witness our past, and read our own story of continuity and transcendence, continuity and transcendence, again and again—there in records of stone, now in records of words, flesh, experience. In humanity, the world of nature comes to expression. It wakens to consciousness, looks at itself, wonders, questions, speaks. In such a context the very question about order depends upon order; the question itself is a witness to that which it asks. But the question, like order itself, takes us beyond ourselves, seeking the future, seeking God.

Why does nature move toward intensity; why does it continually move beyond its past; why does it advance always to a future that leaps beyond the boundaries of the past, yet always in keeping with the preparation of the past? By taking the witness of this movement into account, we can interpret the present, whether beauty or terror, in light of the long history of the earth. Past and present together give plausibility to the interpretation that the world is reflective of a power beyond itself that leads it to deeper modes of complexity, intensity, harmony. Can the source be less than the call? Must not the source of such a call be itself a complex, intense harmony? And does not the movement of the world toward such qualities become revelatory of this? Granted, the revelation is indirect and hidden in ambiguity, but when one takes care to look at the evolutionary evidence of the world, the revelation is there.

To move from consideration of general revelation to special revelation, we must look at the implications of the rise to consciousness in the world. The movement toward complexity is through an increase of contrasts held together in the unity of each actual occasion. In process thought, consciousness follows from an intense form of such contrasting. Why is consciousness a function of contrast? Perhaps this is best explained through an illustration from our own experience of consciousness as a flickering, more-or-less aspect of our existence. We sleep, and are unconscious until we dream, wherein a form of inward consciousness emerges in the image world of impressions, intuitions, feelings within the self. In our waking life, consciousness also varies, from the rote consciousness involved in habitual actions to the perked interest aroused by attention to a situation or task. We experience con-

sciousness as an intentionality directed toward the relations between different things, whether in relation to themselves or in
relation to our own immediate purposes. When contrasts are heightened, consciousness is increased; when contrasts are muted, consciousness lessens.

Habit becomes an interesting illustration of the loss of contrast,
and hence the freeing of consciousness from the habituated activity,
releasing it for other tasks. Habitual behavior is simply the convenience of repetition of activity. The activity, when first begun,
demands a high degree of consciousness. One must master the
coordination of effort involved in balancing a bicycle, or shifting
gears on a car, or correlating fingers and keys on a keyboard. The
consciousness involved is intense, directed toward the contrasts of
body and machine in an effort to synchronize them. Practice after
practice is required, until finally the contrast between body and
machine is lessened—indeed, the bicycle or car or keyboard becomes almost like an extension of the self. Once the activity becomes habit, the contrast effectively decreases, and sometimes we
even speak of performing the activity "unconsciously." The actions
become a rote-like background against which we can direct ourselves toward other contrasts in the renewed creation of consciousness.

Consider the amount of concentration necessary when making a
difficult decision, when studying, or when working. Sometimes we
think long and hard, and grow tired with the effort. In a process
world, it is no wonder we grow tired, for concentration is not simply
a utilization of consciousness, it is the creation of consciousness
beyond our accustomed levels. Always, in the creation of consciousness, there is a contrast between the data at hand and possible ways in which the data might be ordered. There is a contrast
between what is and what might be, between past and future.

If God is truly persuading the world toward depths of harmony
that are reflective and therefore revelatory of God, then surely God
would bring the world towards forms of conscious existence, utiliz-
ing consciousness to achieve a fullness of revelation. The aims of
God pull the world toward complexity and harmony so that in its
own way the world might be reflective of God; the aims of God pull
the world toward the image of God. Whereas the nonconscious
world gropes blindly toward this image, reflecting it but dimly, the

conscious world has the possibility of forming itself clearly in keeping with this guidance toward intensity, complexity, and harmony. But it is not simply that consciousness can guide us toward that image, increasing its magnetic pull as it crystallizes into thought. Additionally, consciousness is itself a means of creating not simply the unity within an occasion, but the unity among occasions as communal existence in the world. In this case, consciousness is not only a means, but also an end: the conscious community can mirror the image of God.

Consciousness holds the potentiality of being the crown and completion of any true harmony in our experience, for it allows the knowledge of relationality to complement and direct the actuality of relations. If God lures the world to reflection of divine harmony, then the divine transformation and reconciliation of many contrasting realities into the unity of beauty is to be mirrored in the world. In God, this unification takes place in the intensity of God's being. In the world, this unification takes place within an occasion, and among occasions. The first unification is only partially reflective of God's own harmony, given the necessity that each occasion must selectively feel its predecessors. There is a necessary negation from feeling that happens as the finite occasion moves toward the simplification of being just this one thing. Given this, the unity and beauty of God, who negates nothing from feeling, requires community for its fullest reflection. The intense "all-at-onceness" of divine harmony receives its counterpart in the "spread-outness" of time through communal existence. Here the limited unification of each single occasion is complemented by the intentional togetherness of many diverse occasions in increasingly complex modes of community. Consciousness in finite existence can become a means of maximizing and intensifying communal togetherness, bringing it to reflection of divine harmony.

In harmonious communal existence, the welfare of all creates the welfare of each, and the welfare of each contributes to the welfare of all. Such is the rhythmic movement of harmony. This movement is optimally attained in consciousness, where harmony on the individual level intentionally depends upon harmonious connectedness on the societal level. The unconscious occasion but dimly feels the wider world beyond itself, and that primarily as a repetition of itself. In the conscious world, where the weight of the future enters more fully into the present, the vision of the future as societal enters into the enjoyment of the individual. Consciousness is thus the crown and completion of true harmony. As the world moves toward consciousness, it moves toward deeper possibilities of reflecting the divine image. Given the continuity of the world and the sense in which human consciousness emerges from the natural world and within the natural world, all of creation can be embraced within the harmony actualized through intensely conscious existence.

In such a context, special revelation of the nature of God to consciousness cannot be seen as tangential to the divine nature, but as integral to the divine nature. If the power of initial aims is the sense in which they offer harmony, and if that harmony is an adaptation to the world of the harmony that is God, then the clearer that harmony is made, the more effective it can be. God, seeking to persuade the world toward the intense harmony of the divine image, will do so all the more powerfully as that intentionality becomes clearer to the world. If God's purpose for the world is an intensification of harmony, then God's purpose for the world inexorably entails revelation of the divine nature in and through human consciousness.

Thus far, there is a possibility of general revelation such that the initial aim of God, while given as the first touch of existence for every single occasion, becomes the vehicle for knowledge about God. The knowledge is ambiguous, telling us about the world as well as about God, but the knowledge is possible. Further, just as we can read the presence of God through the evidence of the world around us, it is so that God is at work within us for our good. We, too, are composed of actual occasions, and we, too, are touched in every moment of our existence by the guidance of God. Just as it is possible to see the trace of God in the world of nature, can we also see the trace of God through God's influence upon us? Can we read anything of God through our own consciousness?

The three following chapters will attempt to do this on the premise that general revelation allows or leads to an understanding of God as the one who is pervasively present to the world, the one who is ultimate in wisdom, and the one who is the power of justice. Inevitably, even though there will be no specific dependence upon the special revelation of the biblical sources, the Christian context in which general revelation is even termed revelation will influence the development. There is no such thing as a value-free interpretation of the world. However, since the thesis is that God's creative work in the world can indicate something of God's nature, lifting the veil of hiddenness to some degree, the initial development of the doctrine of God will work primarily with the dynamics of existence. The further development of the doctrine of God as the answer to the distortions of sin must move beyond general revelation and rely more explicitly upon the special revelation of the biblical texts. This will follow in Part III through the development of christology.

God is revealed in the world. Sometimes, especially in the spring, we encounter a long series of gray and rainy days. To be sure, there is light, but our spirits long for the brightness of the sun. Finally there comes a day when the clouds seem whiter; then they seem as if they are trying to contain a brightness too much for them. Finally and suddenly the sun breaks through. We began this chapter by discussing the hiddenness of God through the sense in which God's presence is at preconscious levels of existence, through the ambiguity that any revelation must necessarily be adapted to the conditions of this world, and through the further complication of the distortions of sin. This hiddenness is no more final than the gray of the springtime skies. General revelation, or the mark of God in the world, is like the light that illumines the world despite the overlying clouds, and special revelation is like the bursting through of the sun. We see that sun not necessarily as it is in itself, but as it is in its appearance to us. Though the knowledge is partial, the sun nonetheless warms us by its lifegiving, lightgiving presence.

5

GOD AS PRESENCE

WE exist in creative response to relationships. This means that existence is through and through relational. Despite this immersion in a world of relation, we sometimes experience a sense of isolation, of watching the crowd, of feeling that there is no real mattering of ourselves in relation to others: loneliness. Who can touch us in our loneliness?

The problem is intensified when we consider the importance of relationships in establishing our own individual sense of meaning. In the illustration of Catherine, it was obvious that her daily purpose and fulfillment were associated with the relationships of her life, whether family, studies, church, or profession. Meaning is found in the concrete relationships of our existence, or it is not found at all. Loneliness, then, carries as its bitter corollary a fear that there is no longer any meaning. In its most intense form, this fear extends beyond daily meaninglessness to an ultimate meaninglessness that reduces one's own life and all life to triviality and absurdity.

Inevitably, however, we judge loneliness to be out of kilter with the way things should be. We measure the hollow places of loneliness by the value of the relationships we wish we had, so that there is a restlessness and discontent with the condition of loneliness measured against the "might be" of our yearning. This loneliness is seldom the total absence of perceived relation; it is rather the experience that known relationships are insufficient to meet our deepest needs. In loneliness, we judge the concrete relationships of our lives as wanting, transient, and without any ultimacy of meaning. It is as if the condition of loneliness takes us beneath the surface of those relationships, so that whether momentarily or longer, we are dissatisfied with them. But we are also dissatisfied with loneliness. Why?

We could almost speak of our experience as if it occurred in layers. The outermost layer is daily existence, but there is a deeper layer—the place of loneliness—where it seems that relationships cannot follow, so that the relationships are deemed insufficient for us. This deeper layer of loneliness does not seem to have ultimacy, for it is itself deemed insufficient. It is as if there were yet another depth beyond the place of loneliness, providing a place of judgment upon loneliness, just as loneliness has provided a place of judgment upon daily relationships.

The experience of loneliness thus indicates at least three dimensions to our experience. There is the surface dimension of everydayness, often experienced as sufficient for the requirement of meaning. Lurking beneath such daily relations is the recurring sense of emptiness, futility, loneliness despite relation. This dimension takes us inside ourselves, forcing us away from the surface of our living. In loneliness, the insufficiency of daily relationships is that they do not seem to follow us here, to the inwardness of ourselves. The relationships are therefore found wanting. But neither is there sufficiency in this inwardness. The lonely self exists in an echo chamber, crying against the prison of its own solitariness for a relation that can set it free. Since the surface relationships cannot participate in this inwardness, and are judged as "surface" precisely through the inwardness, those relations cannot suffice for release from loneliness. Nor, in their insufficiency, can those relations provide the source of the judgment that loneliness is itself a negative state. There is, in the very sense of loneliness as negative, an intimation of yet a deeper dimension to reality that has the power of judgment over loneliness. Loneliness is then like a space between two forms of relation: the daily relationality above, and a depth relationality beneath. The dilemma of the lonely self is its alienation from both forms of relation. The former seems insufficient, and the latter seems inaccessible, or even illusory. Both forms become like the walls of the echo-chamber prison, intensifying the sense of alienation and loneliness.

If only one could rest content with loneliness! Then loneliness might seem more like a great hall than a narrow prison; one could stay the intensifying power; one could hold back the insufficiencies of daily relation and the judgment of ultimate relation, like a Samson braced between the pillars of the Philistine hall. "Loneliness," one could say, "is but part of our human condition, to be accepted in unquestioning endurance." In such a way, one might balance the pillars that hold up the roof of futility and despair, and find protection in the hall of emptiness. But too often we push against the pillars of denied relation, and the chaos of futility, alienation, and meaninglessness falls upon us, and we are lonelier still. The great hall is no less a prison than the narrow echo chamber.

What if the imagery be used in a different way? If loneliness is like a space or room between two forms of relation—the one superficial, the other of inaccessible depth—may we not consider the condition of loneliness not as a room but as a passageway? That is, if in loneliness we have longings for a form of relation that penetrates more deeply into our being than those relations of everydayness, and if this sense of a deeper relation becomes both the judge against superficial relationships and against loneliness itself, may not the loneliness that gives rise to the sense of such a form of relationality in the first place become a mode of access to such a reality? If we intuit such a form of relation through loneliness, might we not go still further, and reach such a form of relation precisely through the prior condition of loneliness? Perhaps the human experience of loneliness becomes an entry point for an awareness of relation to a God who is usually hidden in the dailiness of life; perhaps we can move through loneliness to its further side, and begin to speak of the nature of the God who is for us as an ultimate presence.

How can this be? And what is the import of a God who is an ultimate relation, an ultimate presence? The process conceptuality comes to our aid in laying bare the dynamics by which loneliness becomes a component of our experience, and the sense in which loneliness can suggest the nature of God.

Every moment of existence begins in relationality through the transition of energy from the past to the present. The past *is* present to the becoming occasion. These physical feelings of the past are supplemented by a mental conception of what might be. This conception is the grasp of possibility, or the occasion's response to the moment-by-moment touch of God. God proposes an optimum way of being, and the becoming occasion disposes of this as it wills.

The occasion is responsible for what it does with what it has received. In its becoming, it is alone with itself, determining the value of its universe. This activity can be portrayed as a spiral, wherein the occasion moves from its feelings of the past (including God) into its own integrative activity, intent upon becoming one reality in the midst of its manifold relations. Upon its completion, it bursts into transitional relation again, now hurling its effects upon the future, joining with God and the whole universe in calling that future into being, even as it itself was called into being. In the flashing movement of existence, every momentary act of becoming is followed by transitional relation, and every transitional relation is followed by a new act of becoming, called concrescence. Each concrescence is like a breathing space in a sea of relationality, the aloneness through which one becomes a self in the integration of many relations.

Thus far the model is more descriptive of aloneness in the midst of relation than loneliness in the midst of relation. The difference is crucial, for aloneness can be full of meaning, while loneliness involves loss of meaning. One can be alone, and yet intensely aware of relationships that are integral to the self, both constitutively and valuationally. To be lonely, however, is to experience the devaluation of relations, and an isolation despite relation. The fact that each moment of concrescence is an aloneness with itself is the basis for the further experience of loneliness, but it is not identical with loneliness. To push toward an understanding of loneliness, we need to expand the discussion of consciousness begun in our last chapter.

Each occasion of existence is both mental and physical, with the physical being defined as feelings of the past, and the mental being the capacity to generalize the past and to grasp a new possibility in relation to that past. Very few actual occasions appear to have consciousness, which is the awareness of the contrasts between data in light of some particular possibility for becoming. Consciousness is only one possible aspect of the mental pole. It is a particular development of the mental pole, but is not itself reducible to the mental pole. Consciousness comes about through the strength of contrast between what is and what might be. Thus consciousness is a function of the contrasting integration of the mental and physical poles. It is, therefore, produced through concrescence, and is necessarily a late phase of concrescence. Consciousness cannot be produced in the initial stages of concrescence, for the physical pole is the sheer feeling of energy from the past. Only as the many feelings are integrated can consciousness arise, for the activity of integration is the activity of contrasting.

What provides the contrast? There are two sources, with the first and foremost being a grasp of the "might be" in contrast to the "what is." In order for this type of contrast to obtain, however, the second source must also be present. There must be a wide range of positive feelings (or prehensions) of the past. If most of the past is felt negatively, so that only a narrow sphere of reality is admitted into positive influence during concrescence, then the contrasting activity will be minimal. Consequently, the mental pole will integrate the past with a minimum amount of novelty, and a relative repetition of the past will be assured. The vast number of occasions in our world are of this variety, with the result that there is a basic stability to the natural world. Its rate of change is slow relative to us.

When an occasion is open to a wide range of influences received positively into the concrescent process, then the manyness of influences itself presents a ground for contrast, plus a problem for integration. The more influences allowed, the more novelty is called for. The "might be" comes into play as ways of integrating the many into unity come to the fore. The contrast between the many and the "might be" produces consciousness as a means of integration. Consciousness, then, relies upon an openness to novelty and thus a prominence to the mental pole, a prominence that increases through the intensity of contrasts that the occasion can sustain.

In loneliness, as contrasted with aloneness, the relations that are constitutive of the self are valued negatively. Ordinarily, relations are valued in varying degrees: they range from intense to minimal importance. Further, there is a fluctuation within each relationship, depending upon the immediate purposes of the individual. For instance, a son may be intensely important to a mother, but if the mother is involved in writing, the relationship to the son may well slip to the background of consciousness. When the mother and son are engaged in conversation, however, the values in the immediate experience may reverse. The writing may become background, and the relationship between mother and son becomes foreground. Thus daily existence admits a multitude of relationships, each with its own value, contrasted with the fluctuating purposes of existence. The contrasts of relation are varied. Not so, however, in loneliness. There is a leveling of relation through negativity. There is a painful sameness to all relations in loneliness, wherein the contrasting variability and interest is silenced.

Yet there is consciousness. What is the contrast that produces the consciousness of loneliness? It can only come from the "might be," but the "might be" in the process vision of reality is located precisely in the initial aim from God.

Earlier, we spoke of loneliness as a prison between two modes of relation, the devalued everyday relationships, and the sense of ultimate relation through which loneliness is judged as being askew. We are now in a position to correlate the existential sense with the philosophical model, wherein we can move into the implications for God. Loneliness follows from the devaluation of finite relations. Relationality cannot be negated, for existence is thoroughly relational. But the relationality can be devalued, and in the devaluation, all finite relations are leveled to a sameness. One can, in this process of devaluation, live a robot-like existence, moving in a contrastless world with minimal consciousness. Yet given the propensity of human existence for consciousness, the contrast of the "might be" forces itself upon us, demanding that we visualize a relation that could follow us into our inward processes of existence, meeting us with presence and providing us with meaning.

The "might be" that comes from God is always for an optimum possibility for concrescence, given our situation. God not only begins our existence through the touch that mediates possibility to us, but God also feels us at the conclusion of each momentary existence, integrating that which we have chosen to become into the divine awareness. We are surrounded by God as our source and destiny in every moment. This indicates that the "might be" that comes to us in our devaluation of finite relations is in and of itself rooted in a unique presence, for there is no other reality in our experience that is both our source and our destiny. There is a uniqueness to the aim received from God that goes beyond its content to the uniqueness of its source in relation to ourselves.

This unique source is something that is experienced again and again by each successive moment in our existence. If God is always present in the provision of the initial aim, then there is no contrasting absence whereby God's presence could rise to conscious notice. This would mean that the very constancy of God's presence would paradoxically function to hide God's presence from consciousness. This hiddenness is further emphasized by the fact that the content of God's touch upon each concrescent occasion is toward an optimum mode of existence in the world. Thus God's aim directs us toward the world, not necessarily toward God, and again, God is present in a mode of hiddenness.

When, however, the contrasts of the world are leveled as in loneliness, might it not be the case that a new contrast emerges, touching the edges of consciousness with a sense of the divine presence? Whitehead speaks of a peculiar category known as "transmutation," by which he means the identifying of many occasions by a single characteristic that they all hold in common. As the contrasts of relationality are leveled, they are deemed insufficient, and their very variability becomes part of that insufficiency. We might speculate that in loneliness, we tend to categorize all relations alike, negatively valuing the variability that ordinarily is the source of richness and contrasts. Transmutation occurs, and the many relations are devalued for variability. Is there not then a natural contrast provided between the variable finite relations and the one invariable divine relation? And might not this contrast suffice to begin to lift this divine relation out of hiddenness into awareness?

We have mentioned the invariability of God's presence as one factor that contrasts with finite relationality. There is yet another factor of contrast that follows from strict usage of the process model. Every finite occasion is felt by another as past, since no occasion is effective for another until it is determinate and therefore complete. Upon its completion of becoming, its concrescent energy becomes transitional energy, and the past becomes an object to be felt by the present. Whitehead calls this "objective immortality." Since God concresces conversely from every finite occasion, God's concrescence never ends: God is the only entity whose subjectivity continues even as it is being felt. This is not a violation of the metaphysics; it simply follows from the reversal of the polar dynamics as discussed in chapter three, and elaborated in the appendix. Determinateness, established by all finite occasions *after* the unification process, is established by God through the primordial quality of the mental pole. Finite occasions end in determinateness, thus allowing the transmission of energy. God begins in the determinateness of the primordial vision, so that God's transitional creativity is copresent with God's concrescent creativity. For finite occasions, determinateness is the result of subjectivity; for God, determinateness is the presupposition of subjectivity. Hence God, unlike any other actuality, is felt by the finite occasion during the divine subjectivity, not after—for there is no "after."

If in loneliness the subject's feeling of God shifts from the world-oriented content of the initial aim to the God-derived nature of the aim, would not this peculiar feature, which surely differentiates this aim from all others, play a part in the resulting contrast? And would it not indicate a divine mode of presence to the subject that would differ markedly from finite modes of presence? Two points of discussion might clarify this: the nature of "objective immortality" in the process model, and the account of mystical experience, which could be seen to illustrate the difference the continuing concrescence of God might make in the sense of the divine presence.

"Objective immortality" is the way the past functions in the internal constitution of the present, and therefore continues to "live on" in the present. However, the subjectivity that belonged to each element of the past in its own time of becoming is lost. The easiest way to illustrate this is through some great example from history: Martin Luther King, Jr., created a significant difference in American life that certainly continues in these decades since his tragic death. In that sense, he lives on. But his own subjective reality was cut down in 1968; King himself does not participate in the events that succeed him, even though he critically influenced what those events could be. He is "objectively immortal" in history. The subjectivity belongs to those in the present time who are influenced by him.

Process philosophy says that this illustration typifies what happens not simply with the great figures of history, but in every moment of existence, at every level of existence. Every instant of becoming *is* a becoming through the dynamic convergence of past and future: the past, through many divergent influences demanding an accounting; the future, through a transforming decision concerning how these many influences of the past might be unified. The present is the becoming of a new subject through this process of unifying the past and the future. "Objective immortality" is a critical and technical analysis of the transition that occurs when the becoming subject selectively incorporates aspects of the past into itself. This incorporation is first of all the subject's feeling (or "prehension") of the past, and then a comparison and evaluation of that past relative to the subject's own possibilities for becoming.

It belongs to the process that the present, by definition, signals the objectivity of the past. An occasion of experience feels the past, integrates it evaluatively into its own subjective becoming, and then itself becomes past for some new present. There is a rhythmic movement from subject, to object, to subject yet again—but the movement is of successive units of becoming; it is a process of "perpetual perishing," as Whitehead said, quoting Plato before him.

This process might also be described by the different modes of creativity it suggests. To feel the past and deal with it evaluatively is a subjective mode of creativity, or, in the language of the philosophy, "concrescent creativity." But once this act is completed, it has an effect upon a future, evoking that future into a new mode of becoming. This effect is the transition from subjectivity to objectivity, or the movement from concrescent creativity to transitional creativity. Transitional creativity, or effectiveness for a future, signals the completion of the subjective aspect of existence for that particular unit.

In personal existence, this moment by moment passage of subjectivity is quick and hardly noticeable, like the many distinct frames of a movie that nonetheless yield a sense of singular continuity. The illusion is of an overall subjectivity, but the reality is a series of discrete units of subjectivity, each of which feels and to some extent recreates the subjectivity of the past in each new present. The continuity of the self depends upon the subjective incorporation of one's own immediate and distant past into the present. To put it in more common terms, the sense of self-continuity depends enormously upon that which we call memory. Our yesterdays are objective to our todays; even the self of a moment ago is objectively past to the self of the presently becoming moment. Perpetual perishing characterizes even personal existence.

But there is one momentous exception to this rule. God is the only reality whose subjectivity continues even while God is effective for others. The reasons for this exception are not arbitrary; we have given them in chapter three and in the appendix dealing more technically with the process model. Every finite unit of existence begins by feeling the influences of the past, and concludes by unifying those feelings into one determinate reality, called "satisfaction" by Whitehead. God, as the source of possibility, must be a reversal of this process of becoming, "beginning" in the satisfaction of a unified vision of all possibilities, and concrescing by incorporating feelings of the world into the divine subjectivity. There is thus an essential openness to the divine reality, an everlastingness that is copresent with every finite reality whatsoever. God is before all time, with all time, and beyond all time.

Thus when a new finite occasion comes into existence, it does so through the feelings of a finite past that is now objective, and through the feelings of a God who continues in subjectivity. Every finite element in the occasion's past is completed, finished, devoid of subjectivity; it is present to the new subject only in the mode of objectivity. But God, who is also present to the new subject, is present precisely as subject. In this sense, the occasion's feeling of God is unique. Might not this uniqueness be conveyed to the occasion?

Mysticism offers a number of parallels to our usage of the phenomenon of loneliness, for the mystic tends to move into areas of inwardness in search of the divine presence. If loneliness is a leveling of finite relationality, constituting all finite relations as superficial, there is a parallel sense whereby the mystic at least initially tends to categorize finite relations as insufficient for the soul's needs. The mystic frequently experiences a place of loneliness, a "dark night of the soul," in the inwardness of experience; the mystic, too, speaks of alienation and isolation. The parallel breaks down insofar as the person experiencing loneliness tends to do so not purposefully but meaninglessly. The individual does not seek loneliness, but is rather engulfed by loneliness. The mystic, however, usually intends the mystic journey. There is a purposiveness to the mystical experience of loneliness. The mystic seeks the divine presence on the other side of loneliness, and indeed expects it, or at least hopes for it. The lonely individual is more apt to stumble upon the divine presence, or to sense it as an unnamed and haunting possibility at the boundary of loneliness.

The purposiveness of the mystic is an openness to the presence of God. In account after account, mystics speak of God breaking into the soul in a fullness of presence, so that the consciousness of the mystic becomes entwined with consciousness of God as the copresent one. For the mystic, God's presence is not simply *to* the soul, but *in* the soul. Why not, if God's subjectivity is everlasting, and thus everlastingly copresent to every prehending occasion?

When the continuing presence of God can be conveyed to and in the soul through the influence of God upon the soul (the "initial aim" in process terminology), then we indeed can account for the sense of ultimacy in the divine presence. The depth dimension to the relation to God is based in the tremendous contrasts provided between God and the world—contrasts that are ordinarily hidden in the invariable presence of God, and in the world-directive content of the influence from God. When these contrasts begin to emerge through the peculiar condition of loneliness—or indeed, mysticism—then God as the supremely present one begins to be revealed.

What is the result of the sense of God's presence? Is the world devalued in contrast to the ultimacy provided by God? Following the process model, it is necessary to say that the sense of God's presence must push one back into the relationality of the everyday world. The understanding of God is of one who feels the world in order to offer redemptive possibilities to the world. To have a sense of God is to have a sense of God's purposes toward the well-being of the world. The more surely one is attuned to the reality of God, the more surely one is conformed to the divine purposes. But if the divine purposes are toward the good of the world, then to be aware of the divine presence is to be directed again toward the good of the world. If one laboriously crosses the empty places of loneliness in order to reach God, then one is flung back across those places into the everyday world of finite relationships. Conforming to God's purposes involves being plunged headlong again into a world wherein meaning is constantly being created through relationships. The presence of God releases us from loneliness to presence in the world, and in that finite world, we find ourselves again involved in the creation of meaning.

What, then, can we say theologically about God, based on this understanding of God as presence? If we push the experience and the model further in conjunction with Christian faith, God as presence leads also to an understanding of the faithfulness and love of God. The process model portrays God as giving us birth in every moment through the touch of the divine will for us. The model further portrays God as our destiny since God feels our reality upon the completion of every concrescing moment of our lives. God surrounds our moments, embracing our lives with the ever living divine presence. There is in this an intense faithfulness to God, for the import is that God continually provides presence, and that even in our deepest loneliness we might become aware of that presence.

Long ago the Psalmist cried out in awareness of God's surrounding presence, and the patriarchs and prophets voiced the revelation of God as a guiding presence. As Christians we name Jesus as an ultimate presence of God in human history, calling him Immanuel, "God with us." The process model, working with the dynamics of the experience of loneliness, simply explicates for our own relativity-conscious times what faith has long proclaimed: the nature of God is expressed through presence, and that presence is one of divine faithfulness and guidance.

God's presence is faithfulness because it is unfailing. Existence is impossible apart from the presence of God to us in our beginning and in our ending. God's presence is guiding, because the content of God's touch is directive, making present to us a way of being in the world. In the process model this is necessarily so, for God is the source of possibility for us precisely through God's interweaving of the feelings of the consequent nature with the vision of harmony in the primordial nature. That which God offers us is the best that can be for us, given the circumstances with which we have to work. God's presence to us is therefore also God's love for us, since unfailingly to will the good of the other is assuredly a component of that which we call love. Given this, we can also say that God's presence to us contains judgment, for the initial aim is surely an evaluation of our own past in terms of its possible good, and in terms of the wider good of the world to which we contribute our existence.

To say such things of God goes far beyond the initial experience of loneliness that presses us to say that God is an ultimate presence.

However, the sense in which loneliness is judged to be out of kilter with reality lends an existential basis to the statements. The restlessness in loneliness may give us the means to feel the aim of God, but to feel God as the source of the aim will lead to a renewed valuation of the content of the aim. And always, the aim of God will push us toward relation, creating value in the finite relations that are given to us, working for an optimum good. When in our loneliness we touch God, we know ourselves as also touched by God, and in the knowing, we are open to the pervasiveness of the divine presence. But it is the nature of the divine presence to nudge us back to the world, pushing us toward renewed attention to the content of that touching, guiding, creating aim for our good. The aim inexorably directs us toward our best way of constituting ourselves through and for the world.

As the world again becomes for us a place of importance, the contrasting sense of God as presence may dim to memory. The memory, however, finds its echoes in the world of finite relation—not in hollowness in the prison of an empty self, but in the fullness of finite forms of presence. The inward presence of God turns to the outward presence of God, for the God who is present to us is present to others as well. The God who guides us guides others also; the God who cares for us cares also for others. The whole world is touched by God, and therefore the world can mediate God's presence to us. Divine presence pervades finite presence, launching us into the world again, for its good and for ours. Meaninglessness fades, crowded out by presence, and presence—human and divine—insists upon and achieves the meaning of love.

6

GOD AS WISDOM

THE doctrine of God as wisdom relates to needs experienced as a result of our temporality. Temporality involves us in the situation of "perpetual perishing," wherein the passage of time undermines every achievement, challenges every relationship, threatens every good. Ultimately, of course, the many experiences of loss we undergo in our lifetime are like prophecies of the final loss of ourselves through death. Temporality involves us in uncertainty and insecurity, and can evoke our anxiety and fear.

We might try to answer the problem of time by dwelling not on the past, but on the future. The future, with its lure toward possibility, creates in us a restlessness with present achievement so that the loss of such achievement itself becomes a positive thing, a movement beyond ourselves toward some new goal. Thus the future addresses the problem of temporality by redeeming the past through promises of richness yet to come. We plan a particular future: on the personal level, the possibility of studying this subject, marrying this person, contributing through this profession; on the societal level, the possibility of achieving a just peace, an equitable commonwealth, a healthy and thriving environment. With such futures possible, what difference does the sureness of loss make? Life is worth the encounters with death it entails. And surely both past and future offer compensations for the peculiar loss each offers. Against an improbable future, there is a savoring of the past through its present power in memory. When, on the contrary, the past holds too much pain, it can be transcended by an emphasis on a new future. But neither the past nor the future can be erased. Both impinge upon our presentness in an ambiguous mixture of loss and hope.

So long as the present is experienced as fulfillment, the ambiguity of loss and hope can be interpreted positively. The very edges of the present in past and future sharpen the brightness of the moment, giving it the added delight of giftedness. Because the present moment was not, but is; because it is, but will not be, there is an inherent marvel in its presentness at all. The temporal nature of the present, bounded by a past and future that it will be and was, gives intensity and zest and wonder to each moment—but only so long as the content of each moment is not antagonistic to well-being.

It is impossible, in finite existence where value competes for value and each choice is a denial of other choices, for every moment to be experienced as fulfillment. The temporality that gives such delight also holds terrors, and finite existence is plunged into both. Time is both life and death. The transience of the present can as easily evoke anxiety and insecurity as delight and zest.

Traditionally, the doctrine of God's omniscience has been one powerful way of answering the terror and ambiguity of time. The power of divine knowledge is such that the past and the future are eternally present to God. If they are eternally present, then "past" and "future" are but finite experiences that are swallowed up in God, and by attempting to align oneself with the divine viewpoint one can make peace with the terrors of time.

A problem with this answer is that it answers the problems of time by denying time. Traditionally, the attribute of divine omniscience has been associated with God's knowledge of all things at all times and all places. God encompasses all times in the single totality of divine knowledge. Past, present, and future are but a finite unfolding of that which has, is, and always will be known to God in a single seeing. Consequently, past, present, and future are finite distinctions, perceptions from the limited perspective available to us. In God, all times are as one, and hence known in an eternal insight wherein past, present, and future are forever present in one eternal "now."

Notice how easily this doctrine of God's knowledge addresses the problems of temporality. Is the past lost? But the past is not really past, for it is present in the eternality of God. The pastness of things is perspectival, rooted in our finite limitation. The past only *seems* to be lost. Another way of saying it is that while the past may be lost to us, it is not lost to God. Therefore, the past is as present as God.

How does God's knowledge address the future as threat? In the traditional formulation of God's knowledge, there is no room for contingency. If God knows the future, then God knows it infallibly as that which will take place. It is known to God as if it had already taken place. Will it rain in Chicago on July 9, 2188? God knows that it will! Is there any way, then, in which that rainy day is contingent, or the continuation of the city known as Chicago is in doubt? Is it not as sure as the divine knowledge? Contingency (and with it, the freedom to be otherwise) is but the necessary illusion of finitude, describing not events themselves but our knowing of events. Could we know as God knows, contingency would be eliminated, and with it, time as well. For if we knew infallibly what would happen, precisely as it would occur, then is not that "future" present? And if present, how could it ever become past? The creation of the past depends upon successiveness, upon a future crowding ever anew into a present, rendering that which once was present, past.

Thus the traditional function of God's knowledge in relation to the problems of our finite temporality is fundamentally to deny the reality of time. If God's knowledge is such that the past and the future are continuously present in God, then distinctions are finally not real distinctions, but simply descriptive of our limited knowing. In the denial of temporality, there is neither the perpetual perishing of value nor the threat to the attainment of value. The past is not really lost, and the future will not really replace the present. Nor are the possibilities of the future really shrouded in clouds of contingency, such that the fear of the past is intensified by anxiety over the future. Fear and anxiety should melt away with the comforting knowledge that in God's knowledge, past and future are engulfed in an eternal present.

This interpretation of God's knowledge, phrased in variations of the above by theologians throughout the Christian tradition, creates a tension with our own temporal experience of knowledge. Is knowledge without temporality still knowledge in any meaningful sense? If, in fact, the transience of time is integral to every moment of our experience, can the abstraction of that transience still yield a knowledge of the same thing? For example, a child anticipates the advent of a particular day, so that the days preceding the awaited one take on their meaning in light of their closeness to the longed-for day. Moving toward Christmas, or a birthday, or a summer

vacation, crowds each day of waiting with an importance of anticipation. The experience of transience is so integral to the child's
self-understanding that if the experience is abstracted through a
knowledge that reifies the present, then the present is paradoxically
lost. Time is so integral to human experience that if human experience is to be known at all, it must be known as temporal.

It will not do to say there is a nontemporal knowing of the
temporal. Such a knowing reduces the moments of living to an
empty shell, devoid of any depth understanding of internal reality. It
is more akin to knowledge gained from seeing a photograph, as
opposed to knowledge gained from living the experience that the
photograph symbolizes. There is a capturing of observed time, but
the life that made it worth capturing in the first place is missing. To
know the temporal nontemporally would be to distort the temporal,
and thus not to know it as fully or as richly as its actual experience
demands. Thus a knowledge of the temporal that denies temporality
is not a true knowledge at all. If one looks to such a "knowing" as a
security against the terrors of transience, one is caught in the
dilemma that the security, not the transience, is illusory. A divine
knowledge that denies temporality is less-than-perfect knowledge,
and cannot address the problems of time.

If the above is valid, then it follows that there can be no security
against history as such. Not even divine knowledge can protect
from the sureness of loss, for there can be no divine viewpoint that
obliterates the reality of our temporal condition. Is there no re-
course, then? Is the God discovered as presence, the God who is
before us, with us, and after us, spanning all our times, irrelevant to
the peculiar finite problem of time? How ironic if the God who
answers our spatial alienations through the uniqueness of divine
presence is powerless to answer our temporal anxieties precisely
because the perfection of divine knowledge cannot deny that which
is real.

If we attempt an understanding of God based upon the dynamics
of existence as process, then it will follow that God's knowledge is
precise, knowing all reality just as it knows itself. Temporality is
introduced into the divine nature. But because temporality is introduced into God's nature, there emerges the power not of mere
knowledge, but of wisdom. This wisdom offers trust and hope in the
midst of our histories.

In this model, God's knowledge must be considered in light of the primordial and consequent aspects of God. God's primordial nature is the conceptual vision of all possibilities whatsoever, harmonized in the very process of being known. God's knowledge of possibilities is God's valuation of possibilities, ranking them into harmonies of order, beauty, and goodness. In this knowing valuation, God unifies all possibilities—*all* possibilities. Such a vision calls for symbols and metaphors, for if God's primordial vision is inclusive of all possibilities whatsoever, then this vision goes beyond our imagination. That there are infinite possibilities can be grasped by us, but if we attempt to fill in the content of the possibilities, and then to order them in terms of ultimate complementation and beauty, we stagger at the task. "Infinity" then becomes a symbol for that which is more than we can think. Accordingly, the process model posits an infinite primordial nature in God for the ordering of infinite possibilities into infinite harmony. God's knowledge through the primordial nature is precisely of possibility in infinite modes of suggested existence.

Note, however, the accuracy of this knowledge: it is a knowledge of *that which is possible*. That the possible is ordered into harmony is not a function of the possibilities, but a function of God, conveying the actuality of harmony to possibles without annihilating their nature as possibility. The primordial vision is a knowledge of the possible as possible; it is not a knowledge of the possible as actual—and herein lies the reality of the future in its character of genuine possibility, and therefore contingency. *Which* possibility becomes actual in finite history is indeterminate.

The consequent nature of God is God's feeling of every occasion that ever existed. It is not God's feeling of that which *will* exist, for until a thing is actual, it is only possible. Hence there is a distinction in divine knowledge. Through the consequent nature, God knows all actuality whatsoever. It rains in a city called Chicago on a certain day. Does God know it? How? In the process understanding, God knows it by feeling it, both through the reality of the drops of moisture as they fall and through the experience of wetness as the drops touch the earth, be it upon the pavement, or a leaf upon a tree, or the wet cheek of a secretary rushing to reach shelter from the unexpected noontide storm. Every actuality that comes into existence, human or otherwise, is felt by God in its entirety, just as it felt itself.

The primordial nature of God is God's knowledge of possibility; the consequent nature of God is God's knowledge of actuality; the unity of God, or the integration of the consequent with the primordial, is the wisdom of God and the source of God's redemptive providence for the world. The process model suggests that the fullness of God's knowledge and the dynamics of God's wisdom depend upon the divine reversal of the conceptual and physical poles. Without this reversal, there could be only partial knowledge in God, even as there is only partial knowledge in finite reality.

Our knowledge is always partial for several reasons: First, our own purposes and language distort our knowledge of otherness. We see things "in order to. . . .", thus introducing our own agenda into our consideration of things. Things are known not "in themselves," but "as they might be for us." Further, the very language we use in our knowing "baptizes" that which is known into the human community. Do we know a rock? But rocks are foundations, or seats, or landscape accents, or walls, or combinations of minerals, or witnesses to the vast formative powers of the earth—however we know a rock, the language we use brings that rock into the parameters of human experience. What it is outside our experience is inaccessible to us, so that no matter how extensive our knowledge, we will always live in a universe of essential mystery. The linguisticality of our knowing, together with our sense of purposiveness, deeply condition our knowledge of otherness.

Second, we know through "perspectival elimination." This means that we know selectively, from our own viewpoint. We understand through that which is given to our view, whether actually or metaphorically. In process terms, the many must become one—but this becoming demands the simplification of the many, a sifting of the data presented to us in terms of its compatibility with our sensory system and our categories of knowing. Incompatibilities are eliminated from perception, often irrecoverably. What finally comes to us as knowledge has been transmuted in terms of our own unique standpoint in the world.

Third, the very multiplicity of things-to-be-known introduces a conditioning effect. Each item in our past is conditioned by its companions, so that our knowledge of it is always contextual. Partly this is because we see and understand objectively—we do not understand another subject on its own terms, but only on our interpretation of its own terms. This interpretation includes our perception of its context—but its own experience of its context may be quite another matter. In any case, context conditions all knowledge.

The process model expresses this through the dynamics of becoming. The many energies of the past, together with the guiding energy of God, evoke a new subject of becoming. The new subject becomes *subject* by sifting, contrasting, comparing, and unifying each of these influences in light of its evaluation of its own immediate possibilities. In this process, possibility is turned to actuality, but only through a process of selection: selection of a single possibility in light of the data, and selective evaluation of the data in terms of that possibility. There is a mutual conditioning of possibility and data, until finally the subject simplifies and unifies them into just this one actuality. The manyness of the data launches the process, and the union with possibility completes the process; between beginning and end, there is an enormous elimination and transmutation of data. The implications of this process for those occasions enjoying consciousness and knowledge is that the end result of knowledge is always a transformation of the initial data. There is a connection with what is known, since there is a flow of feeling from "there" to "here," but the connection is not a direct correspondence between knowledge and that which knowledge is about. It is knowledge of the other as conditioned by its context and by the complexity of the knowing subject.

What difference does it make to God's knowledge that God, unlike finite reality, does not "begin" with the manifold feelings of data from the world, but rather "begins" primordially with the unification of all possibility into one mighty divine harmony? The point to be made is that because of this reversal, God and only God can know each unit of actuality precisely as it experiences and/or knows itself.

God, "beginning" in reverse of the finite occasions, is eternally unified in terms of the primordial vision. Since this vision is a harmony of *all* possibilities, there is no actuality that cannot fit into that primordial harmony. Actuality will intensify that harmony, but it cannot destroy it or lessen it. If *every* possibility has been ordered within God's primordial harmony, then no possibility-become-actuality can reverse that harmony. It can only contribute to the ever deepening intensity of a harmony continuously being actualized through God's feeling of the actuality in the world. Thus there is no categorical reason why God cannot feel the entirety of any finite occasion, without perspectival elimination.

The reverse is rather the case. If God's primordial vision is a harmony of possibilities, then the actuality of God acts as an impetus to the realization of the vision in terms of its component parts. That is, there is a primordial actuality to the harmony of God by virtue of God's own reality. The reality, however, is imposed upon a universe of possibles—the possibilities themselves do not strive for existence, but the reality of God strives toward their existence in order that the feelings of harmony in the vision might become intensified by the everlasting actualization of that harmony. How can this actualization take place? Only as the possibilities are realized outside the nature of God, and then received into the nature of God. The fullness of the actuality in the world intensifies the actual reality of the vision of God. Given such a situation, far from requiring selectivity for the divine concrescence, God requires the opposite—a full feeling, or prehension, of the totality of finite reality.

The effects of this for the knowledge of God are simply that God, and only God, knows every reality, every actuality, precisely as it experienced itself. Was the finite occasion conscious? Then God experiences it so. Was it painful? Then God feels its pain, not from the outside, but from the inside. Was it insentient? Then it remains insentient in God's knowledge of it. God's prehensions of the world feel the world in the entirety of every atomistic bit of the world. God's knowledge of the world, then, is absolute and complete, even to the inclusion of its own experience of temporality.

The possibilities of the primordial nature and the actualities felt in the consequent nature thus constitute the knowledge of God. The wisdom of God is not simply God's knowledge, but God's use of that which is known. God's integration of the consequent nature into the primordial nature is the reality of God's wisdom—and it is God's wisdom, rather than God's knowledge per se, that saves us.

In the integration of the consequent and primordial natures, God feels the world as it is and as it might be. God's initial feeling is of the world as it is; God's subsequent feelings within the mightiness of God's own existence is the judgment and transformation of the world into participation in the primordial vision. It is this judgment and transformation of the world that constitutes the divine becoming, or the everlasting integration of the primordial and consequent natures.

We said that God feels the world as it is and as it might be. God feels the world as it is, by enacting an exact transmission of feeling through prehending the entirety of the subject. This will be developed more particularly in chapter 16, when we deal with the possibility of everlasting life. God's feeling of the world as it might be has a double reference. On the one hand, God feels the newly prehended world in terms of its possible transformation into God's harmony; on the other hand, God feels the newly prehended world in terms of the finite harmonies now made possible in the becoming world. The finite harmony will be a reflection of the divine harmony as adapted to the world's condition.

Since the divine harmony is one of enormous inclusiveness, wherein all the world is integrated into God's own being, reflections of that harmony in history will also push the world toward societies with the widest possible forms of inclusive well-being. The degree to which individuals/societies reflect inclusive well-being is the degree to which they reflect the image of God. The degree is conditioned by relevance to the immediate past of the world, by the limitations of finitude, and by the freedom of every actuality to adapt God's guidance to its own purposes. Within these conditions, God prompts the becoming world toward its own best utilization of its past and its own highest creativity for itself and the future. In this sense, the integrative wisdom of God continuously offers redemptive possibilities to the world.

The effect of God's wisdom is that no matter what threats and contingencies we may experience, God is faithful to lead us into a creative mode of dealing with these problems. This follows from the fact that God's wisdom is not a cold calculation of bits and pieces of knowledge, as if God were some gigantic computer knowing all things and feeding information to the world. Rather, God's wisdom follows from the divine feeling, wherein God feels the world and thus knows the world in a coexperience. This feeling knowledge, integrated within the depths of the divine resources in the primordial nature, becomes a redemptive wisdom for the world, a creative wisdom, a faithful wisdom, offering modes of being to us as real possibilities that have been deemed so through the depths of God's ordering in absolute knowledge of that which is and that which can be.

In accordance with this, the previous statement of God's knowledge of the future as traditionally formulated must be revised. God knows the range of possible futures that lie before us, given our total situations. In God's knowledge of our possible futures, God must also know the probable future. After all, while it is inaccurate to name God's knowledge as computer-like, it would be absurd to think of God's knowledge as less than that which we can create through our own technology. God, knowing all actuality in varying patterned responses, knows the combinations that predict the probabilities of our futures. But even for God, the element of contingency is real; that which happens finally depends upon those choices whereby the world, in its solitariness, chooses from among its alternatives that which it will become. And God waits upon the world's decisions.

How does this affect our problems with temporality? A process view can align itself with the understanding that the past is made present in God. However, as will be seen in the development of chapter 16, this is more than simple preservation. Rather, it is a living knowledge of every occurrence according to its own self-experience. Because of the absolute accuracy of this knowledge, transformation of the past from its own perspective is possible in God. Thus God's knowledge of the past is a knowledge transforming the past through wisdom. The past is therefore both preserved and yet transformed through the medium of divine knowledge and wisdom. Our own dealings with the past as loss can become positive and creative as we ourselves reflect this process. For us the past is preserved through memory. But the transformation of the past is not in its memory, but in ourselves. The finite mirroring of the divine process can lead us into creative ways of dealing with the loss of the past.

What of fear of the future? The primordial nature is the source of the future, for the primordial nature is the locus of possibilities. The future is that indefinite complex of possibilities from which we forge each new present; hence the future, as possibility, has its locus in God's primordial nature. Which possibility shall materialize out of the future as a newly made present depends on God and on us, thus contingency is real, awaiting the outcome of finite decision and divine integration of those decisions with the realm of the possible. Since, however, the availability of possible futures to us does depend upon God as well as upon us, we can have a realistic hope and trust with regard to the future.

This follows from the everlasting integration of the primordial and consequent natures of God into the unity of the divine life. This integration constitutes God as an everlasting presence. Note the distinction: one must say God is an everlasting presence, not an everlasting present. The differentiation is that God is the co-presence of all the world within the unity of the divine nature, and the co-presence with all the world in its varied histories. In God the world is resurrected to its everlasting fullness and transformation. Within the single reality of God, then, all that has ever existed continuously participates in the divine adventure, co-present to each other and to God in the unity of God. This mighty God is likewise co-present to the world in the world's own continuous development, the Subject present to every finite subject. God is therefore a Presence, existing in subjective fullness, containing and grounding time through prehension of the world, integration of the world into the divine harmony, and provision of the world's future. God's presence and God's wisdom are the same reality.

From our finite perspective, then, God as presence is God as guidance for our future, or God as wisdom. If God's presence with us is always a guidance relative to our immediate future, then our attitude toward the future can undergo a radical change from that fear and insecurity that was first cited. If we feel the future as fearsome, as a threat to the values we hold dear or the values we hope yet to achieve, the sense that God's wisdom is ever given in guiding aims can allow us to accept the challenges of the future, to dare its risks. No matter what contingencies or wrong choices occur, either inadvertently or willfully, God's guidance is faithfully redemptive. God as wisdom, against the openness and contingency of the future, evokes our trust instead of fear.

Finally, a sense of God's wisdom with regard to our temporality forces us to accept our responsibility for our own future. We can trust God to offer redemptive possibilities, no matter what may transpire—but what it is that will have to be redeemed depends upon the activity of the world. God's redemptive activity conjoins with our own responsively creative activity. It does not obliterate our activity. We become God's coworkers, and the future follows upon the choices of our responsive activity. God invites us into a future that we must create in our response to God. In our awareness of divine wisdom, we replace fear with trust, and move into the contingencies of time. And God waits.

7

GOD AS POWER

DIVINE presence answers the human need of loneliness, and loneliness itself may offer a key to knowing the ultimate presence that is God. Loneliness gives way to love. Divine wisdom answers the problem of insecurity, eliciting trust when the contingencies of time would evoke our fear. Thus God as presence and wisdom answers problems experienced by the individual: loneliness is the alienation of the individual from society, and insecurity falls primarily to individuals facing the problems of the past and the future. What is the importance of God's power for us? What is at stake in our conviction that God is omnipotent?

Whereas divine presence and wisdom answer individual problems, power is related to the societal problem of justice. Justice is the inclusive well-being of society: a society has well-being when its structure insures not only that the basic needs of its participants are met, but that each participant can develop his or her human potential to the benefit of self and society. Interdependence and reciprocity are involved, together with a valuation of the diversity of talent and ability in human existence. A dynamism necessarily infuses such a society, for a society actively attuned to well-being will continuously transform its structures according to the emergent needs. Inclusiveness is involved not simply when the well-being of those within the society is valued, but when the society itself exists in reciprocity of well-being with other structured communities and with the environment.

We ordinarily understand justice to refer not only to the maintenance of good in mutual well-being, but also to the redress of evil and the restoration of well-being to those for whom it has been violated or lost. However, if the first brief description given above seemed visionary, then this second qualification means that a full justice can never be achieved. Too often injustice has crushed its victims, making reparation impossible. How is a broken mind repaired, a lost limb returned, a stunted ability to love reshaped, a murder undone?

Often in our histories persons have been outraged at societal injustice, and inflamed to the point of revolution in order to bring about a just society according to a new vision. The power of that vision motivates the struggle, but it encounters the entrenched powers of past and present. Inevitably, the movement toward what-might-be involves loss of present values and/or lives. If that future vision is made a present reality, then perhaps a wider form of well-being is attained—but those who were lost in the process of its attainment do not participate in the new order. And some, whose well-being depended, in fact, upon the old order, will find the new "justice" to be a most unjust factor in their continuing lives. Historical justice is partial.

The more one begins to consider the problem of justice, the more impossible and visionary any full justice appears to be. Admittedly, the difficulty lies in the perfection of justice visualized, for if one pushes a notion of justice as an inclusiveness of mutual well-being, then plainly the notion becomes an impossible dream. Only if the past can somehow be brought into the present, and only if a sufficient flexibility of vision can allow radical diversities to co-exist in well-being, only then can justice in its fullest dimensions be established. Under the circumstances of our finitude, however, such conditions cannot be secured. Is the notion of justice necessarily to be tailored to a smaller scale so that we might find contentment in lesser conditions?

To do so, however, involves three dangers. The first concerns the very nature of justice itself insofar as it concerns itself with relationships of well-being in society. If the field of justice is restricted to any area or group or time, so that some are categorically outside the range of well-being, then justice is contradicted at its core. The contradiction is like a cancer allowed to exist within an otherwise strong body. Unchecked, the cancer infiltrates the healthy cells; the body sickens, dies. When a body of people constitute themselves as a society of justice, actualize conditions of well-being for many within that body, and yet systematically exclude others from participation, then the so-called justice harbors sickness within it that can destroy the health of the whole body of people.

Likewise, when a society of justice turns in upon itself, ignoring conditions of injustice beyond its border, then justice itself is fed by injustice. In a relational world, no entity, be it cell or society, can exist apart from its receiving and giving to others. The society that turns in upon itself denies the extent to which its very existence is dependent upon other societies beyond its borders. It does, in fact draw from those societies. If it allows injustice to reign unchecked—or if, in fact, its self-concern leads to its fostering conditions of injustice upon other societies, then once again, justice is contradicted. The body is cancerous. Accepted limitations to justice contradict the nature of justice, and hence lead to its decay into injustice.

A second danger lies not with the contradiction to the nature of justice entailed by its limitations in scope or vision, but in complacency. If well-being is the foundation of a society, then the society must be dynamic. A new generation succeeds the old; new technologies replace the old; new problems crowd out old answers. In a society where well-being is acceptably restricted to some, justice moves in a closed, contained channel. The definitions that form that closure and rationalize the restrictions cut off the routes of novelty that could infuse the society with needed dynamism. Instead, the status quo is a valued condition that must be maintained against the disruptions of new perspectives and questions. Insofar as the effort to block out changes of an extensive nature succeeds, then stagnation occurs: dynamism is lost, complacency replaces vision, and justice withers.

Finally, unless a vision of justice holds within it the real possibility of its fulfillment, it cannot inspire the hope that is so necessary to effective action. For example, the summary statement on a society of justice given at the beginning of this chapter is admittedly visionary, but if it is *only* that, then paradoxically it is no vision of justice at all, but a chimera like the grapes forever beyond the reach of the hungering Tantalus of Greek mythology. Visions of justice that have no empowerment within them contribute to injustice through the quenching of hope.

For example, consider the dilemma of groups long oppressed seeking a new society structured for the well-being of all peoples. The longer the group has been oppressed, the more tenuous the hope will be that society will change in openness to their well-being. There is a profoundly existential reason behind women's search for a society in the past, be it biblical or mythical, where women and men together cooperated in the creation of a society for the good of both. If no such society ever existed, where is the hope that a contemporary society of justice between men and women can be realized? The hope must be borne entirely by the future, calling the present to transformation. But a hope with no hold on history teases the heart with too much anxiety. Is the sought after vision realizable at all, if in fact there is no evidence that somewhere, sometime, it was not only possible but real that women and men achieved a society of equality? The realizable nature of a goal is the difference between hope and despair. Hope is catalytic, giving momentum to efforts that can accomplish the goal. Despair is debilitating, draining one's energy into the negative achievement of failure.

Women are but one group seeking a new society that defies past history. Persons with handicapping conditions, rendered "invisible" by a callous culture, claim a place of recognized worth in the world. Third world countries, long under the sway of colonialism or its successor of hopeless indebtedness to countries they themselves have helped to make rich, seek a world of true reciprocity and well-being. African-Americans, caught in a culture so innured to its modes of racist oppression that it seldom deigns to notice its own racism, nonetheless call for the culture's transformation. But what reason is there for any group to think society might be different?

We find ourselves, then, in a strange situation. Justice, to be sought, must be visualized as achievable. An illusory justice cannot inspire the necessary hope. But our finite situation is one where we have never experienced any society of full justice. Even if it could be attained for a present generation, we know that the component of justice that requires redress for past wrongs is simply impossible in many cases. And yet we strive for justice, sometimes against overwhelming odds. Societies traditionally form hierarchical orders, with designated groups kept in menial positions of servitude in order to support a higher standard of living for the privileged. Isn't the system so entrenched in human nature that it cannot change? Perhaps the most that can be hoped for is that one subservient group might climb higher, leaving its slotted position to yet another more subordinate class. The pragmatics of our world mitigate against hope that justice can be achieved for all.

And yet we do work. We dare to dream. We struggle against odds. How is it that we maintain a vision of justice, insist that it can be actualized, and throw our very lives into its achievement? The hope cannot be rooted in our finite experience, for all of our experience denies the full condition of justice. How paradoxical, that we nevertheless experience hope—and how thoroughly necessary this is for the gains that are made and that might yet be made.

But perhaps the power of hope against despair is not paradoxical at all. Perhaps it rests with the nature of God as the power for justice. God is the source of the vision and of the reality; there is a locus for justice in the nature of God. The effect of God upon us is the transmission of vision, along with the conviction of its worth and attainability. God is the source of hope. This is the significance of the doctrine of divine power for us.

To probe the reasons for this, consider again the dynamics of the process model, compared with the dynamics of justice. In each unit of existence, the many become one, giving rise to a new value in the universe. This becoming involves an integration of the felt values of the past—the one, in freedom, chooses those elements best suited to its own ideal of itself, and creates itself by weaving the many influences of the past into its own new unity. This new reality, forged in the freedom and privacy of becoming, is ultimately given again to the many: the individual creation is offered to the future, in part evoking that future into being. Just as this unit inherited from many in its past, now it becomes the legacy for its own future. Its own enrichment, made possible by others, is now given for the enrichment of others.

These dynamics are remarkably similar to a dynamic description of justice. In a just society, the one and the many—the individual and the community—would interrelate in a mutually enriching harmony. The conditions of the society would be conducive to the well-being of the individual, making that well-being possible. As the individual freely develops in a richness of existence, that individual contributes value toward the increasing richness of society. Interdependence in relationality is a basic condition of justice. Acting for the other's good is at the same time acting for one's own good, and the impoverishment of one is the impoverishment of all.

Note the two forms of power involved. There is the power of self-creativity and the power of influencing others. In Whiteheadian terms, there is the "concrescent power" of the subject for itself, and the "transitional power" of the subject for others. In both cases, there are natural limitations to power. In the instance of self-creativity, one is limited by the possibilities of one's nature and of society's structure. A person cannot choose to be a bird or a tree, or to leap tall buildings at a single bound—these do not belong to the possibilities of human existence. There are natural limitations placed upon human self-creativity, and they are fixed. Society's structure further defines possibilities, but in a more fluid way—societal restrictions are based not upon nature, but upon custom. Therefore, these limitations are subject to question and change.

The limitations to power in its transitional, influential mode are even more marked. No one is the sole influence on others, nor can anyone fully determine one's effects upon others. For example, Joan has found a satisfying career in pharmacy, and decides to persuade a friend also to enter the field. She brings all her influence to bear: her own delight with the work, the pressing need for more pharmacists, and the career opportunities involved. Joan exercises her influence upon her friend, but so do others, and Joan's influence is balanced by theirs. Ultimately, of course, it is the friend who determines how influential Joan can be in light of his own self-assessment of visions and possibilities. Joan's power of influence is therefore limited by the fact that she can never be the sole influence, and by the fact that her friend must decide for himself. Hence transitional power is limited both through its context of manyness, and through the self-creativity of the influenced individual.

How do these two forms of power apply to God, and how can such an application give us confidence that there is indeed a realm of pure justice? In process theology, God is described in terms of the dynamics of existence, with the single difference that in God the dynamics move from the mental pole to the physical pole, or from vision to feeling, rather than from the physical to the mental. This reversal of the poles becomes particularly important when considered in relation to the extent of God's self-creative power.

Self-creative power is the ability to integrate all influences in terms of what one wills to be. This decision is limited only by the possibilities defining the parameters of one's reality. But what are the limitations on possibility for deity? Where do we look to find these parameters? In our own situations, we look to the givenness of what it is to be human in the many instances of human beings, and in the shared physical characteristics variously manifested in the genetic make-up of human beings. "Humankind" is a class that limits what any member of that class can be. But if God is one, then obviously there is no class of deities predetermining the limits of what any god can be. The parameters of deity are found within the self-contained possibilities of the single reality that is God. However, it appears that *all* possibilities have their locus in God. The only limitation upon actualization of particular kinds of possibilities would appear to be the constructive limitation of existence itself—for if God is to exist, the possibilities must be unified. Unification is order and valuation in terms of harmony—the terms are almost synonyms with one another. The implication is that for God to exist—for the infinite possibilities to be localized at all—God must be good. God, by self-definition, must be good, for if God were not a unification, a harmonization, of all possibilities, God simply would not be. Yet it is a self-definition, for how this harmonization takes place requires a divine ordering of all possibilities. The very ordering is free in that it is God self-determining the divine existence both in terms of the *that* and in terms of the *how* of unification.

Is there a question then of the beginning of God—of a time when God was not, when there existed simply the sheer domain of possibility, out of which a singular divine entity becomes self-created? But how could this be? It finally comes down to the paradoxical situation that possibilities simply do not exist unless there is a something for which they are possible. If there is no actuality, then there is no possibility. This means that to talk of possibilities pre-existing God is to talk nonsense, so that we are forced to the conclusion that possibilities *are* because God *is*. We must say that

God is the eternally self-created one, created out of the divine concrescent power, self-determined from all possibilities, existing necessarily in goodness. What is God's power relative to the divine existence? Absolute, when considered in relation to the self-decided character of God, and when considered in relation to the primordial nature of God.

But if that's what God's self-creative power would be relative to possibilities, what would God's power be relative to the influences God receives from the world? For if God's existence is relational, then God does indeed receive from the world. And these influences must be integrated into the divine nature. God is not only a mental pole, or a primordial nature, but also a physical pole, or consequent nature. This aspect of God's nature is consequent upon both the primordial ordering that is the self-determined divine character, and the happenings in the universe.

God's power, relative to the integration of the physical feelings of the world into the divine nature, is again absolute—not in terms of what is integrated (save indirectly), but in terms of how it is integrated. What God feels depends upon what the world has become, and this "whatness" is partially the result of God's influence in the first place, but, more determinately, it is the result of the world's decisive utilization of God's influence in its own self-becoming. This would be the world's transitional influence upon God. But how God deals with those influences is sheerly within the control of the divine power. Is God the harmonization of all possibilities in a valuation solely self-determined? Then God will feel the various occasions of the world in light of the divine will toward harmony. Such evaluative feelings mean that God feels the world in relation to God's own harmony, both with regard to finite modes of harmony and with regard to the ultimate divine harmony.

Judgment is inexorably involved in God's feelings of the world, and in the integration of those feelings within the divine nature. The world, felt through the physical pole, would be pulled into a harmonious unification with the mental pole in the unity of God. God, in concrescent power, exercises full control over what will be done with the world in this divine unification, for God exercises unlimited power in the divine self-definition. In this omnipotence, God is the final and full achievement of justice.

The many for one and the one for the many: justice involves a rhythmic interdependence; justice involves a mutual enrichment and harmony. In Part V we will develop an argument for the resurrection of the world in God so that the world, felt by God, would be understood to participate subjectively in the divine harmony. Insofar as that interpretation is coherent and consistent with the process frame of reference, then it will build upon the omnipotence of God with respect to the divine concrescence to make the notion of God as justice more concrete. God is heaven, and heaven is God. The many finally enjoy the unity of the one, each contributing what value has been achieved and benefitting from the values of others in the transformation of judgment and harmony. Justice is not an illusory dream; justice is as real as God.

If God exercises omnipotent power over the integration of the world within the divine nature, thus everlastingly overcoming evil in justice, what is the power of God for us in relation to the temporal order of things in history? How, if at all, does this transcendent realm of justice address our finite experience of the mixture of justice and injustice? Can it provide us with a vision of justice in history?

In a process universe, everything affects everything else: to be for oneself is also to be for others. To know concrescent power is also to create transitional power. The power of becoming issues into the power of influence. That which one is, one is for the universe. This is no less true for God than for the most insignificant portion of actuality: to be is to have an effect. As God feels the world and pulls the divinely recreated world into divine justice, this actualized reality of justice itself gives rise to God's feeling for optimum modes of justice in the becoming world. Therefore, God's continuous influence upon the world is always in terms of specific modes of order for the diversely becoming world that reflect to whatever degree possible the divine justice. This reflection is limited by what the world can or will bear but it is an influence toward increasing orders of well-being. God leads the world toward an achievable goal of justice. That the vision of justice is achievable is due to God; whether or not the justice is actually achieved is due to the world.

The justice that is inherent in God's influence for the world may be controverted. This follows from the very structure of existence. That the many are for the one and the one for the many is simply part of the order of things. How each one participates in this order depends upon the self-creative decision of each entity.

Because of interdependence, injustice is possible. Given the denial of responsibility on the part of the one, the many will suffer. However, it is also interdependence that makes justice possible. Given the nature of reciprocal existence and the requisite of order for a world, this order may manifest harmony of the one and the many in justice. Whether or not it does rests with the responsibility of the world. That it can, in specific modes suited to time and place, rests with the influence of God. God and the world together are responsible for the reality of justice in the world. The power of God makes it possible, and the responsive activity of the world makes it real.

Given the role of God's power in the achievement of justice, and given our increased awareness of our own responsibilities in an interdependent universe, there is a ground for hope despite injustice. The dynamics of existence make injustice possible, but only as a perversion of the interdependence that allows the growth of order in the first place. Interdependence, working smoothly as the many for the one and for the many, is the divinely created basis of order, and therefore is the foundation of the universe. To work toward justice is to work with the dynamics of reality. Divine power assures it. Further, inasmuch as the mode of justice that is seen relative to any situation is a mode that is suited to the world through the creative ordering of God, then that mode of justice is truly achievable. Once achieved, it will be surpassable, opening up still further modes of justice. This is necessarily the case in a process universe. But that it is achievable is also the case, based upon the reality of a God who orders all possibilities in justice, and fits possibilities to the world in a realistic fashioning of optimum modes of existence. Since modes of justice are thus grounded in reality, and are really achievable, then hope is appropriately a component in all our efforts toward achieving our visions of justice. Hope is catalytic, and ultimately is the most important ingredient in the struggle for justice, insuring the perseverance that brings justice about.

The reality of God's power relative to the world is such that there is ground to hope for the achievement of justice. This hope is due to the concrescent power of God as the locus of full justice in the transformation of the world, and to the faithfulness of God's influential power. God influences the world in keeping with the divine character, and thus leads the world toward modes of justice. So we address the evils of our existence in the hope that they can be overcome.

Part Three

GOD AS PRESENCE

God in Christ:
A Process Christology

8

JESUS

GOD of presence, God of wisdom, God of power: a discussion of God based on general revelation can lead to an affirmation of such a God. However, it would be foolish to pretend that such conclusions about God are drawn strictly from a disinterested perspective, as if all persons at all places could derive such opinions concerning God based on an analysis of the world. All knowledge is conditioned by perspective, and when a consideration of God based on a process analysis of the world is done from a Christian frame of reference, then that frame of reference, including its texts and traditions, influences the resultant analysis and conclusions. General revelation, it must be remembered, is a *Christian* category. It speaks of a way of interpreting the world of our experience apart from explicit reference to biblical categories, yet with a faith stance that seeks the unity between the world of nature, human nature, and God.

The Christian perspective in our treatment thus far is apparent in the traces of redemption that are included in the analysis of the previous chapters: God as presence answers alienation and loneliness with love; God as wisdom answers the loss of time with trust; God as power answers injustice with empowering hope. This vision of a redemptive God of presence, wisdom, and power comes from the biblical revelation of God's presence in Jesus of Nazareth, named the Christ. Special revelation, or the understanding of God as given through scripture, is prior to general revelation, providing the key whereby we name our interpretation of God in the world as "revelation" in the first place.

Thus all Christian theology, whether explicitly or implicitly, is dependent upon and informed by the biblical texts that are fundamental to the tradition. Process theologians often leave this dependence implicit, primarily drawing upon it explicitly when illustrating the unique compatibility between its philosophical vision of God and the dynamic, relational biblical vision. Here we will make the relationship between the philosophy and the bible more explicit by drawing first from biblical notions of Jesus, and then treating them from a process perspective.

Special revelation, as indicated in chapter 4, takes place through intensifying the image of God in human consciousness. While Christians see this occurring in an ultimate sense in Jesus, this revelation could not occur apart from the long history of revelation in Hebrew history. How does God create that amazing people, save through a covenant that reveals the divine nature? Whether the covenant is considered through the dim recesses of the past recorded as a relationship with Adam, Noah, and Abraham, or through the giving of the law through Moses, or through the call and response represented by the prophets, always the covenant is at once revealing and creating. Through the covenant, God's will toward justice in relationships is revealed. Through the people's participation in the covenant, justice in relationships is enacted in society. Faithfully, God lures the people into being a people who will reflect the divine character as inclusive well-being. Insofar as the people become a society of justice, the image of God is created in human society; insofar as they fall from this ideal, the image is distorted. Always the constancy of God is like a lure, drawing the people into relationships that exhibit justice, and therefore fulfill the covenant.

The revelation includes divine wrath against injustice, but of course this simply intensifies the revelation of God as love. Justice in the Hebrew scriptures is seen in the concrete caring of the people for each other within society in well-ordered relationships. When the people act against justice, they act against love: the disadvantaged are cheated and downtrodden still further, the stability of a just society is undermined; all become impoverished in spirit. If God is indifferent to human society, then of course we cannot expect any divine response to such a situation. Instead, the Hebrew scriptures reveal the intensity of God's care for human well-being, and the prophets thunder down divine wrath against injustice. Only a God of inclusive love could exercise wrath when love is violated.

But more often than not, the wrath revealed in the scriptures is human as well as divine. Consider one illustration of wrath in the thirteenth chapter of Hosea: "Samaria shall bear her guilt because she has rebelled against her God," writes the prophet. "They shall fall by the sword, their little ones shall be dashed in pieces, and their pregnant women ripped open." The actions are clearly those of warfare. Humanity, not God, devised the atrocities mentioned. Assyrians wielded the sword and decimated the towns and villages. How is it *God's* wrath?

When injustice is a violation of relationships, not only between neighboring persons but also between neighboring nations, then violence follows as the most concrete form of that violation. The warfare is part and parcel of the injustice being decried. Violation *is* violence, and breeds yet further violence. It is not that first people are unjust, and then in an entirely unrelated action people also experience warfare. Warfare is itself the violation of relationships of caring, revealing instead the invidious and corrupting network of injustice.

God acts with the world as it is, leading it toward what it can be. The aims of God will transcend the given, but must also reflect the given. What kinds of aims can God give in a context of violation and violence, when the world has determined its own course? It may be that the slight avenue of transcendence open is that the cause/effect relationship between violation and violence may be seen in such a way that both will be denounced. The magnitude of the effects of injustice as warfare can serve to reveal the evil of violated well-being at any level. Thus even though the momentum of violence has built to an irreversible destruction, the very naming of that destruction as God's wrath may well be the result of God's grace. It indicates a redemptive and religious interpretation of the political event, rightly associating the enormous violence of war with the "small" violence of tolerated injustice in the internal social fabric of the nation. To make such a connection is to move toward reform; the judgment of wrath is therefore the opportunity of grace. It opens the door to a better way.

In the book of Hosea the better way follows immediately upon the above text. "Return, O Israel, to the Lord your God, for you have stumbled because of your iniquity. Take words with you and return to the Lord. Say to him, 'Take away all iniquity, and receive us graciously, that we may present the fruit of our lips. Assyria will not save us, we will not ride on horses; nor will we say again, "our

god," to the work of our hands; for in thee the orphan finds mercy.'
I will heal their faithlessness; I will love them freely, for my anger
has turned from them." There is a double play in the critical phrase
found in the midst of this passage: "In thee the orphan finds
mercy." On the one hand, it could refer to the suppliant Israel's
expectation that God will grant mercy, but on the other hand, it
goes to the heart of the justice of God, and only because of this is it
an apt description of God's readiness to receive the confessing
people. God's love is a justice that is measured not by the well-being
of an elite, nor even by the well-being of the many, but by the well-
being of the least valued in society. Justice is an ordering of social
relationships so that none is without help; it is therefore measured
precisely by the condition of those without protection, symbolized
in the text by the orphan. God's justice flashes like a jewel against
the contrary ways of injustice, demanding the well-being of the least
till there be no "least." The people's naming of this reality, in the
exigencies of their own suffering from injustice, is the turn toward
grace; their living this reality is the well-being of justice. Divine
wrath turns the evil of human injustice into a call for justice;
judgment is the opportunity for salvation. In the painful conditions
of direst human need, God's nature is revealed as a love that is just,
and a justice that is love.

The revelation through the person of Jesus builds upon the revelation given in the Hebrew scriptures, and is impossible without
those scriptures and the Jewish people who wrote them. Christian
history builds upon Israelite history, not to supersede that history,
but to create another path from it and alongside of it. The richness
of Judaism made Christianity possible. The revelation of the nature
of God, seen and still seen through this people, was also given
through the person born of this people, Jesus. Through this one, yet
another people are given birth, so that they, too, might begin to
reflect the image of God in the creation of just societies that
embody love.

How can such a singular revelation be given? Bear in mind the
dynamics of God's aims for the world in process thought. The
harmony of God is adapted to the conditions of the world. Continuity and novelty mark each aim from God. The preparation of the
past makes a particular aim possible, so that there is continuity.
Transcendence of the past in the direction of increasing reflection of

the harmony of God makes the aim novel. The past and the future unite in the aim, leading to the creation of the present. Through these dynamics, it would be possible for one person so to reveal both the nature of God and the nature of what we are called to be as human beings that we could call this person "Immanuel, God with us." Incarnation is coherent in process thought, given the following historical conditions.

First, the past must be such that there is a readiness for this revelation. The "fullness of time" is absolutely essential, for all aims must have some continuity with the past.

Second, the content of the initial aim toward incarnation must be a full communication of the nature of God. In general revelation, as noted earlier, there is a hiddenness to God since aims adapted to the world are generally more reflective of the world than of God. An aim toward incarnation must overcome this, although in continuity with the preparation for such a revelation. Therefore, the aim of God must communicate the essence of God's self-created character.

Third, the initial aim would have to be adopted fully by the recipient. Usually, the aims from God are adapted by the world. Incarnation would require a full conformity to the aim, for to the degree that the recipient deviated from the aim, to that degree incarnation would fail. In process terms, this means that God's full communication of the divine nature in the initial aim would have to be met by a full acceptance of that nature in the subjective aim of the finite occasion. To use an expression fully developed in several process christologies, the finite occasion would be "co-constituted" by the divine and human aim.

Fourth, if all of this is to be achieved by a human person, incarnation cannot be a once-for-all happening, but must be a continuous process. In process thought a person is not one actual occasion, but a series of many, many occasions. For incarnation to occur, there would have to be an assent to incarnation in every moment of existence. Incarnation would have to be continuous.[1]

---

1. The unique ability of process categories to illumine christology, particularly in terms of the Chalcedonian creed, is an important contribution of process theologians (notably John B. Cobb, Jr., David Ray Griffin, Schubert Ogden, and Norman Pittenger). Chalcedon held to the two natures of Christ, divine and human, even though there was no way to give rational explanation for how mutually contradictory qualities (such as infinitude and finitude, omnipotence and limitation) could combine in one person. With a process metaphysic of

Notice that in no way would such an incarnation do away with the humanity of the one through whom incarnation took place. To the contrary, the humanity of the person would be highlighted. If human nature is perfected in a just society, and if God's aims flowing from the divine character are always toward love and justice, then any person in whom full incarnation was a continuous reality would always be living in the perfection of love and justice. The injustices of society that act as original sin demanding conformity would have to be refuted, the future as loss would be transformed to trust, and the present would be marked by relationships of inclusive well-being as a continuously enacted norm. In short, the humanity of this person would be brought to perfection.

Furthermore, incarnation in a process world could only take place through the cooperation of the individual. The dynamics of incarnation are no different from the dynamics of any actual entity. The difference is in the content of the aim and the quality of the response. Incarnation would be cooperative, bringing the full freedom of both God and the world to perfection. Therefore, neither through the dynamics of the aim nor through the content of the aim is there any abrogation of the full humanity of the one manifesting the nature of God for us.

Jesus is born in "the fullness of time" in Jewish history. His people have over a thousand years of the covenant behind them, deeply ingraining them with the awareness of God's nature as love and justice. Furthermore, Jesus is born at a time when the people were deeply restless in the bonds of political oppression; expectations were high for a redemption wrought by God. Some expected a single person, a Messiah, to be appointed by God to break the bonds of oppression and bring in the reign of God, reestablishing the nation of Israel. Many expected this to be a cataclysmic event, overturning the natural order in a re-creation of the world according to divine love and justice. The resurrection of the dead would signal the advent of this new order.

All of this is in the past of Jesus. But the aims of God transcend the past, and can bring about deeper reflections of the divine

---

internal relations, the contradiction disappears—a process world is an incarnational world. The problem set for process theologians is not to explain how Christ can be both human and divine, but to explain why Jesus of Nazareth is a unique manifestation of God with us.

harmony than the past alone makes possible. That this happened in the case of Jesus is evidenced by the use the apostle Paul makes of the phrase "much more" in the fifth chapter of Romans. Again and again he turns to this superlative to speak of the abundance of grace received from God through Christ. He writes, of course, from the viewpoint of the resurrection, as do the gospel writers. The resurrection becomes the lens through which the story of Jesus is viewed; through the resurrection, Jesus is seen not only as the expected deliverer from oppression but as the manifestation of God for us.

We, too, look through that lens to know God. In the light of the resurrection, we encounter the early church's remembrance of the life of Jesus in the pages of the gospels. Contemporary theology gives us an "archeology" of the texts, showing the layers of remembrance and interpretation that represent Jesus and his effects, with Jesus' preaching of the reign of God as the fundamental base. Jesus' use of parables is essential to this preaching, and often these parables point toward a reversal of the expected or established order of things as a mark of God's reign, along with a demand for action that is appropriate to the reign. Since the established order of things embodied systemic oppressions, whether of Israel by Rome, or of persons marginalized from mainstream society on the basis of health, wealth, or position, the reversal of the social order was essential to the coming of God's reign. Jesus' actions as recorded in the gospels show that Jesus not only called for a reversal of values, but also that he himself *is* such a reversal. Therefore, through his own reversal of values as well as through his proclamation of such a reversal, he reveals the nature of God and of God's reign.

There is a great reversal of the established order in Jesus' relationship to others in society. We read of Jesus' acceptance of the lame, the blind, the deaf, and of his ministry marked by healing. Scholars of the New Testament period tell us that at the time of Jesus there were many communities established for the purpose of anticipating the coming reign of God. A mark of many of these communities was a purity that excluded all of those with physical handicaps. In contrast to this, the gospels portray Jesus as calling out to those who were lame, blind, deaf, leprous. Not exclusion, but an inclusion that frequently included healing was his attitude. The justice of God in the Hebrew scriptures is marked by the well-being of the least; Jesus joins his message of God's imminent reign with a healing acceptance of those who had been shunned for their physical misfortunes.

Reversal is also evident in that Jesus called sinners to himself, accepting them even prior to their repentance. The story of Zaccheus tells us, "He has gone in to be the guest of a man who is a sinner." The result of Jesus' graciousness is that Zaccheus did indeed repent and reform: "and Jesus said to him, 'Today salvation has come to this house, since he also is a son of Abraham. For the son of man came to seek and to save the lost' " (Luke 19:9–10). Thus, Jesus accepted the unworthy, apparently heedless of his society's disapproval of such people. The sin of Zaccheus was not only his extortionary work in tax collecting, but also his association with the oppressor, Rome. Exclusion of such people, not consorting with them, was the proper behavior of the day—as, indeed, it appears to be of every day and every people. But Jesus reached out in acceptance toward the one who was shunned.

There is also a reversal with regard to women. The gospel of John speaks of Jesus' encounter with a woman from Samaria, and here the proscriptions against her would have been on three counts: she was a woman, and therefore not considered a proper participant in theological dialogue; she was an outcast due to her lifestyle ("you have had five husbands, and he whom you now have is not your husband," John 4:18); and she was of the despised half-breed people, the Samaritans. Yet Jesus entered into a spirited dialogue with this woman, discussing the nature of God, and of worship, and of salvation. The disciples, returning from the town, are portrayed as astounded. Jesus overturned the accepted boundaries of society in his openness toward women.

There is also an important note of judgment in this breaking down of the accepted social standards that worked ill-being for the people and denied the nature of God's justice. We can see this by focusing on one particular gospel story, the account in the seventh chapter of Luke. Jesus is portrayed at dinner in the home of Simon the Pharisee. During the meal, "a woman of the city who was a sinner" enters, and begins to minister to Jesus in a strange way: she "began to wet his feet with her tears, and wiped them with the hair of her head, and kissed his feet, and anointed them with the ointment." The host is indignant: in the text, he is depicted as despising both the woman and Jesus— the woman, because she was "a sinner," and Jesus for not having the discernment to cast her aside. Evidently this indignation was not voiced—that would violate Simon's dignity as host. Despite his reserved silence, the text goes on to say that Jesus answers him.

The answer is both a judgment and a response to Simon's needs. Just as in the Hebrew scriptures judgment is an opportunity for salvation, even so Jesus' judgment holds the possibility of a richer mode of existence for Simon. The judgment begins with a parable of two debtors, one owing a large amount, and the other a small amount. The creditor remits the debts of both, whereupon Jesus asks Simon which of the debtors will love the creditor more. The answer, of course, is the one who was forgiven the larger debt. His gratitude will be correspondingly great. The woman, with her fullness of gratitude and love, is a woman who is acting in the knowledge of forgiveness; Simon, with his small love, is unaware of his own need for forgiveness.

Consider Simon's plight. If he excludes the woman from his home and the presence of Jesus, he will preserve his well-ordered world. The woman disorders his world, reversing its comfortable and exclusive structure. She ought not to be there. But she is, and Simon's own guest receives her attentions. Doesn't this mean that Simon's own exclusiveness is not appropriate? Isn't his own self, along with his valuation of the world, brought into question? His felt need is to condemn the woman for her way of life and Jesus for accepting her; this would re-establish his world, and reaffirm his own self-constructed worth. At the same time, of course, it would refute God's call to an ever-new order of inclusive well-being, denying God's reign.

In a world constructed through love and justice, the welfare of one affects the welfare of all. To despise the welfare of another is to lessen the welfare of oneself. To lessen the welfare of oneself, in turn, impoverishes the whole. Inexorably, a society of true justice is a society of true love, requiring an extension of well-being throughout the society. By excluding the well-being of the woman from his concern, Simon was impoverishing himself in two ways. On the one hand, he had so drawn the lines of his self-concern that he was in fact a small self—defined by small loving. This diminution of himself was an impoverishment to society: the woman would be ignored or excluded by him, not enriched. On the other hand, Simon's self-limitation was such that he had foreclosed the avenues of his own growth. His exclusion of the other was the reinforcement of the smallness of himself. Had Jesus answered the man at the level of his felt need, and played the part of the gracious guest who conforms to the host's expectations even though those expectations are not shared, then the man would have been left in his smallness. He would have been gratified, no doubt, by the confirmation of his exclusive world, and he would have felt a pleasant affirmation of himself, but he would never have noticed how restricted and impoverished that self was. Nor would he have seen that those restrictions involved him in guilt that placed him as well as the woman in deep need of forgiveness.

Jesus responds judgmentally, revealing Simon's true need. Through the brief parable and through direct confrontation ("you gave me no water for my feet, . . . you gave me no kiss . . . you did not anoint my head with oil") Jesus reproves the man. This very act of judgment against him is witness to Jesus' love, for by awakening Simon to his true need, Jesus provides the catalyst for change. Suddenly Simon has the opportunity to see his smallness, and to break out of his exclusive prison to an inclusiveness of being wherein he can reach out to others, enriching and being enriched in the realization of justice.

Jesus calls the woman and the Pharisee to a new mode of life. If Simon responds to Jesus' judgment, then he must let go of his preestablished values. Letting go of one world, he must participate in the creation of another. But if his security is built up out of the very predictability of a world, if his strength is based upon the absoluteness of order and value, how can he let go? How could we? Likewise, Jesus calls upon the woman to "go and sin no more." The implication of the text is that she is a prostitute. Her very livelihood depends upon one mode of life; if she gives it up, where will her next meal come from? How can she live in a world that allows her no other route to physical sustenance? How can she dare to let go? How could we?

The Pharisee requires his preestablished world for the sake of what he perceives to be his psychic survival; the woman requires her preestablished world for the sake of her physical survival. Jesus confronts them both with the demand for a new order. He dares them both to enter a new future. He turns their worlds upside down, and the overturning is fearsome and dangerous, calling for the terror of sacrificed security. It is as if he asks them both to walk upon water, for all surety and balance and safety are gone when the foundations become fluid. How can they dare such a thing?

The foundations of the new world of God's reign are simply the foundations of the interdependence of love, working itself out as justice. If love always looks to the real needs of the other, then love cannot predetermine what those needs will be, and how those needs will be met. Love must always take its boundaries from that-which-is and that-which-can-be; there is an openness of vision in an interdependent society of love and justice that cannot be restricted by past situations, even though those situations might have been valid responses to love in their own time.

Ideally, such openness and risk may all be very well, but in the real world, how can we dare this? In the gospel account, the daring seems to follow simply from the presence of Jesus. Jesus, embodying that kind of love, becomes the new foundation. It is as if the active presence of Jesus is a reassurance offered against the terror of an insecure future, as if the old foundations of the ordered world can only give way because of the dynamic reality of this person. Part of the terror of a new future is the fear that it may not be a possible future: what if we let go of the past only to find out that the future we dared cannot be? Where are we then in terms of security? Will not our last condition be worse than our first? And so we imprison ourselves in the past against the terror of a new order. Jesus calls the man and the woman alike to a new order, but his very call to them is from his embodiment of that order. Jesus *is* living in love; Jesus *is* openness to the other; Jesus *is* himself our judgment, calling us to our true mode of being. Jesus, extending a call to a new order, is himself that order, the instantiation of God's reign, and therefore a true witness to its real possibility. Therefore, he becomes the ground of our daring to attempt such a future ourselves, and finding, in the process, that it is God's future for us. Jesus becomes the firmness in the water, and we, too, can walk.

No matter which gospel text we take to consider Jesus, we are confronted with one who consistently manifests the love to which he calls others. He breaks down all partitions that divide humans from each other; he embodies a love that is just, and a love that therefore variously exhibits judgment, affirmation, service, or sharing, depending upon the context of love. He is a radical reversal of the established order of his day insofar as that order mitigated against the well-being of all peoples within societies, and among nations. But this is the life that reveals the nature of God for us; this is the life that offers a concrete vision of the new society to which God calls us. This is the revelation of God to us for the sake of conforming us to that divine image. If we see in Jesus a revelation of God for us, then the way Jesus loves is the way God loves. The metaphorical text of Hosea, "in thee the orphan finds mercy," is given countless embodiments in the actions recorded of Jesus. The irony, of course, is that the unexpected reversal of society's exclusive standards is what we should expect to see in any revelation of God, if we have taken the revelation initially given in Hebrew scripture seriously. The reign of God is the full love that is justice, not simply in personal relations, but in the depths of a society structured according to patterns of inclusive well-being.

To see the life of Jesus as God with us, incarnate in him, is to lift all that we see in that revelation to ultimacy. Consider the implications of this by looking again at the story of the Pharisee and the woman. The reality of Jesus, living the love to which he calls others, enables the others to trust the viability of that kind of living and to dare to create such a society. But Jesus is the incarnation of God: does this not imply that such openness in love and justice describes the very foundations of reality? If *God* is this kind of love for us, what is there left to fear? God relates to all reality, calling each element in the world toward reflection of a divine image that is love and justice in relationships. Since it is God who so calls us, and since God, in keeping with the divine nature, exerts this lure throughout existence, then our actions in accordance with love and justice are in conformity with the direction of the universe. To act in love is to act *with* creation; to act against love is to act *against* creation. If God is the love we see in Jesus, then all God's actions are in accordance with love. Insofar as the future to which we are called is one lived in love, the future receives its ground in God. All finite forms of security to which we cling against the uncertainties of love are revealed as false securities. When through Jesus we see God as love, then the confidence Jesus could inspire in the woman and the Pharisee is shown to be a confidence grounded in the nature of God—and thus a confidence that is appropriate to every person in every situation calling for ever-new forms of particular love.

Jesus reveals the nature of God as love, and the nature of God's love. Theologically, how do we translate this revelation of God into an understanding of God as God? There are two considerations involved: first, we must see that the fullness of the love revealed in Jesus is attributed to the nature of God, but second, we must be careful to preserve the "Godness" of God. The fullness of the love that Jesus reveals includes an openness to others that crosses the boundaries we define to divide us, a judgment that opens us to the richness of forgiveness and growth, inviting us to togetherness in giving and receiving. How is this love God's love? Jesus, as a human being, manifests this love. Therefore, the love is not alien to our humanity—difficult and challenging, yes, but certainly a possible mode of being human. When we translate the qualities to our understanding of God, do we then make God human too? Do we fall into the problem of anthropomorphism, of describing God in human terms so that what we are saying of God is essentially no more than we can say about humanity? Does the "Godness" of God disappear?

Process theology contributes to resolution of the dilemma with its metaphor of the "actual entity" as a model for reality. Human beings are constituted by many actual entities, as are all the other things we see in our environment. The description of the actual entity is more basic than the description of the human being. Furthermore, the dynamics of the entity are the route whereby differences can be expressed. While the dynamics are the same for all entities, the content selected and unified in each entity accounts for the differences of things. The same dynamics will enter into the description of entities in a human being and entities in a puff of smoke—or the singular entity which is God, as noted in chapter 3 and in the appendix. The import of this for theologians struggling with the problem of anthropomorphism is that now we have a model that is more basic than the human being for a discussion of the reality of God.

The clearest example of the way the model helps in overcoming anthropomorphism is in the problem of the sexuality of God. Naturally the biblical texts speak of God in masculine or feminine terms; our language has no other way of expressing personality. Given cultural understandings of the role and rule of males in the ancient Hebrew world, the gender most often chosen in discussing God was male, reflective of the patriarchal culture. Yet the use was not exclusive; God was also imaged through female roles such as bearing, nursing, and rearing children. However, again and again the texts suggest that while male and female imagery can be used of God, God transcends sexuality and gender. Hebrew scriptures portray God as beyond sexuality; in this respect, God was totally unlike the fertility gods and goddesses of other religions. Nonetheless, given a continuing patriarchal bias, the Christian tradition has tended to reduce God to maleness, such that doctrines of God are not only anthropomorphic, but andromorphic as well. When the model for understanding God is humanity in general, and maleness in particular, then it is too easy to project all features of humanity, including gender and sexuality, onto God even when those features are clearly inappropriate to the singularity of deity.

We can avoid this since process thought portrays things such as sexuality and gender as belonging to composites of entities, whether animal or human, and not to an entity per se. For example, the soul/mind of a man or woman will draw from specific bodily experiences. The gendered nature of the mind is then derivative from embodiment. It becomes part of the interpretive grid used in interaction with the world. Since it is part of the grid through which one sees and understands, it can itself remain "invisible." Just as wearing tinted sun glasses "colors" the world we see, so that we are surprised to see the "real" colors when we take the glasses off, even so we are habituated to the difference our gender makes, and hence read it explicitly or implicitly into our interpretations of the world. But our glasses, we can remove; our gender, we cannot! And so we are dependent upon the differences among us to adjust our interpretations, and hopefully to see more clearly. Process thought becomes one way to make the adjustment.

By discussing God in terms of an actual entity rather than as a series of entities such as are required to constitute human beings, we can utilize the dynamics of the model to express the nature of God in nonanthropomorphic terms. Those features that belong distinctly to physical existence, such as the sexuality of Jesus or any other human being—stay clearly within the realm of composite entities, which is the only place where they can occur. It is impossible, in process metaphysics, to translate strictly human features to deity. If one were to talk of embodiment at all for God, one would have to talk of the whole universe, for God feels all reality precisely as it felt itself. Therefore God, analogous to the human soul, "inherits" from the entire created order with a fullness not possible to any finite human being. The universe, then, would function analogously as God's body. But how could one establish a divine gender on such a basis? Clearly, God is neither male nor female. By the fullness of God's feelings of the world, God includes male and female within the divine nature, but by the singularity of the divine reality, God transcends both. The gender of Jesus, then, is not a revelation of the gender of God, but becomes the vehicle in a patriarchal society of reversing society's valuation of one gender above another. Jesus as masculine denies masculine "privilege" by redefining a togetherness of male and female in a new society of equals.[2] The reign of God does not confirm society's injustices, but overturns them toward inclusive well-being.

If the model precludes ascribing the gender of Jesus to God, in what sense does the fully human Jesus become revelatory of God? How does the metaphor of the actual entity help? Consider Jesus' openness to others in relation to the sense in which God, through the consequent nature, feels every reality in the universe precisely as that reality feels itself. What is added to the philosophical statement by the biblical revelation is that the divine openness to all is love. Jesus reveals the character of God as love. In Jesus, openness to the other is in the mode of love; in God, openness to the other is an unimaginable fullness—a feeling of the other regardless of place, position, or power—with a force toward the other's well-being. Every feeling of otherness requires an emotive form; the revelation of God in Jesus identifies that form as love. God is love.

Jesus loves in judgment, refusing to affirm actions or desires that cut against the well-being of the self or others. Such love is stern and strong: stern in its determined will toward true well-being, and strong enough to withstand the anger, ill will, or defensiveness called up against such judgments. How is God like that on a process model?

2. I owe this insight to Elisabeth Schüssler Fiorenza's analysis in *In Memory of Her* (New York: Crossroad, 1983).

Jesus loves with a mutuality that invites giving and receiving—he gives, seemingly unendingly, but he also receives in a way that is so simple it often escapes our notice. The Samaritan woman gave him water, and he drank; Zaccheus gave him food, and he ate; the woman gave him perfume and service, and he received. In these simple modes of daily interdependence, Jesus gives and receives, receives and gives, in the reciprocity of love. Is God's love reciprocal, too? How can this be? Such questions require us to move beyond the discussion of Jesus' life to his death and resurrection.

The fullness of the revelation of God, reversing our personal and social structures of injustice with the shocking force of love, does not stop with the life of Jesus, but continues through the crucifixion and resurrection. Here the many reversals of expectation manifested in Jesus' acts and words culminate in two final reversals: that love should meet first with death, and then, against all hope, with life.

9

CRUCIFIED

AT the heart of Christian faith is the strange symbol of crucifixion. Instrument of torture and violent death, the cross nonetheless speaks of God's gracious salvation. Is this not a contradiction? How is it that death becomes a symbol of salvation? The query has echoed through the Christian years, finding varied answers, none of which has ever been lifted to the level of dogma in the church. It is as if the closer one approaches to the heart of Christianity, the deeper the mystery becomes.

Among the questions entertained concerning the cross is that of God's presence. If Jesus is God incarnate, is God present on that cross? And for the most part, theologians have recoiled from such a statement. "Patripassionism" became the despised name of an early century heresy suggesting that God did, indeed, suffer on the cross. The dominant interpretation was that God turned away from Jesus at that point, leaving him to suffer sin, evil, and death vicariously for us. In such a case, God's revelation in Christ would be limited to the life and resurrection of Jesus, while the cross simply reveals God's wrath against sin. In the twentieth century, however, there has been renewed interest in the suffering of God, particularly as represented by Jesus' crucifixion. Process theology represents one way of probing the mystery: what does it mean, that this one who incarnates God dies on a cross? For we cannot adequately account for the judging and transforming power of the love manifested in Jesus without looking at the cross, too, as a revelation of God.

Surely to see the crucifixion as part of revelation is in keeping with the theme of reversal so powerfully manifested in the parables and acts of Jesus. The reign of God is not an extension of our own forms of worldly dominion and power; it is not designed to exalt the powerful at the expense of the lowly in class systems of privilege and exclusive well-being. Rather, the parables use humble images of God's reign—salt, leaven, fish, fields, laborers, housewives—and shock us out of expectations of a military reign of might and privilege. Expectations are reversed. Likewise, Jesus as the revelation of God keeps company not with the professionally religious, but with outcasts and other socially suspect persons. Reversal is revelation. Why, then, should we be surprised that the theme of reversal continues with the most profound reversal of all, God on a cross? The cross was a great shock to the disciples, a reversal of all their expectations concerning the rightful culmination of Jesus' presence, proclamation, and person. But precisely in this most profound reversal, God may be most profoundly revealed.

I propose to look at the revelation of the cross by considering the words each of the four evangelists attributed to Jesus while on that cross. No evangelist includes all seven sentences, and this essay is not intended to give a composite description of what Jesus said and did while dying. Such a description is not possible, since each of the gospel accounts weaves the story of the church with the events on the cross in such a way that multiple purposes are served. The gospels are already an interpretive account of the encounter with Jesus; furthermore, interpretation builds upon interpretation. Matthew and Luke each expand upon the words of Mark, recording their own respective interpretations. And throughout the centuries the gospels continue to demand interpretation as they bring each reader/hearer and the church as a whole into encounter with God's revelation in Jesus.

Written separately, the gospels have nonetheless come down to us as a whole, severally and together inviting us into our own response to God's reign. And one response is to consider in wonder the composite effect of the words associated with the cross. This is not to deny the integrity of each evangelist's terse interpretation of what was happening on that cross and captured in the words attributed to Jesus. Rather, it is to recognize that the whole may not be reducible to its parts; we can see something in the togetherness of the gospels that is not so clearly apparent in each separately. And if a reversal of expectations is a mark of God's revelation in each evangelist, then perhaps there is justification in seeing a new form of this reversal in the composite words of the cross.

These words are the crowning manifestation of love in the life of Jesus. One could deeply admire the love that Jesus manifests prior to the cross, for Jesus loves consistently. He encounters moments of fear, such as in Nazareth when he was nearly stoned; he experiences weariness and thirst, such as at the Samaritan well. He knows hunger, for he sent the disciples to buy food. Such weakness does not prevent his loving, but after all, such weakness is common to humanity and can be endured by strong people. And Jesus surely knows the presence of God with him, in him—is he not the revelation of God? Perhaps love is easier for Jesus. The cross disallows this mitigation, precisely because Jesus continues to love not only in the grip of death's pain, but also in the agony of a sense of Godforsakenness.

The earliest evangelist, Mark, sounds the theme with the terrible words, "My God, my God, why have you forsaken me?" Matthew repeats the sentence—and it is the only sentence given by two evangelists. The words invoke the twenty-second Psalm, where the sense of abandonment and the sense of trust are coexistent, eventuating in a confident proclamation of the eschatological reign of God: "For the kingdom is the Lord's, and God rules over the nations." Since often the first sentence of a Psalm was used as a symbol for the Psalm as a whole, this sense of trust as well as abandonment, and a continuing proclamation of God's reign, could be indicated in that agonized cry. Yet even this deep meaning would not preclude the immediate dimensions of spiritual pain also expressed in that cry.

The power of pain is its ability to force out all other sensibilities, claiming its own screaming reign in the soul. Pain has the power to crowd out the sense of God's presence as hunger, thirst, and weariness could not. The cry of abandonment signals the pain of body and spirit; the force of physical pain claims full sway in the sense of Godforsakenness, even though trust continues. Without that empowering sense of God's presence, can Jesus still reveal the love of God?

The remaining two gospels, Luke and John, record other words from that cross. John begins with the words to Mary and the

disciple John, "Woman, behold your son! Behold your mother!"
There is most likely a symbolic reference to the beginning of the
church in this passage, but deeper than this symbolism is the simple
word of caring to his mother. In the midst of the pain of death, there
is love given forth as comfort and care.

Luke's words continue the theme of love despite suffering. "Father, forgive them; for they do not know what they are doing" is a
word of forgiveness extended to those who are carrying out the
crucifixion. On the cross, in the midst of Godforsakennesss, Jesus
still loves with the strength and insight to perceive the needs of
those around him. That love embraces not only a mother and
disciple, but the very ones who are killing him. How is there room
in Jesus to respond to the needs of others when his own needs
pound out his death?

Yet again Luke records another word, this time of comfort to the
thief, and we might feel undone at the depth and inexhaustibility of
the love of Jesus. Neither spiritual nor physical Godforsakenness
weakens the strength of his loving. On that cross we see that the
power of love extended by Jesus is the very love of God, stronger
than death. The seeds of resurrection are sown on the cross as love
refuses to succumb to the distortions of pain or the terrors of death.
Jesus continues to love, through deepest pain, in a great reversal of
what one would normally expect.

Does God love so strongly even in the midst of pain? How can the
revelation on the cross say less? Through the cross we see not only
that God's love is stronger than death, but that God in love endures
the pain of death, and that God's love is unconquered by death.
That God should endure pain is surely a reversal of religious expectations!

The dynamics of the process model force a strict application of
the revelation on the cross to the nature of God. This can be
explained by considering a tragically common illustration of evil. In
a poor section of the city, a young man knocks down an old woman
in order to steal her purse. As she falls, she breaks her hip. On the
basis of the revelation of God in Jesus, God is open toward us; God
feels us with love. This love is or can be a judgment that wills our
well-being, and the crucifixion of Jesus is involved in the revelation
of this. How is this applied to the young man and the woman? How
is it applied to God?

In a process universe, God launches every occasion of existence with an aim toward its good. This aim is one that is shaped to the particularities of the occasion. The earlier discussion of revelation suggested that the aim reflects not only God, but the conditions of the world. In relation to that young man, God feels his whole past world, and fashions an aim for him that gives him the best possible way for going beyond that world. To say the phrase, "best possible," describes the limitations of the aim, for clearly, that which is absolutely best—say, for instance, that the young man shall suddenly become a model of industry and virtue—is not immediately possible. Were God to give such an aim to the man, the man would have no hope at all, for there would be no realistic way beyond the power of his past. Despair would increase the evil of his lot.

Assume that the man has not experienced much human love, that he is exposed to violence, that he has not had practice in trusting others, let alone in empathizing with them. In short, while his life is necessarily relational in an ontological sense, it is nonrelational in an emotional sense. The man lives as if he were an island in the universe, with all relationships appearing as the sea that isolates him. Violation and violence have become his pattern of existence, reinforcing his isolation.

Is he responsible for this situation? To a degree, he is, and to a degree, he isn't. While he did not create the situation into which he was born, he perpetuates it every time he resists the possibility, however slight, to begin to transform and transcend his world. Given the enormity of his situation, the possibilities for transcendence will likely be small—sometimes the best in a particular situation is bad from any other standpoint. If that best is actualized, however, the next "best" will be better, building on the first and leading further into transformation. The man is responsible, as we all are, for actualizing or modifying the best that is given in each moment.

Responsibility is a matter of degree due to the relational role of the past. Determinism and freedom intertwine in a relational universe. As noted in chapter two, we are not responsible for a past we did not create, and we cannot avoid that past. Inexorably, we feel its weight. Our responsibility lies in what we do with the past. If the press of society is such that what the man in our illustration can do is little, then his responsibility is correspondingly lessened. When his alternatives to change that past are wide, then his responsibility increases. However, every response he gives is in itself a force that he adds to the past, and that will affect his next moment of response. Responsibility is therefore made more complex, for he is not only responsible for what he does in the present, but he is also responsible to some degree for what *can* be done in the present. One might say that responsibility increases with age, for our own dealings with the past as we created that past add to the width or narrowness of our possibilities in the present.

The man's habituated acceptance of violence is his own responsibility, albeit shared with a society that was conducive to that mode of being. The man is bent on robbing the woman, regardless of its effect upon the woman. God's faithfulness would be manifested in the given alternative to regard the woman. If the character of the man is such that he is, at that moment, incapable of seeing her as a person with her own needs, deserving respect and care, then the aim of God will be toward a step that might eventually lead toward such a capacity. The aim, fitted to the occasion, may simply be to do that which is within the young man's possibilities, which is to refrain from this violation. And the young man ignores the possibility, contradicting the aim and nature of God and relational existence. He violates the woman.

God feels this young man precisely as the young man feels himself; this is entailed in God's openness to the world through the consequent nature. But God not only feels the man in his own self-constitution, God feels him in light of what could have been possible had the man actualized the initial aim given him by God. God feels the actuality and the might-have-been together. This means that God feels the man with more pain than the man feels himself, for God feels the disparity in a way that the man himself has rejected. Could the reality of the pain of God be revealed in the crucifixion of Jesus?

Consider what the divine experience might be given God's openness to the woman. The woman, too, responds to a past; her past includes the effects upon her life of poverty. Her fixed income barely extends to cover the rent for her room, let alone the luxury of food. Relationships are impoverished, for her husband is long since dead, and her children are grown, too involved in fighting their own battles with poverty to give much assistance to the old woman who is, after all, irritable and quarrelsome much of the time. God feels the pain of her existence, both in the way she experiences it and in relation to the might-have-been that has marked her personal and social alternatives along the way.

The young man dashes toward her, and the woman experiences the shock first of fear and then of pain as she crashes to the ground. Oddly enough, her thoughts circle in a frenzy about the loss of food—how can she buy supper now, with her money gone? But her situation is far more dire, for her bones are brittle, and break in the fall.

To write about such things and read about such things in a book on theology may seem strange, but no theology can afford to ignore the concrete reality of such facts, for they happen, and they happen daily in all their ugliness, in all their pitiableness, in all their pain, in a world too far from being the reign of God. God feels the world. If God feels the world, God feels *this* world, not as an abstraction, but as a reality. God feels *this* woman's pain, both in the impoverishment of her body and of her spirit through the past and in the sharp terror and agony of the present. Is it not true that God is crucified?

Notice the severe implications that follow from the fact that God feels the effects of the society upon both the young man and the woman. Society is always felt by God directly as personal, and only indirectly as impersonal. For instance, we might hear of the above crime, feel a momentary pang, and then dismiss it from our personal lives—it becomes another impersonal fact in the cold cruel world. We impersonalize the society. Impersonalization need not be dehumanization, for impersonalization may be one of the ways of coping with social evil. The society, bearing the weight of the past, has a force greater than an individual within that society. When society perpetuates evils, one can bear with it on the grounds that society is impersonal, and therefore less culpable and therefore perhaps more bearable. Since God feels the society through every individual within the society, God feels the effects and the perpetuation of the conditions conducive to such effects. God therefore feels the society personally, through each individual within it. The mitigation of distance that allows us to leave social evils unaddressed can be no mitigation in the feeling of God. God feels the effects directly, both as given and as received. God can only feel the society as impersonal insofar as God feels our own impersonalization of it. Thus for God impersonalization is indirect; personalization, direct. This means that the sins of society are directly sins against God.

If God is in Jesus, then God reveals through him that every sin is a sin felt by God and is therefore a sin against God. Every pain is felt by God, and is therefore God's pain. The dreadful truth revealed in the crucifixion of Jesus Christ is that the world crucifies God. We crucify God. Each pain we feel and each pain we inflict enters into the reality of the God who is for us.

Process theology gives expression to this revelation through the consequent nature of God. In God's supreme openness to the world, God feels each actuality, and in the feeling re-enacts the actuality of the world within the divine nature. My pain, in being my pain, is also God's pain.

The incredible reality revealed on the cross is that God's love does not cease in pain, not even the pain of death. We easily assert that God continues to love us in *our* pain, but what the theology of the cross, expressed in process terms, requires us to acknowledge is that God continues to love in *God's* pain. The theology pushes us even further to illumine why this pain is the price of our redemption.

The answer is deceptively simple. God fashions possibilities for us that will lead us toward reflection of the divine image. These possibilities must be real for us; they must be ways in which we can actually go, given the reality of who and where we are. God must know us and our situations in order to know what possibilities will be truly *our* possibilities. How well must God know us in order to give us the appropriate possibilities? Will an objective knowledge do? But what of those hidden realities within us, indiscernible to the most penetrating objective eye—what of those aspects of ourselves that are hidden even to us? God knows us well enough to give us the possibilities that can lead to our transformation because God knows us from the inside out, as well as from the outside in. God feels us as we feel ourselves, even including those depths that we do not allow into conscious feeling. God's full openness to who we are involves God in the pain of who we are, symbolized most profoundly in the revelation of God in Jesus on a cross. But this unsurpassable truth of God's knowledge is the means whereby God knows precisely what possibilities will be redemptive for us in the next moment of our existence. Through God's crucifixion, God provides us with a resurrection fitted to us in a love that demands our well-being. Who would think of a God whose love involves God in our pain? Revelation comes through the reversal of our normal expectations.

The event of God's love revealed on a cross has been interpreted both in scripture and in the long Christian tradition as providing the grounds for God's justification of us, despite our sin. Justification, in turn, has often entailed a penalty for our sins—a penalty paid by Jesus, the God-man, suffering for us and in our stead. The process explication of the cross as the revelation of the nature and role of God's love in providing our redemption is not alien to these more traditional notions. As noted in chapters two and eight, violation involves violence. Very simply, Jesus' proclamation of the reign of God was refused by the ruling powers, who answered radical love with an intent toward pain and death. Jesus suffered the results of sin, even as God suffers the results of sin. Precisely through this suffering, God makes resurrection possible. Thus God's identification with us in our sin, pain, and death is the ground and means of our salvation, both in history and in the everlastingness of God. This is justification, acceptance, forgiveness, and redemption, making new life possible for us in every moment. Such a justification is a reversal of the justice we consider after the fashion of law courts, for rather than meting out the measure of our sins, this justification is all mercy and grace. God feels us completely, in all our conditions, and through the radical love of such presence, provides us with forms of resurrection.

10

RISEN

THE edges of God are tragedy; the depths of God are joy, beauty, life. Resurrection answers crucifixion; life answers death. If Jesus reveals the nature of God in his life and crucifixion, he most surely also reveals God through resurrection. Here the reversal theme, so pronounced through Jesus' life and teaching, is brought to its most awesome expression: death is reversed by life. The public defeat of death on the cross is refuted by the power of resurrection.

Curiously, the New Testament speaks less about resurrection itself than about the results of resurrection. If we wish to talk of the way Jesus reveals God in his life, we can point to nearly any text in the gospels to see the content of that revelation. Likewise, to speak of God revealed in the crucifixion draws us to the long passion narratives that form the crux of each gospel. But if we wish to understand the glory of the resurrection, we are turned back. Not a single gospel account describes the details of the resurrection. There is no privileged discussion about the exact event. We must look instead to the results of resurrection, whether recorded as resurrection appearances, or in the faith and zeal of the disciples as they proclaim the dawn of the new age heralded by the resurrection of Jesus. The resurrection itself is hidden from our view.

If the immediacy of the resurrection is hidden, the results are not. In fact, the resurrection might be considered through the metaphor of the sun. We cannot look directly at the sun, for the brightness would blind us—our eyes are not suited to that strength of light. Yet the sun, which we cannot see directly, illumines all else, and in its light we make our way in the world. We cannot look directly at the resurrection because it is not given for us to see. Nevertheless, it illumines the entire landscape of the New Testament. The resurrection is the confirmation of Jesus and all that he revealed in his life; it is the reversal of the judgment of death. It is the catalyst that transformed the disciples, releasing the power that led to the formation of the church.

The resurrection, like the life and crucifixion of Jesus, functions as far more than a mere historical account of what happened to Jesus. Rather, the whole complex of the life, death, and resurrection of Jesus is like a mighty metaphor, leading us to deeper understandings of God and God's ways with us. Like a beauty whose depth defies any one description, the resurrection yields interpretation after interpretation, each adding a different facet to the mystery of God's presence in Jesus. This multiplicity of meanings is already functioning in the New Testament, where Mark interprets the resurrection as a vindication of Jesus' death, and a prelude to Jesus' transformative return to earth in judgment. Matthew, who includes appearances in his account of the resurrection, interprets resurrection not as preparation for a new presence of Jesus on earth in apocalyptic judgment, but as preparation for the new presence of Jesus in the church. For Matthew, resurrection culminates in the commission to the disciples that now they, like Jesus, shall teach the reign of God. Luke views the resurrection as occurring in two stages, the first on the third day following the crucifixion, where Jesus is raised to a new form of earthly existence and is eucharistically present to the disciples in the breaking of bread, and the second as an ascension into glory. The critical period in between is a time when the risen Christ instructs the disciples in their mission, which is then empowered by their reception of the Holy Spirit following the ascension of Christ into glory. Thus the synoptic evangelists interpret the resurrection in terms of a coming judgment, the creation of the church, and the empowerment of a Spirit-filled imitation of Jesus' way of life.

We have already established that process christology is revelational christology. In Christ, we see God for us, and the revelation culminates in the resurrection. One of the appearance stories begins to indicate the depths of this revelation. In the gospel of John, Thomas plays the role of the misunderstanding disciple, first with regard to the raising of Lazarus, and second with regard to the resurrected Jesus. In both cases, Jesus' answer to Thomas underscores the purposes of God. In the second account, Jesus has appeared to ten of the disciples, Thomas being absent. Upon being told of the appearance, Thomas scoffs, claiming that he will not believe until he sees the marks of the crucifixion on the one the others claim is Jesus. Accordingly, Jesus appears again and invites Thomas to touch the scars. His response is not to touch the scars, but to proclaim, "My Lord and my God," recognizing at last the presence of God in Jesus.

In the account, the scars of crucifixion mediate the truth of resurrection. But the scars belong to the preresurrection existence; the scars are the result of pain and death, yet they are present as well in the resurrection. The transformation of Jesus that occurred in resurrection is no absolute and new beginning. Rather, the transformation is fashioned through the experience of crucifixion. Transformation bears the marks of the process leading to the very need for transformation. There is a continuity with the pain of the past in the resurrection life, for the pain of the past adds its shape to the resurrection. The resurrection power of God does not annihilate the past, it transforms the past. That which was, is affirmed, but given a new dimension, a new context, a new direction.

The dynamics of the process model can help us to express this. God feels the world, precisely as that world feels itself. But God's feeling of the world cannot be an end in itself, any more than any finite occasion can be constituted simply by feeling the diverse elements of its past. Unification is required, and that unification is decisive and, to varying degrees, purposeful. God feels the world in order to transform the world into the unity of God's own character, and this happens in a twofold sense: God transforms the felt world within the divine nature, and God makes finite forms of transformation possible in history. God's feeling of the world can be crucifixion; God's transformation of the world, both within the divine nature and in history, is resurrection.

The model can be illustrated by continuing our story of the injured woman. God feels her in that moment of pain as she falls to the sidewalk; God feels her as she feels herself—pain, fright, and worry all woven together in the instant of panic. Her suffering is God's suffering as well. But this moment of co-experience at the edges of God is but the beginning of God's feeling of the world. In the process dynamic, every feeling must be integrated with all other feelings in terms of what the subject shall become. With God, the divine character is primordial, occurring eternally through the valuation of all possibilities in harmony. God does not decide the divine character on the basis of the felt world, but on the basis of God's primordial decision concerning possibilities. The feelings of the world must be integrated into this character. This means that the woman in pain must somehow be integrated with God's own vision of the togetherness of all things in love. This integration is the transforming power of the resurrection.

God feels the woman in relation to all other feelings in God—feelings of the young man, feelings of the woman's past, feelings of all the world—and primarily, the woman is felt in relation to the eternal love of God. But, as we shall argue in chapter 16, the woman-in-God participates in God's evaluative integration of her; she co-experiences with God this dynamic process of judgment and transformation of herself deep into the depths of God's being. This is *her* resurrection, moment by moment, accomplished by the power of God who *is* resurrection.

This resurrection is hidden in God, but the results of it are given to the world through the providence of God for the world, given in the process model through the initial aim that launches every finite unit of existence. God's accomplishment of the woman's transformation relative to God's own experience yields new possibilities for her continued finite existence. But the possibilities for her history must be shaped as much, and often more, by the relational factors of that history as by the resurrection in God. The initial aim must be marked *both* by the reality of the woman's context—her age, her place in society, her past creation of herself in her personality and character— *and* by possibilities for her transformation. The possibilities for her transformation are those elements deeply within the resources of God that can apply to a finite form of transformation, mirroring in a finite way the divine transformation.

God feels the resurrection of the woman both as actual within the divine nature and as possible for the world. The one will be perfect; the other will be an adaptation of that perfection to particularities of finite existence. There is a "best" for the woman, even in her harsh circumstances, and this "best" will bear the marks of both the world and God, leading her toward transformation.

The marks of pain cannot be abstracted in resurrection. Imagine the possible modes of resurrection that might be given to the woman. Perhaps the most immediate would be the simple expedient of unconsciousness, blocking out the immediacy of pain. As we try to imagine further transformations open to her, we must be guided by the resurrection nature of God, which according to the revelation of Jesus is a depth and strength of love. It is possible that the woman might be taken to a hospital to receive care, and in that context encounter others who also need care. It is possible that because of her own pain, she might empathize with another in his or her pain; receiving care, she might give care. We might further speculate along the path of the reality of love to consider the possibility that upon release from the hospital, her attitude and actions with her family might be different.

The possibility of such paths would be finite reflections of the redemptive power of God, leading the woman toward a finite mode of resurrection living and loving. If the woman actualizes such possibilities, she will experience a transformation of her pain that is nevertheless purchased through pain. The shape of her sensitivities will be direct inheritors of the scars she has received, and will bear the imprint of pain transcended. Whether or not this happens would depend upon a complexity of circumstances, primarily the response of the woman to the opportunity. Her habituated responses might hinder her movement into transformation, or keep her transformation to a low level—but insofar as it occurs, she will be living in the power of the resurrection, made available to her through the character of God. That God *is* this power is revealed by Jesus in his resurrection.

The revelation of God that takes place through Jesus' life, crucifixion, and resurrection is one that takes us to increasing depths of the divine nature. In the life of Jesus we see a manifestation of God's love—openness transcending boundaries, judgment making possible forgiveness and salvation, mutuality in giving and receiving. The quality of God's love is given expression in Jesus. In the crucifixion we encounter the raw power of this love. Its source is beyond all finite means of sustenance, for neither physical nor spiritual pain can destroy this love. God's love is self-generated in God's own self-definition. God's love endures through pain and death, inexorably reaching toward the well-being of the other. In resurrection, the resources of love are revealed, but the resources are not separate from God's love, as if God surveyed the resources and brought them to bear as so many bandaids for the world's ills.

Rather, God *is* the resource of love. In process terms, the primordial nature of God—God's own valuation of all things in a togetherness that is beauty and well-being—provides the great resource whereby God is the power of resurrection. But of course God *is* the primordial nature; the vision is not outside God, but is the very self-creation of God. Therefore, the final revelation of God in Jesus is to reveal the nature of God's love as transformative, which is to say the nature of God as transformative. God is not only the power of resurrection, God *is* resurrection. Resurrection depends upon the reality of God, not simply as that which God can do, but as that which God is.

Jesus expresses the nature of God through his life, crucifixion, and resurrection, taking the revelation progressively deeper until finally we are led, not simply to a description of God but to the mystery of God as God. And that mystery is an inexhaustible love, manifested in a power that both confirms and transforms the world.

In concluding the chapter on the life of Jesus, questions were raised that could not be addressed until after a consideration of crucifixion and resurrection. Jesus' love toward others involved components of openness, judgment, and mutuality. How do these qualities translate to God without reducing God to humanity? More specifically, since the element of openness was dealt with at the time, how do judgment and mutuality apply to the love of God for us? And finally, there is still the question of the problem of sin as defined in chapter two. How does the revelation of God in Jesus answer the problem of sin?

The love of God is such that God desires our well-being. The transformation process whereby the world is integrated into God is a judgment against that which separates any reality from well-being, and a transformation into the depths of God's love. This will be developed more fully in chapter 16, but what can be said at this point is that just as the gospel allows us to understand the consequent nature in terms of love, it also allows us to understand the concrescence of God as a judgment according to love. The result of this transforming judgment is the final reconciliation of all things in the depths of God. The world, transformed through divine judgment, is made a participant in the divine nature. If the actualized primordial vision of God can be understood to be a harmonious togetherness of all things, then the mutuality that we see in the life of Jesus is no less than a revelation of this divinely achieved togetherness in love. God is love. What the model tells us in abstract terms, the gospel tells us concretely through Jesus. The model gives the dynamics, and the gospel clothes the dynamics with the shape of love. The profound nature of this love is revealed by Jesus. The model aids us in understanding it, not simply as embodied in humanity, but as qualifying the reality of a God who holds all things together.

How does this revelation bring about salvation, addressing the problems of sin? The answers must be both personal and communal, since the development thus far indicates that the individual in God is always felt relative to a context. If the ultimate aim is the transformed togetherness of all things in God, then historical answers to the problem of sin must always contain both personal and social implications, thus mirroring in finite form the complex nature that is God.

The problem of original sin and the demonic originates in the power of the past over the present. On the personal level, we can experience elements in our past as overwhelming us, cutting off all alternatives. We easily succumb to those elements, incorporating them into our lives, and conforming ourselves to the image of that which ensnares us. On a social level, human communities are a complex bonding oriented toward the perpetuation of the community. The boundaries of the community are more or less fluid, since communities are sustained not only by their members, but by their interaction with wider societies and environment. Insofar as a society perpetuates itself by depending upon the ill-being of any, whether within or without its own boundaries, it is to that degree demonic. How does God in Jesus answer these problems, delivering us from this form of sin?

There is a threefold answer. On the personal level, the actuality of Jesus in history places Jesus in our past. If there are demonic powers threatening to overwhelm us, there is also Jesus. Jesus is a counterforce to the demonic through the simple power of his presence in our past. Jesus is the alternative whom the demonic denies.

Secondly, the power of the crucifixion shouts a witness against the power of the demonic. In revelation through the crucifixion, we encounter the reality that God's love endures all pain, without being conquered or overwhelmed by it. This revelation, when we experience it, defies the ultimacy of the powers threatening us. God, too, experiences those powers—the crucifixion says so. God, too, experiences our terror at the threat—the crucifixion reveals it. But God, experiencing with us, endures the threat unconquered, transforming it in the divine nature into resurrection possibilities for us. Because God endures the threat with us, and because God is stronger than all threats, we, too, can endure, and look for the form of resurrection fashioned for our immediate moments.

The third way in which Jesus offers salvation from the demonic addresses the social dimension of the problem, and is presupposed by the two forms of salvation particularly involved in the personal. This is the way of proclamation, which is inherently a social phenomenon, continuously creating a society that is itself called to be a counterforce to the demonic. In the example of the high school student, the boy succumbed to the powers in his environment and perpetuated them. How is the power of Jesus in the past efficacious for him? How is he to take hold of the nature of God revealed in the crucifixion, deriving from this revelation the power to contribute not to the perpetuation of the demonic, but to its transformation? His problem is that the negative past dictates violation as a way of survival, obliterating all other alternatives. How is Jesus a saving reality in the immediacy of his life?

The answer, of course, is that there is no apparent way in which he experiences Jesus as salvific. But God gives initial aims in every moment, and God knows the alternatives created by grace in the incarnation. God knows the necessity for a finite hearing, a finite seeing; this, after all, is the whole burden of incarnation. In God's care for the whole world, there must be an extension of the incarnation in a society that can become the embodiment of God's force toward inclusive well-being. This society as the church will proclaim the power of God for new life, not through words alone, but through living words, offering resurrection alternatives to persons and society. The counterforce to the demonic offered in the life, crucifixion, and resurrection of Jesus will be made present as the church proclaims it with its life. As the church is faithful to its own mission of proclaiming the resurrection through structures that promote inclusive well-being, the power of resurrection can be mediated to the larger society. Only such action will truly affect the situation of our high schooler, providing a social context for personal transformation.

There is also sin in response to the threat of the future as death. Again the situation is personal and social, requiring both personal and social answers. Death is threefold, striking at our physical, emotional, and spiritual existence. Our lives, our relationships, our meanings, are all subject to the cancellation of death. How does Jesus save us from the imprisoning walls we build against these threats?

Jesus reveals God as the power of resurrection. The future contains forms of death that frighten us, but the future is not obliterated by death. Rather, the future is resurrection as well. To know this through Jesus is to live into the future, looking for the forms of resurrection God gives us. God is stronger than all our deaths, and this strength is imparted to us so that we can live and die our many deaths. Through resurrection, Jesus is in our future and therefore opens us up to our futures.

Again, this power must be mediated to us through the force of living proclamation. The salvation accomplished through God in Christ takes place in history, and must be mediated to us through our own histories. This must happen through the faithfulness of the church in proclaiming its witness to the resurrection. As the proclamation is heard, that word enters into the immediate past of the hearer, demanding a response. God can then weave that proclamation into the rest of the hearer's past, adapting a relevant initial aim that will lead to transformation. The touch of God that begins every moment of existence can increase the resurrection power for each individual's future. As resurrection becomes applied to one's own personal future, the wall against the future will crack. The distortion will face its own denial, and transformation can begin. Jesus, by revealing the nature of God as resurrection, is the means of salvation from the forms of death. Proclamation makes that salvation a present reality.

The societal problem of the fear of death becomes in fact the promotion of death. The nuclear arms race is an awesome illustration, as nations, fearing economic or physical annihilation, amass weapons that can not only annihilate us all together, but undo creation as well. Who can deliver us from the power of this death?

Social problems require social resolutions; again, the power of the church as a society embodying and calling for an openness to life and mutually assured well-being, not destruction, must factor into the complex answer to societal fear and promotion of death. God addresses social problems through the social means of the church.

The ambiguity, of course, is that the church is not immune to the problem—the church, like the larger society, has a blighted history of seeking to save itself in cherished forms against alternative forms it experiences as threat. The church, like the larger society, has relied not on the power of resurrection and life, but upon powers of oppression and death, such as witchhunts and sexism, anti-Semitism, racism, and inquisitions of various sorts. How, then, is the church to be a social force proclaiming resurrection from the fear of death to the wider society?

The humbling answer derives from the image of crucifixion as well as of resurrection. If God is in Christ, then in crucifixion God identifies with us in all our agonies for the purpose of releasing us and raising us, giving us new possibilities of resurrection life. The church has a clear means of identification with the larger society, for we as church have likewise participated in death-dealing modes of preventing death; we can identify through our own historic experience. It is not as the pure society that we address the wider society, but as a society that can itself tap into the healing grace of God, showing in our own corporate life the better way of resurrection. Drawing on the power of God through trust, hope, and love, we are called to illustrate that which we proclaim, so that we might be a force used by God in calling the wider society to the mode of resurrection life that God ever holds before it.

There is also the problem of sin in the absolutized self. It occurs both personally and socially: personally, according to the description given previously in chapter two, and socially as any society treats others, within or without, as objects for its own disposal. The most heinous consequence of a society existing as the absolutized self is genocide, experienced in our own century as the horror of the Jewish Holocaust. But any society that exists through the oppression of others is engaged corporately in the sin of the absolutized self.

In chapter two we described the sin of the absolutized self in two ways: through viewing all others as objects for the self, or through viewing the self as the object for all others. In the first instance, the absolute subject, there is a distortion of the reciprocity of interdependent existence. In the second instance, the absolute object, there is again a denial of the way things really are. Both forms of behavior are imprisoning, cutting one off from the resources of relational existence. How is there deliverance from this form of sin?

We could look to the crucifixion as giving a salvific revelation against the power of the demonic; resurrection gives a saving revelation of God against the power of death. On the personal level, we look to the life of Jesus for the primary answer to the sin of the absolutized self. It is as if the Jesus who looks at Simon or at the weeping woman turns from the page to look into the eyes of the reader, inviting our own response.

How can this happen? Proclamation re-presents the life of Jesus. But the life of Jesus reveals the nature of God as the one who is for us in love. The God who encounters us through the pages of a gospel encounters us still in the faithfulness of the everlasting divine presence. As the church proclaims the gospel, God is unveiled. The living God encounters us in love.

Judgment and salvation are simultaneously present in the encounter. The clarity of love in the gospel is a judgment against every failure to embody love—and the failure is equally great in both forms of the absolutized self, whether as subject or object. But the very process of receiving this judgment is relational. This means that the judgment has broken the absolutization by establishing relation. Further, since according to the gospel the judgment is given through love, the encountered relation is one of an acceptance of the self that demands the well-being of the self. The encounter burns through the false absolutization, opening a way for further relation. Brought into the circle of relation, one finds the prison of the absolute self already broken. Judgment is salvation.

To deal with the problem of the absolutized society, we need to consider one further dimension of the salvation received through the revelation of God in Christ. Every aspect of this revelation is a call to community. In his life, Jesus created a community of equals, drawn from various walks of life, but united in their relation to him. Resurrection radicalized the community still further, turning it into an extension of the incarnation, now modeling within itself and in its proclamation a new way of being together. Just as Jesus touched and transformed others with healing love, even so the community that bears his name is called to do likewise in the world. The church is called to witness by its life and words to a social mode of communal well-being. Insofar as it does so, it can be a counterforce in the wider society, influencing that society with judgment and transformation.

The salvation that comes through the full revelation of God in Jesus' life, death, and resurrection addresses the personal and social evils of our time. But while we may speak of the social and the personal separately, in actuality they are deeply interwoven. To experience the power of God personally is to be called into the corporate structure of the church as the body of Christ; likewise, to be a part of the church is to become a mediator of the power of God, both socially and personally.

There is one final aspect of the salvific power of God's revelation in Jesus that we must mention. When we realize that Jesus reveals the nature of God, and when we see that this revelation bespeaks God's purposes for the world in pulling that world toward reflection of the divine image, then our approach to the world is radically altered in the direction of hope and love and trust. For instance, consider a vision of reality that sees the world as a place of blind chance, where forces beyond our control are always buffeting us, where every plan of reason is as a tiny grain of sand attempting to be as a full dike holding back the sea of chaos. What hope is there in such a vision, how can it move us toward actions of love? How can it lead to the creation of meaning? Or consider a vision of reality wherein not blind fate, but stern determinism governs the unfolding of human life. As it has been, so it shall be; every cause inexorably produces its effects, and if we but knew all the causes adequately, we would see that the world is precisely as it should be, precisely as it must be. How is there, in such a vision, any catalytic motivation to deepen the forms of human justice? Would it not be the case that one should simply accept the inevitable, drifting along with the ruthless tides of determinism? Consider again a vision of reality that sees isolated, self-sufficient existence as the supreme value: would not such a vision lead to self-aggrandizement, to a utilization of others in the service of the self? In such a vision, would there not tend to be strict hierarchies of valuation, wherein human beings were valued only insofar as they were deemed self-sufficient—with

the richest, of course, then being the most human, and the disadvantaged being excluded from humane consideration?

How one considers the nature of reality profoundly affects one's
actions with respect to the self and society. Jesus reveals the nature
of God, and this revelation is of a relational reality—of openness, a
judgment toward justice, mutuality: love. What happens matters,
and the deepest form of human existence is in the responsibility
of relationality oriented toward mutual well-being. The well-being
of each enters into the well-being of all. If this is indeed the way of
God with the world, then action in accordance with this revelation
is not only reasonable, it is required. As we respond to God in trust,
then we dare to hope that love can be enacted in our lives and in
society. We will move upon the strength of this trust, hope, and love
to contribute our own efforts to building our lives and society in
consonance with the vision.

To say this in a process understanding is to speak of the internal
effect of our visions of reality. How we think about reality is internal
to who we are, not external. Our visions of reality are incorporated
into how we are, who we are, what we do. Hence when Jesus gives
us a vision of reality that changes the world for us, giving it and us
an importance of mattering, then that vision is internalized, changing our entire orientation toward life. The vision of reality given us
through Jesus is salvific, changing our self-constitution, catalyzing
our actions in and for the world.

Finally the revelation of God in the world is the presence of God
in the world. In process terms, God is revealed through initial aims.
As was noted in the discussion, in the usual course of events the
aims are cloaked in ambiguity. In Jesus God's aim comes to full
expression, and the life of Jesus is such that we see Jesus embodying the full character of God. In Jesus, God is present to us.
Because of Jesus, we know that God is always present to us. The
singular power of this revelation of God's presence is perhaps best
expressed by turning again to the gospels and looking at the disciples.

The disciples experienced the presence of Jesus directly, but
their overwhelming response was not one in which there was any
apparent primacy to faith. Rather, the disciples seemed forever to
misinterpret Jesus—in his death they fled from him, and in his
resurrection they were dubious. Nor was their response one of

glowing hope, for they frequently misplaced their hopes, looking for self-aggrandizement in illusioned places of esteem and honor. Finally, of course, they fell into despair at the trial and crucifixion of Jesus. The one unfailing response that appears throughout the gospels is the response of love. The deepest power of the revelation of God in Christ is the generating power whereby love calls forth love. This love is the basis of the resurrection and the firstfruit of the resurrection, becoming the ground for trust and hope. The presence of God in Jesus is ultimately the creative power of love, giving birth to love which, in turn, gives birth to love yet again. This response of love called forth by the presence of God is the birth of the church. Like the disciples, the church through the ages frequently fumbles in its trust, falters in its hope; but insofar as the church senses the revelation of God for us as an ultimate presence, an ultimate love, the church, too, answers with its echoing form of love. In love is the renewal of trust and hope.

Part Four

WISDOM

Christ in God:
A Process Ecclesiology

11

IDENTITY THROUGH FAITH

IN the cathedral of Notre-Dame in Paris, the light glows golden upon the old walls, so that the ancient stone seems strangely soft. The light leads the eye upward, beyond the stone, to a burst of spiraling light, magnificent color: the great windows of Notre-Dame. In a splendor striving to foretell the glory of the heavenly Jerusalem, where "the walls are enhanced with all manner of precious jewels," this earthly Jerusalem tells the story of the church within the drama of creation, fall, incarnation, ascension, and judgment. In stone and glass the tale is told, and the deep tones of the organ fill the cathedral with sound, that the medium of music shall join in the magnificent telling.

In the midst of this, there is a strange incompletion. Not all of the windows participate in the telling of the story; some have only the bare outlines of color in a slim border, with the inner portions of the window but a faint translucent green. They await their transformation into history, when they too shall spring into the vibrancy of color through which to tell their portion of the story that is the church.

In this incompletion, a profound note is sounded. By speaking of incarnation, of the sense in which God is in Christ, christology begins. In speaking of ascension, of the sense in which Christ is in God, christology is completed through its very incompletion. The fullness of christology waits upon the church, as God mediates the benefits of Christ to the world. This appropriation of Christ is the ongoing completion of christology; it is also, of course, the doctrine of the church: ecclesiology.

Part III presented the dynamics whereby God was present in

Christ. God not only affects the world, but the world affects God. God is present to the world, and the world is present to God. That return dynamic must now become the focus of discussion in order to develop a doctrine of the church.

Recapitulating the process model, God fashions aims for the world by integrating the actuality of the world within the divine nature. God's aim toward harmony will necessarily enter into the initial aims given to the world, but each particular aim is also conditioned by what has happened in the world. Otherwise, there would be no relevance to the aim, and no real persuasive power. God works with the world as it is, luring it toward what it can become. The reality of the world conditions the relevance of the possibilities God can make available for the world. Jesus Christ, as the fullness of divine revelation in history, makes a difference to the kinds of aims now relevant to history.

The divine movement from the actual harmony in God to the possible harmony for the world can be illustrated through music. In listening to a piece of music, be it a symphony or a song, one hears not only the single note but the pattern that the whole is forming. Each note, in relation to those that have preceded it, is affected by the pattern that has been created. In turn, it joins in creation of the pattern. This participation in the pattern is both a realization of beauty and an anticipation of beauty. If the music suddenly stopped, the listener attuned to the harmony could nevertheless feel the possibilities for continuation of the harmony. The more deeply one knows the actual harmony, the more sensitive one becomes to the possible harmony. Actual beauty includes movement, change. Because it does, actual beauty suggests new forms of possible beauty.

God, creating actual harmony, is supremely attuned to the pattern of the divine creation. God is also supremely attuned, through the feelings of the consequent nature, to the reality of the world. In wisdom, God transforms the world into the divine harmony; in wisdom, God feels ways in which the becoming world might benefit from and participate in its own reflection of divine harmony. God fashions initial aims for the world.

In the primordial nature, God contains all possibilities in the harmony of a divine ordering. Through the divine nature, possibilities are ordered into beauty. This beauty, however, is ever being manifested anew as the contrasting actualities of the world bring now one possible combination, now another, to the actuality of divine realization. The actuality of the world through the consequent nature provides the contrast whereby the primordial vision comes to light. Harmony, not in vying patterns but in complementing patterns of infinite beauty, inexhaustible, mark the reality of God in the unity of the consequent and primordial natures.

Insofar as the world is concerned, the way this marvelous harmony can be reflected to the world is intensely dependent upon what the world has done. If the actualities of the world distort the harmony offered by God, then God's integration must overcome this distortion. The kind of aim that can then be given the succeeding world is limited to a corrective harmony. It is as if the edges rather than the depths of God's harmony are then able to be reflected to the world through initial aims.

The corrective movement of transformation of the world in the harmony of God will be discussed fully in chapter 16. For now, it is important to see the relation between the actual divine harmony and the ways it may be offered to the world as possibilities for the world. There are two considerations: the relation of the actual world to the harmony of God in terms of distance or correspondence, and the accessibility of harmony to the world, again in terms of distance or correspondence.

In the illustration previously used of a young man who steals from an old woman and injures her, the distance from divine harmony is obvious. If God holds the many together in complementing, enriching beauty, the young man violates that beauty in his violent disregard for the woman. God feels that action, transforming it in judgment through divine wisdom. That reality is integrated and transformed within the primordial vision, moving through successive stages from disharmony to harmony. However, the distance of the man from harmony in his finite circumstances deeply affects the mode of transformation that can be given him by God. Divine wisdom must fit the edges, not the depths, of harmony to him. Thus the initial aims given him persistently offer the first steps toward redemption. The aims must match the man's readiness and resources. The man will not receive an aim from God that he suddenly become a great philanthropist; that aim is not a real possibility for him. But he may very well receive an aim from God that might lead him to open himself to another's welfare, even in a slight way. Remorse at the sight of the woman's pain, or even awareness that the woman's pain matters—these steps toward transformation are slight, and but dimly reflective of the divine harmony; distance makes them so. Again and again, such aims may be fitted to the man until, in his own moment of choice, he actualizes such an aim. The next step offered will build upon this, going slightly beyond the first. In these two steps, the second aim will be more reflective of divine harmony than the first, for the first is akin to those movements in God wherein the evil is felt in its starkness, and transformation begins, whereas the second step is reflective of a further stage in the divine transformation of evil. Thus what God can offer to the man depends upon the man's realities in their relation to the harmony of God, and upon the man's responsiveness toward God's guiding aims for transformation.

Consider now the same dynamics in the opposite case of not only a consonance with the divine harmony, but of the actual manifestation of that harmony in history. Consider Jesus. Jesus received the divine aim to manifest God's nature for us; he actualized this aim, conforming himself to it, thus becoming the incarnation of God's will toward good for us. What must be the effect of this in God, both in relation to the actualization of divine harmony and in relation to the possibilities now made relevant to the world? Jesus manifested the divine nature in our history. In him the harmony of God is mirrored in the world, not dimly but in all of its wonder for us. The depths of God, the intensity of divine beauty, the vortex of divine harmony, all receive expression in Jesus, making him the Christ, anointed with God's presence and manifesting God's presence in, to, and for the world.

Sometimes, as we look at the night sky, a single bright star will appear. In its brightness it transforms the night; every star in the sky is changed in relation to this new appearance. It is as if this one star, in unparalleled beauty, crowns the entire beauty of the night. Christ in God is like that bright star, illumining the actuality of the primordial nature through the beauty of his manifestation of that nature in our history. Through Christ the depths of God are touched for the world; new possibilities for reflecting divine harmony in human history shine out for us. The church is born.

How is this wonder appropriated in the continuing history of humanity? How is the church related to Christ in God, such that it can be identified by the image, "body of Christ"? What is the concrete nature and function of the church, born and guided through the wisdom of God? Traditionally, the church has been defined through such qualities as unity, apostolicity, holiness, and universality; what do these terms mean if we understand the church in relation to Christ in God? Particularly problematic is the notion of universality, for we are intensely aware of the integrity and value of religions other than Christianity. Does the sense in which we understand Christ in God do justice to other modes of achieving harmony? These are the questions to be addressed in developing a doctrine of the church.

The individual presupposes the community. It is the community that brings the individual to birth, not the individual who creates the community. "The many become one, and are increased by one," is a paradigmatic Whiteheadian phrase, indicating the sense in which the many energies of the past together evoke the existence of a new subject. The subject, emerging from the community, contributes to that community, whether by perpetuating or transforming its values. But without the many, there is no basis for the existence of the one. The individual presupposes community; Christian existence presupposes the church.

Within this context, consider the sense in which the community, through its proclamation of the gospel, gives birth to new participants in that community. Jesus proclaimed the reign of God; the church proclaims Jesus, the embodied reign of God through whom we, too, are opened to the challenging yet grace-filled reign of God in our lives and society. The church proclaims this gospel, as did its Lord, in incarnate form, or clothed in the particularities of its own culture. This creates a fundamental ambiguity in the proclamation, for were it not given in cultural terms, it would not "speak to our condition," in a cultural language we can understand. At the same time, however, the gospel challenges the very culture through whom it speaks, calling it to the norm of the reign of God. Thus the proclamation the church gives is also a proclamation under which the church must itself constantly stand, in openness to the radical reign of God that can speak through all cultures, and therefore challenge all cultures.

Imagine one individual, a young man named John, who hears the church's proclamation of the gospel and is moved toward response. By responding positively to the gospel, John changes the pattern of his personal past. He may well have had a knowledge of the gospel simply through its effects upon the culture, but that knowledge had not been of determinative importance in John's self-understanding. Now the gospel realigns the meaning of his past; it enters his past through his present response. If the gospel is felt as a judgment of that past, John's positive response may be felt as an overwhelming repentance. Alternatively, the gospel may be felt as suddenly giving meaning to a past that hitherto defied meaning, and the response may be in feelings of joy. If John's past has been shadowed by encounters with death, the gospel may spell life, and John's response may be one of comfort and triumph together. John hears the gospel, responds to it in light of his own particular needs and perspective, and in the process changes his past. This opens him to God's future.

Remember that God fashions aims for us in continuity with our past, such that the transformation offered is relevant in light of that past. As John adds Christ to his past, Christ enters into the relevance of the transformative aims that can be offered to John. The resources of Christ in God are, in the wisdom of God, fitted to John's particular situation. Speculate as to the dynamics by which this takes place; slow down the rapid succession of events that constitute John, and cast those events into a detailed analysis of the process whereby they come into being.

John feels his past in a new light. His understanding of Jesus changes the pattern by which he evaluates existence. Jesus is now part of John's personal past, through the power of proclamation. God, who feels us in every completed moment of our existence, feels John's responsiveness to the gospel, re-enacting or resurrecting this response into the divine nature. Since Christ is now in John's relevant past, the integration of John in God can take place in such a way that John moves into that constellation within the depths of divine harmony made actual by Christ. John's reality participates in Christ in God. This integration of God's feelings— feelings of John in union with Christ—results in a new possibility being given to John for his next moment of finite existence. The possibility that is fashioned for him is made possible through Christ in adaptation and application to John's finite situation. Thus a

christly repentance, a christly joy, or a christly comfort and triumph may be the immediate possibilities for reflecting the divine
harmony that are given to John.

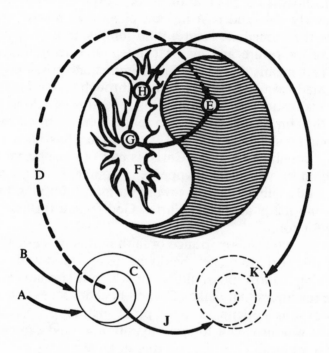

A = proclamation of Christ in John's past

B = God's initial aim to respond positively to the proclamation

C = John's constitution of himself in a positive response

D = God's prehension of John

E = God's re-enaction of John in the consequent nature

F = Christ in God

G = God's integration of John with Christ

H = the Christly possibility now made relevant to John in his next moment

I = John's reception of this possibility as the initial aim

J = John's feelings of his past

K = John's union of past and possibility in his new constitution of himself

Consider, however, that whichever one of those possibilities is given to John comes to him in the form of an initial aim that he may then actualize. In the minuteness of the process analysis, many successive entities are involved in John's person, and not simply one. Each entity is the re-creation of John, ever newly responding to an ever newly enlarged past in light of an ever newly given possibility for the immediate future. Who John is, in each instant, is a function of his future and his past, integrated in the unity of the present. This means that when John's immediate possibility for the future is made available to him in and through Christ in God, then John's actualization of that aim is his reception of Christ for him. Through the aim, Christ enters into John's identity. If our future is a part of our present identity, and if the future has been uniquely provided through Christ, then Christ is part of our present identity. The medium by which this happens, of course, is divine wisdom. Through God's subjective aim toward harmony, unifying John with the harmony made actual by Christ, God feels a further mode of harmony for John.

Notice the intense importance of faith in this process. God does not force the world to reflect the divine nature; God waits upon the world, giving it those possibilities for which it is ready. Faith provides the readiness that makes Christ's benefits accessible to John. Apart from John's openness to the proclamation of Christ, there is no feasible way in which John's integration in God can be aligned with christly possibilities; faith is therefore necessary.

Faith, however, does not appear in a vacuum. Faith presupposes grace in this model. That is, the proclamation of the gospel and God's aims to respond to that proclamation through faith precede John's response of faith, and in fact make that response possible. Since John is responsible neither for the proclamation he hears nor the aim God gives him, these elements, both of which make faith possible for him, are entirely gracious in character. John's positive response in faith depends upon this prior grace, and is inexplicable without it. Nevertheless, John's response *is* his response. This means that insofar as he responds positively to grace, he constitutes himself through faith; insofar as he responds negatively, he is responsible for refusing grace. The decision is ultimately his own. In this model, faith is a response-ability, and therefore a responsibility. It takes place within the encompassing reality of grace, which makes faith possible. By grace and through faith, John participates in the benefits of Christ. In so doing, his identity is formed through Christ.

We began this account of personal responsiveness to the gospel by affirming that the individual presupposes the community. To focus only on the individual response to God through Christ risks a distortion of the situation, for the church is not a collection of individuals who all happen to come to faith; rather, it is through the community's faithful proclamation, in word and deed, that individual responsiveness is made possible. Because of God's gracious action through the proclamation of the church, John is brought within the sphere of faith. John's identity as a Christian, therefore, is inexplicable apart from the identity of the community called church.

Throughout the centuries and throughout the earth there are those who have responded to Christ in faith. Each one, like John, has been united with Christ in God; each one, like John, has received a christly possibility for the immediate future, formed in conjunction with her or his personal past situated in time and culture. With the union in Christ, each one, like John, has an identity formed through faith in Christ. The church is the community of all those whose identities have been so formed through faith, and the church is the community through whom the proclamation is given that makes possible in time this hearing that makes for faith.

12

ONE, HOLY, APOSTOLIC CHURCH

JOHN, Tuyet, Maria, Ti-Fam, Kwasi, Kuang-ming, Masao—these and countless others share an identity formed through Christ in faith. Each is brother or sister to all others in the family of God called the church. The church, however, is more than the contemporary members—it extends into the long past; it will extend into the future. What is the nature of its existence throughout time since its foundation in Jesus Christ? An answer is suggested by looking at the traditional dimensions by which the church has been described for two thousand years: unity, holiness, apostolicity, and universality.

Apostolicity is the sense in which the church is continuously affected by and responsible to its past, beginning with the testimony of the apostles to the life, death, and resurrection of Jesus. Unity comes to the church from its future, because of the dynamics of identity in Christ. Holiness is the present result as the church exists in faithfulness to both its past and its future.

Apostolicity has been interpreted in various ways throughout the history of the church, but a central element in any interpretation is the constant testimony to the resurrection. The first apostles were those who were witnesses to the resurrection and who had been with Jesus in his teaching ministry. Their apostleship also involved proclamation of the resurrection and a continuance of the teaching of Jesus. Whereas Jesus preached the reign of God, however, the apostles preached Jesus. Jesus embodied God's reign, and made openness to that reign a present possibility. Thus the apostle's proclamation of the resurrection included within it a call to the reign of God through identification with Jesus Christ.

Proclamation of the resurrection was never simply verbal. Just as in the ministry of Jesus, so in the ministry of the early church proclamation involved service, or the embodiment of that which was proclaimed. Healing was united with preaching in the book of Acts. There is ample evidence not only in Acts but also in the epistles that the proclamation of the word within the community was in a context of love: edification of the church in body and spirit was essential. The ideal of the church presented to us is of an egalitarian structure wherein people were clothed, fed, and cared for in communal ministries of well-being.

How could it be otherwise? The ultimate Word is not a paragraph, but a person. If Jesus is the Word of God incarnate, then the heart of proclamation is relational and communal, not propositional. In order to be true witnesses to God's fullness of action for us in Christ, we too must be living words, embodied proclamations, living in community that which we proclaim. If the telling of the gospel is simply the recitation of words, then we have lost the gospel.

This implies that there is both a constant and a relative pole to proclamation. Insofar as both are present, the church is apostolic. The constant pole is the unchanging referent for the church in the life, death, and resurrection of Jesus Christ. God is for us, calling us and enabling us to reflect God's image in communities of love and justice. But to preach such a message is to be gripped by the message, formed by the message. This brings out the relative pole of proclamation, or the sense in which its effect in us leads us to the living testimony written in communities open to the reign of God.

Consider the necessity of keeping this pole of proclamation fluid, conformable to the specific needs of a time. Suppose that a small group of believers decides that the demands of love and justice require that they form a community ministering to the poor of a certain neighborhood. They research the specific needs of the area, and investigate the civil/cultural/political structures contributing to this poverty for the purpose of influencing systemic change. They explicitly carry out these activities in the name of Jesus Christ.

In the process, they find there are internal needs of the group that also require attention. Some of these needs are directly related to the planned mission, but others are rooted in problems stemming from the group's past, whether as individuals or as a whole. So the group develops specific internal ways of ministering to each other, as well as external ways of ministering through word and action to the surrounding community. The worshiping component of the group remains central. However, the way of worship soon begins to reflect the depth of concern the individuals feel for the society around them. Intercession mingles with praise. In the renewal of the specific forms of worship that evolve, the people feel themselves energized for the full proclamation of the word to the society.

Their ministry is so successful that they decide to make sure it is preserved. They decide the way to do this is to draw up a careful and precise record of the way they do things. This record includes detailed instructions as to the organizational format, the worship activities, the kinds of ministries, how to do them, and an analysis of their internal needs and how they are addressed. This descriptive account could be read as a formula for success, for in fact it was a record of success. Surely success achieved once could be achieved again, if the same format were followed precisely! But of course the living word—that which in essence must flow from the responsiveness to needs and situations that surround us—would become a lifeless word in its translation to mere marks on paper. Description would become rule, and the reality of love and justice extended to real people in real societies by a specific group of Christians would be endangered. No subsequent society could exactly duplicate the conditions of the first society in which ministry took place. Hence, no society could be truly ministered to in precisely the same way.

Try to imagine what would happen if the description of that ministry were in fact turned into a rule for imposition on another community. Imagine that the same group that began the ministry was suddenly transferred to a totally different area. All of the members are magically transferred to a suburban community of middle-to-upper class people, many of whom work in the various professions. If the group utilizes the same forms and methods they developed before, will they still enact love and justice? If a mode of worship totally integrated into the kind of ministry they are living is copied verbatim in the new situation, will not their worship become increasingly separated from their living? Obviously, the ways in which they minister in the second location will be most like the ways they developed in their first location not by a mere copying of the first experience, but by responding as freshly and lovingly in the second instance as they did in the first. The record of the past incorporated into their documents will be useful as a history of who they have been, but they must transcend that record if they are to be faithful to their call to minister. Ministry in the second location must be tailored to the specific needs encountered there. Likewise, the new work will uncover different kinds of needs internal to the group; it might well require a different organizational structure. The new ministry will surely affect the content of prayer and worship if the group retains its faithfulness to the proclamation. Faithfulness to the proclamation of God's love toward us will require that the group be responsive to change, willing to let go of former ways in order to develop ways that are appropriate to the changed circumstances.

And is this not the way of the reign of God? The great reversal themes in the teaching and life of Jesus call for a radical openness to God's rule. Our structures, no matter how inclusive their original intent, tend to harden toward their own preservation and perpetuation, rather than to be continuously open to the needs of inclusive well-being. The structures are to be in the service of love and justice. Openness to God's future calls upon us indeed to create structures, but always to submit those structures to the critique of the demands of God's radical love. Faithfulness to the past, when that past is the revelation of God in Jesus Christ, calls upon us for a radical openness to new and unexpected forms of inclusive well-being, God's reign.

Apostolicity, therefore, is a continuity with the past that nevertheless has an essential openness to it. In every generation and in every Christian there must be a faithfulness to the content of the gospel: our words must point to the Word who is a person, living, crucified, risen. Therefore, our words must also take the form of ever new interpretations of ways in which we can enact love and justice. Word and deed together constitute the church's faithfulness to its apostolic tradition. Constancy and openness form the dynamism whereby the apostolic church witnesses to the world.

With such a definition, it is clear that the church as a whole, and not only a specific class within it, is called to apostolicity. To be an apostle was to be an eye-witness to the resurrection; in a primary sense, this refers to those named by the apostle Paul in I Corinthians 15:58. Approximately six hundred persons are included in this account. Since it is on the basis of these appearances that Paul counts himself an apostle, presumably all six hundred or so persons were eligible for apostleship—the number is not restricted to the list of disciples named during Jesus' lifetime. Indeed, a Roman woman, Junia, is named an apostle in Romans 16, so clearly apostleship is a category extending beyond the original disciples.

It is said, certainly with the justification of historical common sense, that no one beyond those early Christians is an eye witness to the resurrection, and hence all apostleship since that time is derivative. For some Christians, this is restricted still further by naming only the ordained as standing in the direct descent of the apostles by virtue of the laying on of hands. Yet given our identity in Christ, and the faithfulness of God, there is a profound sense in which we are all immediate witnesses to the resurrection. There is no Christian who has not experienced deep trial of some sort or another—indeed, to be human is to hurt. The trial may be social—the experience of oppression, or the helpless agony of seeing environmental destruction and international ruthlessness—or personal, through some deep pain of body or soul, for whatever reason. But we also experience the faithfulness of God, who fashions modes of resurrection for us. These modes of resurrection, reflecting the communal nature of God, have social dimensions. It may come through a renewed dedication to plunge into efforts to bring about profound social change, together with some hope concerning the effects of this effort. It may come through the personal ability to endure, trusting to God's ability to work, moment by moment, toward a transformation that will, amazingly enough, deepen our humanity—albeit through a way that leaves nailprints on our hands. In as many ways as there are needs, God in faithfulness works resurrection for us, in us, through us. And the good that is wrought is never for ourselves alone, but brings benefit to the community, as well. In such ways as these, we are all eye-witnesses to the resurrection. And we are all called to the apostolic witness.

Apostolicity requires a faithfulness to Jesus Christ and an openness to new ways of acting in love and justice. Actions impelled by continuity with the apostolic past will lead us into the newness of how we may minister today. Through faithfulness to the past, we will be open to the future. It is at just this point that we must look to see the basis for the unity of the church. In process thought, apostolicity involves the church's relationship to its past, but in a way that is continually open to newness, to the future. This openness provides the basis for the church's unity in the following way.

Remember the description of the initial aim of God. It comes to each one of us as a real possibility for our immediate future. When we gave the example of John coming to faith in Jesus, we outlined the dynamics whereby his whole identity is changed by that faith. Christly possibilities are available to him. The kinds of aims God can give John are radically changed by his faith in Christ, and we can truly say that John's identity is formed by Christ. Christ is mediated to him through the initial aim.

The initial aim shows us our immediate possibilities for the future. This means that John actually experiences the benefits of Christ coming to him as his future. Insofar as John conforms himself to those aims, he incorporates Christ into his personality. John becomes an extension of Christ's incarnation in the world.

The very notion of identity indicates why this must be so. Who we are depends upon our past and upon our future possibilities. If John should decide to go to seminary and prepare to become a minister of the gospel, John's whole identity in seminary is not only a function of his life experiences to that date, but even more importantly, his identity is informed by his hopes and plans for the future. Ordination to the ministry—something that, for John, is still three years in his future—is the most dominant influence upon his identity. John talks about his entrance into ministry as a response to a call, as if he were forming his identity in obedience to a future responsibility. Is not the genuineness of that call rooted in the initial aim of God, coming to John as a possibility for his future? And isn't that aim informed by the christly possibilities made relevant to John through faith? John goes to seminary, and in time he is ordained to ministry. But all the while, his identity has been forming in obedience to the future, in obedience to God's call in Christ. This illustration of John's identity formed in response to the call to ministry is but one instance of what takes place in every moment of our lives. In every moment John is responding to the call of God, forming his identity in response to that call. John and each one of us are who we are precisely in the way we combine our past and our future in the present. When that future is made possible through Christ, then our identities are formed through Christ. But this formation always comes to us as the future.

Consider the unity that is created if many people share in an identity formed through faith in Christ. The unity we see in a family group stems from its past. Brothers and sisters, by sharing the same parents, share the same family identity. Their common past, whether by birth or adoption, defines them as family. For the family that is the Christian church, unity comes primarily from a shared future. Just as the sharing of a past creates a real kinship, even so the sharing of a future creates a real kinship. If John's identity is formed through Christ, and if Kwasi's identity is formed through Christ, and if Ti-Fam's identity is formed through Christ, then all three share in the same identity and become brothers and sister to one another even though they live so widely scattered in the world. Christ, as the source of their identity, is also the ground of their unity, creating in them a bond as real and as close as family, creating them as the community of church. This unity and community comes to each from the future, through the initial aim. The future, mediated by God through Christ, is therefore the basis of the church's unity.

Focus now upon the content of the initial aim in order to see more clearly how the unity of the church can be realized. A christly possibility is one that conforms to the nature of God, revealed so clearly in Jesus as an accepting and transforming love, willing and accomplishing our good. Just as the love of Jesus was intensely responsive to the needs of those around him, even so the content of christly aims will reflect a loving responsiveness to the well-being of the world of which we are a part. The aims from God push us toward care for the world. this push toward well-being stems from the character of God; it must therefore be an unfailing component of every christly initial aim.

Suppose that John, in his travels, meets Masao, a Christian from Japan. They wish to experience their common bond, their unity as members of the one body of Christ. How shall they discover this unity? Shall they begin an exhaustive analysis of their pasts? In the past, they will discover their common bond as witnesses of the resurrection, but if they have been obedient to their apostolicity, they will also discover much diversity. Each will have been open to

God's call in their own specific cultural context—for if God works with the world as it is in order to bring it to what it can be, God's aims reflect a contextual well-being, conditioned by what the world in any one location can bear. As John and Masao come together, God's aims for them both will reflect that new togetherness, and the new possibilities that togetherness brings forth. The way to discover their unity in Christ is to look to the leading of God with regard to the immediacies of the world around them. In an orientation toward God's reign, their unity will become apparent, almost as a byproduct of responsiveness to the one God leading us in ways of well-being. The future, not the past, clarifies the unity of the church.

There are many implications for the many different types of churches in the world. We not only see Protestant, Roman Catholic, and the various forms of the Orthodox churches, but each of these bodies subdivides into various ways of being Christian community. Our usual response is to bewail our diversity, decrying the scandal of so many people who disagree with our own way of seeing things. But has anyone ever joined a church which she or he believed to be false? Has not every member of every congregation chosen, to some extent, to join or remain in that congregation because it seemed to be God's leading, however culturally conditioned? How, then, can looking to the past alone show us our unity? While the past will indeed reveal the constancy of our apostolic proclamation—we all preach Jesus, crucified and risen—the past will also reveal the many ways in which we have been called to live out that proclamation, as well as the many ways by which we have dishonored that proclamation by failing to honor the diversity it allows. The past will also show God's gracious faithfulness to us despite our great failures. The crucifixions we have inflicted through our refusal to see many forms of God's reign have nonetheless yielded new modes of communities, each itself manifesting the power of God's resurrection. Churches sown in dishonor—and who can call the wars and persecutions of the Reformation era honorable for any one of the churches involved?—have nonetheless born honorable fruit. The past, with its faithful and unfaithful diversities, will not show us our unity. Only as we look to the future, and discern the way in which God calls us to further acts of love and justice in the world will we begin to know the rejoicing that follows when we find a sister or brother in the many communities of the family of God.

The unity of the church flows from the future by the grace of God, who mediates the benefits of Christ to us.

Notice, however, that this unity is essentially experienced through the relative pole of proclamation. Unity comes through the future aspect of apostolicity. As we are open to the call of ministry, to that living proclamation of the gospel, we are also open to our unity, our bond of kinship in Christ. The union with Christ creates the unity of the church, from which the church moves to mission. This apostolic witness, in turn, is the basis of the message whereby persons may respond to Christ in faith, thus realizing christly possibilities and creating anew the conditions of church unity. Apostolicity and unity are interrelated aspects of the church, a moving rhythm between the past and the future, wherein the church in the present is ever formed anew.

To speak thus about the unity and apostolicity of the church raises the question of the church's holiness. In the description thus far we have outlined the conditions for goodness, beauty, holiness. Is the church in its concrete reality indeed holy? Is the holiness of Christ in God communicated to the church? Is the church "without spot or blemish," as the letter to the Ephesians claims?

Just as we discussed God in Christ and Christ in God, even so the church must be discussed in both a temporal and everlasting dimension, in the world and in God. Only so can full consideration be given to the question of the holiness of the church. Insofar as the church is in God, it participates in the nature of God, and hence in God's own holiness. God transforms the community of the church in the integration of the consequent and primordial natures, and in that divine process God welds the church into true holiness. In God, the church is purified and transformed. A full discussion of this must await the chapter, "The Reign in God," but it is important to indicate here that this holiness that qualifies the transformed church in God is not tangential to the kinds of holiness to which the church is called in history.

Thus far, every description of the process dynamic has been an enormous simplification. We speak of one occasion, the wealth of its past, and God's feeling of that occasion and integration of the occasion with Christ in the depths of divine harmony. But the process happens again and again and again. Not one occasion, and not simply one series of occasions, but every occasion whatsoever is felt by God and integrated according to divine wisdom into the primordial harmony. Everything affects everything else in this process universe. God adapts aims to the world in light of this intensity of complex interrelationships. Therefore, what the church accomplishes is felt by God and dealt with by God in transforming wisdom. God blends the whole church everlastingly with that constellation we call Christ in the primordial nature of God. The church is made without spot or blemish by God in God, and there is an effect of this action continuously presented to the world. The effect is in the multiplicity of aims given to the individuals of the church, each aim being given in light of all the others. Thus the very aims of God, reflecting the divine holiness of the church, tend toward a communal form of that holiness on earth.

Insofar as the church manifests holiness it must do so in its communal structure. The holiness of the church exists in the communal nature of the church. Again, to use the metaphor of the light and prism, that single holiness that is the church in God is reflected through the prism of God's purpose for the world, breaking into the many rays of holiness made possible for the world. The rays, however, complement each other, since they all spring from the same source, which is the church unified with Christ in God. Further, the rays complete each other, for only in togetherness do they truly demonstrate the unity of their source. Just as the harmony of colors in a rainbow bespeaks their initial unity in the single ray of light, even so the communal actualization of God's purposes in the world bespeaks the initial unity of that purpose in God's divine integration of the church with Christ in God.

For instance, John, identified with Christ, feels the call to love and justice relative to the plight of poverty-stricken older persons in his town. Fixed incomes in an inflationary age, no opportunities for employment, isolation and loneliness, and the apathy that accompanies the sense of not being valued, of being tangential to a society— all of these problems seem to afflict these aged people, complicated by the fact of physical problems. Yet the people elicit John's love, and he earnestly desires to see more just conditions for them. However, while some of the problems may be met on a personal level, others, such as poverty itself, are societal problems. How can John address them? His openness toward the people, his invitation to mutuality with them, and his active love toward them may be great, but John alone cannot create conditions of justice for these people. His single individuality encounters the weight of society, and while his lone voice has some effect, it must be reinforced by other voices if the necessary political and social changes are to be enacted. John may work personal wonders with the people, but the counterweight of the force of habitual ways of doing things works against him.

Joan is also identified with Christ, as are Catherine and others in John's church. They, too, receive aims for love and justice in concrete forms. As John shares his vision for the people with his sisters and brothers in Christ, the vision gains in power. The communal force of the larger society can be countered by the communal force of the church, seeking love and justice for those aged people. Furthermore, within the church itself the communal identity in Christ will create ways of addressing the needs of the aged within the church. These people will be invited to participate in the openness and mutuality of the community in Christ. In community, the holiness of existence in love and justice becomes real. The common identity in Christ requires this. Insofar as the church lives from its identity in Christ, it becomes a holy community.

By so defining holiness, the interrelationship between apostolicity, unity, and holiness becomes apparent. If apostolicity relates to the church's continuity with the past, and unity relates to the church's creation from the future, then holiness is the effect of apostolicity and unity held together in the present. In holiness the many are as one; in holiness, apostolicity receives new expression; in holiness, and only in holiness, does the actualization of the community of Christ occur.

To make such a statement obviously creates a problem, for is our local church community really holy? The problem is associated with our usage of the word, holiness. We are accustomed to think of holiness as a rarity, assigning the quality to individuals in the past of particularly saintly character and deeds. Alternatively, we make holiness an ideal somehow associated only with the future, such as applies to the church with Christ in God. However, to dissociate holiness from the church in the present is a dangerous thing, for it tends to allow justice to be an abstract quality, and love to be a sentimental devotion to the past or future. If holiness is associated primarily with a few individuals in the past, or if holiness is assigned only to a realm transcendent of time, then the church is relinquishing its identity in the present. The church's unity can only be expressed through holiness; the church's apostolicity depends upon concrete holiness; holiness is thus the actuality of both unity and apostolicity. Without such holiness in some degree, there can be no church.

The church is called, by its identity in Christ, to be love and justice, to be openness and mutuality, and in the living dynamism of these qualities, continually to move into deeper forms that manifest these qualities. Always the forms of love and justice are relative to the actual conditions in the world, working transformation. This is the identity of the church, and the holiness of the church. Holiness must be a present quality, or the church loses hold on its very identity.

Holiness will be appropriated by degrees. The initial aim is adapted by the occasion into the subjective aim. This constitutes the freedom and self-creativity of the occasion. The adaptation of the aim is not necessarily in either/or terms. Rather, it can be accomplished through modifications that are closer or further from the aim given by God. This means that the community called church will continually be actualizing its identity in a more-or-less reality. The church in and of itself is fluid, not fixed. It will be more or less holy, and thus more or less itself, according to the ways in which it individually and corporately adopts the aims it receives from God. God is faithful in leading the church toward ever deeper forms of love and justice, and waits upon the church to actualize the specificities of love and justice, to be holy. By the grace and power of God, the church is without spot or blemish in God; by the exercise of its own finite responsibility, the church may mirror this holiness in the world, brightly or dimly, according to its choice. In its choice is the measure of its holiness, and the measure of its identity with Christ as community, as church.

Holiness is relative to the circumstances of the present. Since holiness is a present quality, it must be concrete. If it is concrete, it is relative to the particularities of circumstances. This relativization of holiness becomes a guard against both pride and judgmental intolerance. In fact, this relativization of holiness becomes a basis for the diversity and ecumenicity of the church. Consider the situation: the call to the church is to manifest its unity and apostolicity in holiness, which is to say the church is called to the enactment of love and justice, openness and mutuality. Given the relative nature of these enactments, no one concrete achievement can be normative for the others. In fact, this would work against the continuous achievement of still further realizations of these qualities. This means that no single achievement can exhaust love and justice, and that every single achievement contains within itself a dynamism that leads beyond itself. Pride would be the tendency to take one's own achievement as an end in itself; judgmental intolerance involves the further step of using one's own achievement as a way to measure others. Since holiness requires many forms, true holiness negates pride, and with it, judgmental intolerance. Further, the communal nature of holiness reinforces the interdependence of the many and the one for the achievement of love and justice. Gratitude for such interdependence, and for the God whose aims reinforce it, crowds pride from the space of holiness.

Holiness is very much a "here and now" matter, but there are many "here's," and many "now's," which means there must be many ways to manifest holiness. No one shape is exhaustive or determinative. If there is no diversity in the church, no variety of ministries, no incorporation of those varieties into forms of worship, then holiness is lacking. Without holiness, the identity of the church is to some degree in question. Thus the very diversity of the church can and must express the holiness of the church in faithfulness to unity in Christ. Uniformity, on the contrary, is against the nature of holiness, and therefore a denial of the church's unity in Christ. The church's unity, coming to the church through the future, must be expressed through diverse actualizations of holiness. Given the togetherness of unity and apostolicity in holiness, true apostolicity is being recreated in many ways. Apostolicity multiplies itself in diversity, and denies itself in sheer uniformity.

The churches recognize their unity in Jesus Christ in and through their diversity. Each church proclaims Christ's life, death, and resurrection, with this proclamation taking an incarnate form as an enacted word, and an interpreted deed. Thus the incarnation of God in Christ must be completed by the incarnation of Christ in the church, through the means of Christ in God. This incarnation, if it is faithful to the proclamation, will be in the many forms of holiness, each form pushing beyond itself. The unity in Christ calls for a diversity of forms, and the diversity of forms bespeaks the unity in Christ.

13

THE SACRAMENTS

IF the church is to have a diversity of forms, what of the role of the sacraments in the church? Do not the sacraments argue against that diversity of forms? Are not the sacraments uniform in nature, transcending the relativity of time and space, thus requiring but one interpretation, one mode of administration?

The uniformity of the sacraments no more mitigates against the diversity in unity of the church than does the uniformity of the life, death, and resurrection of Jesus Christ. There are many interpretations of Jesus Christ, but only one person Jesus Christ. Further, the one person necessarily gives rise to many interpretations, since the one person is experienced in the relativity of many cultures, many times, many encounters. Each interpretation is reflective of a multiple reality, so that we might say that the varying interpretations of Jesus are ways in which Christ has influenced the interpretation of one's own best way of communal being in a particular culture. The constancy is the groundedness in the gospel. Jesus, crucified and risen, reveals to us that God is for us. The relativity is the power of that gospel as it impacts persons, wherever and whenever those persons live. This is cause for the church to rejoice, since this diversity reflects the power of God in human history.

The sacraments participate in constancy and relativity. The constancy is in the ritualistic profession of the life, death, and resurrection of Jesus Christ; the relativity is in the way in which that profession is received, experienced, understood. The ways we interpret the sacraments are reflective of the ways in which we understand our experience of relationship with God and each other through Christ. Again, using the metaphor of light, the one light passes through the prism, breaking into many rays of color. The rays, because of the unity of their source, are creative of a new unity through their togetherness in diversity in the loveliness of the color spectrum. The sacraments, like Christ, are one, and are interpreted in light of the encounter with Christ. The many interpretations can be creative of a temporal unity in the diversity that is community.

The sacraments are essential to the life of the church, both because of the constancy of proclamation they provide, and because of the very means through which the proclamation is made. We are a linguistic species; we express ourselves in words, and guard the words from generation to generation through oral or written traditions, as if we could defy the shifting nuances and changes of language. We continuously interpret ourselves in dialogue with our past through the texts we have accrued, or with one another, or in the interminable monologues we construct within ourselves—we are a word-afflicted species. On the one hand, the word liberates us—because of our words, we transcend one time, one place; through the words of our communication, we establish communities. On the other hand, the word binds us—we are tied to the word, almost trapped inside it, till some would reduce humanity simply to linguisticality, like some web spun from a spider that traps the spider first of all. There is also the sense in which the binding word divides—we construct our shibboleths for one another, defining acceptable versus unacceptable communities, and then use our words as reason enough to destroy one another. We are a linguistic people, caught within the ambiguities of our worded existence.

In the midst of our wordiness, there comes a living word, the Christ, in all the concreteness of embodiment and relationality. Yes, we interpret that Word, too, and are invited to do so—but the sacraments, themselves interpreting that Word for us, remind us again and again that we cannot tie that Word into our texts and textuality, for the Word is no abstraction—the Word can be touched, tasted, and it is this concretely embodied word that finally frees and nourishes us. Not abstractions of countless texts, but the living relationality of Christ, enacted now in community, is that to which the sacraments call us. The proclamation is made in the reality of bread, wine, water. We repeat the words telling of the life, death, and resurrection of Jesus Christ as we participate in the sacraments, and the beyond-words power of the Word is conveyed in the wordless Word of bread, wine, water. God is communicated to us: God is for us, concretely, here, now.

Thus in all the ambiguities of our linguistic being we have a constancy in the concrete re-presentation of the Word that is the foundation of our existence. From that Word, given now in these elements, many of our own words follow, reflecting the interaction of the Word with a culture, a philosophy, a time. The constancy gives rise to the relativity of many interpretations, and this is good. If that constancy were lost, then our words would spin from one interpretation to another, weaving webs of abstractions, till finally the very reason for our words would be lost, and no identity in Christ left to be proclaimed. The sacraments ground us in the embodied Word of Christ.

The sacraments, like Christ, do what they proclaim. Christ proclaimed the reign of God, and embodied it, opening its possibilities to those who identify with him. Likewise, the sacraments proclaim Christ, and make Christ present, creating community among those who participate in Christ through the sacraments. We will consider this first through the sacrament of baptism, and then through the sacrament of the Lord's Supper.

Through baptism, the community encounters its own transformation through its incorporation of another member. Just as a mother gives birth to an infant, even so the community gives birth to those baptized into it. Faith begets faith. The community has proclaimed faith in Christ, identity with him, and therefore openness to the reign Jesus proclaimed. Through the faithfulness of the church in proclamation, and the faith of the church embodied in that proclamation, one comes or is brought to the community for incorporation into that faith. Adults come through the faith already born in them through the proclamation, confess that faith, and receive baptism. The children of the community are brought through the faith of the church to be embraced by the church in baptism. In both cases, baptism is into the life, death, and resurrection of Jesus Christ; baptism is participation in Christ, and therefore identity with him.

How is baptism into the life, death, and resurrection of Jesus Christ? The answer is both symbolic and literal, with the symbolic answer being the deeper of the two. Remember that we are a worded people, so that words have a forming power. Christian baptism builds upon the symbolism of Christ's own baptism, which in turn builds upon the baptismal practice recorded of John. John gave a baptism of repentance that would ready persons for the coming reign of God, purifying them as they waited expectantly for that reign. Most likely John held an apocalyptic view of the reign, expecting it to break into and through the Roman oppression of Judaism, bringing liberation and purity. His baptism of repentance for the forgiveness of sins was a purification that then allowed deeds of justice that would anticipate God's reign.

Jesus' baptism is twofold. On the one hand, he participated in the baptism of John that Mark records as Jesus' reception of God's Spirit. In the following three years of ministry, Jesus proclaimed and embodied the reign of God, despite his increasing isolation as the disciples failed to understand him. Mark then recounts the second baptism as the baptism of his death. This death is both a cup from which he must drink, and a baptism with which he must be baptized (Mark 10:38). It is as if the baptism of Jesus begins in the wilderness with John, and continues until its completion on the forsaken hill of Golgotha. Through this extended period, this God-in-Christ identifies with our condition, drinking it fully, immersed in it completely.

We, too, are baptized, but in keeping with the great reversal theme of common expectations. Jesus identifies with us in his baptism, and we are identified with him in ours. The verb is intentionally passive: it is God, acting through the community of faith, who makes this identification possible, and God through the community who actually baptizes. The person simply receives the baptism that is given.

What happens in this baptism? We are made one with the life, death, and resurrection of Jesus, whose own three-year baptism is his anointing as the Christ. Since we are made one with him, his person and work are now effectively joined to our lives, so that christly possibilities are available to us through all our days. Our identity may be formed through our identification with him, so that through him, we may be made open for God's reign.

But this formation does not happen to us in isolation. Indeed, the community is essential to the process, and the process is essential to the community. In the actual rite of baptism, the congregation's role is critical. They participate in the baptism by their own response of faith and faithfulness, for the community is asked to receive and support the baptized one. Through the communal as-

sent, the effectiveness of baptism begins—and that effectiveness is
to span our lives. The community is bound by its vow to nourish the
one newly received, that the faith so nascently born might grow.
But by the community's embrace of this new participant, the community is changed, transformed even if ever so slightly by its new
incorporation of this member. As the infant faith is nourished
(whether in child or adult), this baptized one participates in the
work of the church as a sign community, proclaiming and open to
the reign of God as inclusive well-being. And through this participation the church itself grows in faith, enriched by the contribution of
this one, even as the one is enriched by the contributions of the
many. For the church is a community of the baptized, each one of
whom depends upon the support of all others and is vowed to the
support of all others. Baptism is the continuous generation of the
community, creating the very reality that it proclaims: unity with
Christ for the sake of the reign of God.

Such a view of baptism is deeply related to the ministry of the
church, for baptism is itself an ordination to ministry, a call and
empowerment for openness to the reign of God. The community of
the baptized are themselves bound by a word—that word of their
identification with Christ—and liberated by a word, for through
identification with Christ they are freed to serve. As the church
develops a structure to facilitate this service, some will be called to
give order to the structure for the sake of freeing all to serve as a
total community. Through this order of the ministry within the
community, the whole community is to be given structure and
empowerment for their ministry in the wider society as a sign of
God's reign.

Like Christ's own baptism, Christian baptism into Christ is instantaneous and a process. As instantaneous, it takes place when
the community and the one to be baptized are bound together by
the Spirit through word and water. As a process, it is the constant
living from that baptism in the resurrection life of the community.
Baptism spans the life of the community ill its own ultimate incorporation into the fullness of God.

The elements of apostolicity, unity, and holiness discussed in our
previous chapter have relevance for the sacraments, for they find
their deepest expression in the life of the community precisely
through the sacraments. In baptism, the constant pole of apos-

tolicity is expressed through the re-presentation in water and word of the life, death, and resurrection of Jesus Christ. The relative pole is embodied in the contemporary congregation and the one to be baptized: here, now, this word of the gospel interprets this community as it increases through this new sister or brother in Christ. At the same time, the community interprets the gospel through its own mode of enculturated being, giving expression to that gospel in this unique place and time. The relative and the constant together create this community as apostolic in its essential constitution.

The unity of the church comes particularly to the fore, for this community is united in faith, creating the new bond with the baptized one. In giving and remembering baptism, the identification with the life, death, and resurrection of Jesus opens the community in its members and as a totality to the christly aims that conform it to God's own purposes. Thus baptism is an essential expression of the unity of the church.

The holiness of the church is likewise embodied in this sacrament as apostolicity and unity are recreated in the present moment. This is sacred space, sacred time, creating an openness to an exercise of the generosity that embraces another for the creation of inclusive well-being. Baptism embodies a love that generates acceptance of the other, and love that opens itself to its own transformation through inclusion of the other, and love that seeks to turn inward growth to outward service. This is the holiness that is expressed through the togetherness of apostolicity and unity.

In speaking of baptism, the emphasis has been upon the community. The supposition throughout, however, in keeping with a process vision, is that it is God who acts in and through the community. God's mode of action in history, whether through the sacrament or in any other way, is through the "initial aim," God's touch, God's providence for each occasion. Using the community's openness to God's reign, God gives aims for the intensification of community for the purpose of generating love and justice. The particularity of baptism, giving it its sacramental quality, is its ritualistic representation of who Jesus is for us. Time after time, through all the ages and cultures through which Christianity has traveled, this ritual has inaugurated our incorporation into and as the body of Christ. It is a "holy habituation," with the conformal strength that repetition brings. By faith we claim that God ordains this rite, that through it the apostolicity, unity, and holiness of the church might be brought to creation and re-creation time and time again.

The Lord's Supper likewise contributes its own "holy habituation," also functioning to re-present the apostolicity, unity, and holiness of the church. But whereas baptism is the sacrament of inauguration, the Lord's Supper is the sacrament of culmination, bringing the anticipation of the fullness of God's reign into the present. In both the Hebrew scriptures and in the New Testament, the fullness of God's reign is symbolized by a great banquet, a heavenly feast. The feast is an apt symbol, for hunger shall be no more when God's reign is fully established. In the gospels, the multitudes eating on the hillside on the multiplied loaves and fishes are symbols of the messianic banquet that is to come, and in a number of parables the reign of God is likened to a great banquet, a marriage feast. The apocalyptic vision of John concludes the New Testament with "the marriage supper of the Lamb," signifying the accomplishment of all things and the final fullness of God's reign. Hence the humble meal of bread and wine, the Lord's Supper, is a proleptic participation in the fullness to come. If baptism brings Jesus' life, death, and resurrection into our present, the Lord's Supper brings the culmination of all things into our present.

And yet this down-payment on the future, this token of that which is to come in unspeakable fullness, is like baptism in that its center is the cross. It is closely aligned with baptism—indeed, in the passage already cited from Mark, both baptism and eucharist are symbolized in the coming cross: "Are you able to drink the cup that I drink, or to be baptized with the baptism with which I am baptized?" It is only through the fullness of God's identification with us, given most deeply on the cross, that we can be identified with God. In process terms, our forms of resurrection, whether in history or in God's everlastingness, are purchased by the depths of God's knowledge of us. Without God's identification with us in our crucifixions suffered and perpetrated, our resurrection would be impossible. Hence the great banquet symbolizing our participation in God's everlasting reign is deeply connected with the suffering and resurrection of God in Christ.

The cup of wine and the loaf of bread look forward to the great marriage feast of the Lamb, and backward to Jesus' meal with his disciples on the eve of his passion. Is it not possible to see in this togetherness something of the great reversal theme so prominent in Jesus' teaching? The eschatological marriage banquet is a feast of joy and final triumph, culminating the years of all history—the Passover of Jesus' last supper is a meal of betrayal and misunderstanding, culminating the years of Jesus ministry. That the one should be a symbol for the other is the mystery of crucifixion and resurrection, conjoined, like the tragedies and triumphs that mark our existence.

In that Passover meal Jesus presents the bread as his body, and the cup as his blood. In the book of Mark, it is just that, with the additional words concerning the cup that it is "My blood of the covenant, which is poured out for many." The starkness here is in keeping with the theme of the increasing suffering of Jesus as he is isolated through the disciples' misunderstanding and eventual falling away. In Matthew, the evangelist adds the words that the blood of the covenant is "poured out for many for forgiveness of sins" (Matthew 26:28). The Lucan evangelist gives the most elaborate account of all, directing the disciples to "take this (the cup) and share it among yourselves," and saying of the bread, "This is my body, which is given for you; do this in remembrance of me" (Luke 22:17, 19).

Covenant, forgiveness, sharing, remembrance: these are the descriptive words of the Supper. In a yet earlier account of the actual practice of eating the Lord's Supper, the words recounted of Christ are the identification of body and bread, and the identification of cup and covenant; both are to be done "in remembrance of me," proclaiming "the Lord's death until he comes" (I Cor. 11:24–26). Are not all of these words that create community?

The apostle Paul illumines this in his injunction to the community to celebrate the Lord's Supper in a seemly fashion. The church at Corinth came together for the Lord's Supper, but far from being an occasion of love and community, there was an unequal distribution of food so that some were hungry, and for some a drinking of too much wine, leading to drunkenness. How could this be either the solemn remembrance of Christ's cross, or a joyful anticipation of the great sharing in the resurrection? Rather, the church as the body of Christ was profaned, and the community disrupted.

The right administration of the sacrament of the Lord's Supper, therefore, is one in which there is the remembrance of Christ's death as that covenant that purchases our redemption through forgiveness and new birth. This remembrance is itself a means of sharing with one another alike, proleptically anticipating the culmination of this covenant in the everlasting community of God. Through this covenant, this forgiveness, this sharing, and this remembrance, the community is created anew. In the sacrament the community stands between the times, drawing them together in memory and hope, and hence sacralizing the present. Eating such a meal, it is nourished for its mission of inclusive well-being, and becomes once again the anticipatory sign of God's reign in the midst of history.

From the above, it should be seen that the "proper administration" of the Lord's Supper is less a matter of *who* administers the supper than *that* it is administered, and *how* it is administered. The community must be nourished in memory and hope, so that its present existence may be one of sharing and love. The community may and indeed must insure that there are those who can make the memory of the Lord's death and the hope of God's everlasting reign of justice present; the community must insure that the equal need for nourishment in the body of Christ is observed; the community must participate in this meal regularly and show forth the fruit of its nourishment in mission. Hence the community may educate and set apart some who can insure that the sacramental gifts are given, but the church must remember that those who are ordained to word, sacrament, and order are for the sake of the community, and not the community for the sake of those who are ordained. *That* the sacraments are administered is more important than *who* administers them.

How is God present in this sacrament? It is clear from the Corinthian account that God's presence does not prevent the misuse of the meal. What, then, is the function of God in this sacrament? How does a process perspective contribute understanding? Just as in baptism, process thought suggests the presence of God through God's providence in the initial aim, and through the use that can be made of the power of repeated symbols. The focused content of the Lord's Supper is remembrance and anticipation, a holding together of the origin and end of faith. Through this focus, and the common sharing of the community in these elements of bread and wine, the aims for each are reinforced by the others. There is an openness to christly aims, to conformity to God's providence. Can God not use this openness to strengthen the bond of community and therefore strengthen the force of the community for God's purposes in society? God is present in the sacrament as God is always present, through the divine faithfulness in luring us to our future. But the sacrament of the Lord's Supper becomes an occasion of focusing us to the presence of God, opening us more fully to one another, and therefore to God. Through this nourishment, we are sent into service.

Apostolicity, unity, and holiness are evident in the Lord's Supper, just as in baptism. Apostolicity is maintained by proclaiming the life, death, and resurrection of Jesus, recreating that event in memory. Unity is created by our participation together in these elements, wherein we appropriate our identity in Christ and therefore our kinship with one another. Holiness is in the resultant sharing in love, strengthening ourselves and one another for the community's works of love.

The communal nature of the sacraments is multidimensional. First, there is the focus on the present community, as outlined above. Second, the sacraments relate us to the full community of the church, past and future. Third, they are an impetus to the societal witness of the church in the creation of communities of love and justice. The sacraments generate the power of community with the past and the future through the present creation of apostolicity and unity. Through apostolicity, the sacraments bespeak the community of the past, and of the many who have preceded the community of the present in this same act of participating in the sacrament. The very ritualized repetition of the sacrament gives it a power in this process universe, for it strengthens the being-made-present quality of the past through prehension. Each repetition of an act gives it increasing power relative to the present, propelling its influence into the present, whereupon a conformal feeling of that influence re-enacts it, making it present once again. Therefore, the ritualized expression of the sacraments implies an intense power of continuity with the past. In illustration of this, we could simply point to the intensive resistance that is raised whenever ritualistic aspects of the church's worship are changed. The intensity of repetition gives the past much greater power in the present. The positive aspect of this power is that through the sacraments one can sense the community of the past, and thus make it present. Hence the communal aspect of the sacrament increases the community of the present by giving it the dimension of the past as well.

The communal aspect of the sacraments also relates to the church of the future through the dimension of unity. Christ is the source of our unity and community, mediated to us through our future. This openness to Christ is at the same time an openness to the future, but to be open to the future is to anticipate it. Since our community comes to us from the future through Christ, one can appreciate not only the present creation of community, but also the many who will succeed us in this creation of community. Furthermore, for those in the future, we will function as the apostolicity of proclamation in the past, and hence we will be made present to them in the sacraments, even as our past is made present to us. Therefore, the community of the future is made present through the sacrament, increasing the intensity of the present community.

This communality of the church in the sacraments is holiness. The presence of one to another, whether in relation to past, future, or present, is for the enrichment of each in and through the many. The upbuilding of the church in love is essential to the nature of the sacraments. This holiness is internal to the church, insofar as it is the effective binding together of the many as one in the identity of Christ, and external to the church insofar as it must have an effect on the society of the fuller culture. In a process universe, everything affects everything else.

Insofar as the community extends the identity of Christ, it will be the body of Christ, and holy within itself in its internal relations. There will be love, justice, openness, and mutuality within the community as the many participate together in christliness. However, the dynamism of these qualities pushes to new forms. Love and justice contradict themselves if static, and hence cease to be love and justice. If the church is dynamically embodying Christ, the inner holiness of the church must have an outward effect. The church must be a catalyst for love and justice in society, looking toward inclusive well-being. Again, we have come full circle, for the holiness of the sacraments in their creation of community pushes that community to the transformation of ever increasing and intensifying forms of love and justice. This, of course, is the expression of the church's unity with Christ, and the continuous creation of the church's apostolicity in proclamation.

14

UNIVERSALITY

THE emphasis upon the church's witness in the larger society raises the question of the fourth dimension of the church, universality—or, as it is also called, catholicity. Broadly, the term is taken to mean that Christian faith can be expressed in any culture at any time; it is not inherently restricted to the cultures of its origin or primary development. The vibrancy of the church in places that historically have not been primarily Christian, such as Africa, gives strong witness to the universality of Christian faith.

That Christian faith is expressible through many cultures should not be surprising, given the central role of incarnation in Christian faith. The nature of the God who is before, with, and beyond creation was revealed in and through Jesus of Nazareth in all the fullness of his particularity. Jesus spoke Aramaic, and used thought forms thoroughly immersed in the worldview of his particular culture. Yet we who come to God through him, even though our thought forms and suppositions concerning the world are far different from those of his time, are nonetheless called to be "little Christs," to quote the words of Martin Luther. We, too, by virtue of our union with Christ, are called to manifest God's nature and purposes in time, creating history in God's image. Our western rather than Judaic culture is not an obstacle to our being a sign of God's reign in the creation of communities of inclusive well-being. Rather, western culture is simply one more form through which God calls the world to justice. The incarnational God who is revealed in Jesus of Nazareth calls upon us to reveal God's nature in and through every society. Consequently, Christian faith may be expressed in every culture—the church is universal in nature.

Two important points follow from the universality of the church. First, while the church may take form in any culture, and will reflect that culture, it is called to do so transformatively. Second, the existence of the church in many cultures serves to relativize the church in each culture, including, of course, the church in cultures long associated with Christianity. Such relativization means that no church can be normative for all others; to the contrary, all forms of the church stand under the norm of the reign of God.

With regard to the transformative work of the church, while it is true that every particular church will weave patterns that are unique to its own culture into its form of existence, it is also true that the church must do so critically. Can this particular pattern express well-being for the whole community? If so, then the cultural form can become a new voice for expressing the gospel of salvation. Does this particular pattern perpetuate ill-being for members of the community, contrary to the love of the gospel? Then that pattern must be transformed by the gospel, until it can become a channel of God's grace and social-spiritual well-being for the people.

The transformative work of the gospel is a many faceted and open process. Its effects are on the church as well as on the culture, as aspects of the culture are taken into the church, and aspects of the church affect changes in the culture. For example, the Christian church has taken root in many African nations, and been radically affected by African culture. One indigenous form of that culture is the strong sense of the ancestors—those who have died, but who together with the living create the continuous community. The analogous belief in Christianity as it developed in Europe was the "communion of the saints," or the fully gathered church in God. In Africa, however, the belief is central, not peripheral, affecting daily life, and it has unique aspects not included in the traditional notion of the communion of the saints. The understanding of the legacies of the ancestors is a shaping factor in the African church, and through that church, becomes a gift to the wider church in many lands and cultures. The African church will revitalize and transform the traditional western sensibility of the communion of saints.

Well-being is mediated through this transforming fusion of the ancestors and the communion of saints in several ways. The African church can recognize the gracious work of God in their culture through the many pre-Christian generations, and so know the affirmation of their culture as yet another channel of grace. Also, through the gift of the African church (and, by extension, the church in every land), the solidarity and vitality of the whole church is strengthened. The mutuality of love, whereby one gives as well as receives, and receives as well as gives, becomes an affirmation of the participation of the new form of the church within the continuously transformative history of the whole.

The transforming effect of this fusion is not limited to the church, however, but affects the African culture as well. The presence of the ancestors as the fullness of the presence of God intensifies the demand for right relation in the human community, calling that community to the norm of God's justice. This norm mandates the well-being of the present community, so that it might become a right unification with the gathered community in God. Since the well-being of the gospel is physical, social, and spiritual, the community of the church is called to bring health and wholeness to the wider African society. God speaks to the people through the culture, and in so doing, makes possible the continuing transformation of the culture.

The universality of the church, whereby the church can grow in any culture, relativizes the church in every culture, and this is itself a great gift. Consider the problem of the church. The church is that people called in and through Jesus Christ to be a sign of God's holy and gracious reign. The church is faithful in this call insofar as it knows itself to be under the norm of that reign, judged by God and called by God to ever-greater forms of justice and love. The great temptation to the church is to begin to think of itself as the already given reign of God. In this case the church equates its particular cultural form with God's everlastingness, raising the finite to the infinite, and then falling into the idolatry of worshiping itself rather than God. Such a church never looks for norms of justice beyond those it already instantiates, never looks for transformation, never opens itself to learn from God through another person or culture alien to it. But when the church so absolutizes itself, it fails miserably to be the sign among peoples that God has called it to be.

One of the great gifts of the cultural diversity in the church is that this very diversity calls each form of the church to account. How can the church absolutize one form of its existence, when there are clearly many forms? Because there are many, the church is better able to worship the one God who calls the many forms of the church into existence, rather than falling into self-idolatry. Among the dangers of idolatry is that of universalizing the particular, or treating the culture as if in fact it, rather than the gospel, were universally valid. When the church recognizes that each one of its particular forms is a unique way of integrating Christian faith and culture, then it is much less apt to idolatrize itself.

A further gift of the diverse nature of the universal church is the great possibility of spiritual growth. Particular churches can learn to see themselves through each other's eyes, and to recognize the many-splendored gift of the gospel. This amounts to an openness to the novelty of God's transforming grace, and to renewed wonder at the magnificence of God, who can work through so many means of grace in so many cultures. Such a church is not only universal, but holy, one, and apostolic as well.

Just consider: if western Christianity were the *only* mode of Christianity, then there would be no means of noting the particularity of the way we express faith. But as Christianity has moved into other cultures, and given rise not only to communities open to God's reign, but to theologies drawn from the cultural experiences of Africans, or Koreans, or other countries new to the gospel, then we see more clearly that the western mode of expressing faith is but one mode. Each culture, drawing from the life, death, and resurrection of Jesus Christ, manifests its own unique incarnation of the gospel. In this rich diversity, the universality of the church is celebrated.

The question that is particularly important to the issue of universality is not the rich diversity of Christian communities throughout the world, but the relation of Christianity to other religions. Indeed, for much of Christian history the universality of the church had the connotation that Christianity is the only faith acceptable to God; "there is no salvation outside the church." It was fairly easy to maintain such an exclusive view so long as one never encountered other faiths in their own integrity and beauty, but the twentieth century has brought us all closer together. It is no longer so easy to follow the path of caricature in describing other religions, or to look for those aspects that are similar to Christianity so that we might name the other religion good. We are today in a situation of radical religious pluralism. What, then, does this mean for the Christian understanding of Christ as the means of salvation?

There have been various Christian efforts to answer the question.

Early responses called for an investigation of other religions, with the supposition that God is revealed imperfectly there, but perfectly in Christ. Christianity would then be the superior religion, but other religions would be acceptable to the extent that they mirrored the Christian witness. Among the difficulties of this view is the fact that one cannot isolate a component of religion from its total complex. A notion of grace in Mahayana Buddhism, for example, may on the surface seem similar to Christian notions of grace. But as one explores more deeply, it is less easy to interpret Mahayanan grace like grace in western Christianity. The leaves of the plant may be similar, but the root system that supports the leaves belongs to a different plant species. We distort the richness of Mahayanan "grace" by ripping it from its native soil and comparing it with Christian grace. It must be understood in its own context—but that renders its similarity or dissimilarity to Christian grace less relevant.

Another approach to other religions was to view them as various cultural vehicles organizing life and value, acceptable and good as sociological phenomenon. But deep within the human soul there is a place of openness to God. While the person might actually worship in temples, say to Lord Krishna in Hinduism, if the heart of the worshiper truly desires God and the good, then God receives the worship as if it were given in the name of Christ. The persons are then considered "Christian" in God's eyes, albeit they continue to consider themselves followers of Krishna. This approach takes the pluralism of religions no more seriously than the first.

On the other side of the equation, there are religious scholars who hold that all religions are incommensurable, somewhat on the grounds sketched above noting the difficulties of translating "grace" from Mahayana Buddhism into Christian categories. In this view, there is indeed a valid religious pluralism in the world, but hardly any hope of dialogue among religions—for how can we leap out of our faith languages to hear and understand each other? Rather, each faith exists solipsistically in its own universe and there are as many universes as there are faiths. There is neither a transcendent norm to which any religion is accountable, nor is there any possibility of linking the various religions through dialogue. It would seem that the only transcendent reality is the scholar, who views impartially the solar systems of faith.

What can a process perspective contribute to the conversation? How is the gospel both expressible in any culture, any time, and yet affirmative of religious pluralism? At the outset, we must recognize that there is no neutral standpoint for consideration of religious pluralism. Not even a secularist point of view can bring an impartial consideration, for there are as many implicit and explicit biases to secularist views as there are to religious views. In fact, there is some advantage in addressing the question from a specifically religious standpoint, since there is at least an insider's understanding of what it is to be constituted by religious commitment. But because religious commitment does influence one's approach, it is best to attempt to see how that commitment shapes one's views, and to be clear that there need be no "universal" acceptance of the view. It is simply a voice in the dialogue.

The particular bias informing a Christian process perspective is that regardless of what religion is under consideration, God is operative in that religion. This builds a distortion into consideration of religions such as Buddhism, for which a "no-god" stance is deeply important to the salvific nature of the religion. Notions of God, from a Buddhist perspective, involve us in an essentially dualistic stance, which is by their definition part of the human dilemma that must be religiously solved. While process thought can help us address the issue of religious pluralism, then, it is clear that its answer is fundamentally oriented toward the Christian self-understanding.

Consider the nature of God developed thus far in the theology. In this process universe there is an interrelationship between God and the world, such that the world receives from God, and God from the world. God provides the world with possibilities for harmony that are reflective of the divine nature. The harmony of God is the unification of all possibilities in a togetherness that is beauty. This harmony of possibles becomes a harmony of actuals as God receives from the world, integrating the world into that divine harmony. Obviously, the harmony of God is one of ever-increasing intensity through the integration of the world. The world matters to God in this vision of reality, for what the world does becomes the actuality that God integrates into the divine harmony. The world determines what God shall deal with in the divine nature, but God determines how the world shall be dealt with in terms of the divine character. Insofar as the world actualizes possibilities that reflect the divine harmony, the world contributes positively to the richness of value in God, deepening the divine intensity. Insofar as the world acts in a way destructive of value, God's action must be transformative. The harmony in God is not lessened, but it will be less than it could have been had the world acted differently. God's will toward the world is for the intensification of harmony in it. This intensification in turn leads to intensification in God.

In Christ God's universal aim toward the good for all stands revealed. However, we have emphasized again and again that the universal aim must be relativized in order to be made concrete. The harmony in God is one; the harmony in the world must be many. Since all temporal modes of harmony come from the one divine source, this common source is reflected in the communal nature of temporal harmony. There is a balancing and blending effect, whereby what is good for one is tempered by the good of the other in an intermeshing network of communal good. This becomes important, for in Christ we see not simply an abstract revelation of the nature of God as an absolute good viewed far off—to the contrary, in Christ we see God *for* us. God in goodness bends to our condition, fitting divine harmony to the human situation. In Christ we see the universal made relative. God shapes our redemption according to who and where and when we are. This means that the source of redemption is always God, but that the shape of redemption varies by the will and boundless grace of God, who bends to our condition, shaping redemption according to the uniqueness of every particular human situation.

There would be commonalities in such a relativized redemption. Insofar as people share a common culture, a common tradition, a common time, the communal nature of harmony would be illustrated in a common faith and a common mode of experiencing redemption. One might even say that although there would be diverse forms within the basic commonality, the marks of "sameness" would be strong. We could imagine that adherents to the faith in that community would be so impressed with the apparently invariable elements of their faith that they would name their faith "universal." In fact, of course, these elements would be invariable and therefore universal only relative to the varieties and forms within the boundaries of that faith. But if one looked beyond the boundaries, then of course the so-called universal elements would begin to show that they, too, were relative to quite finite boundaries of geography and tradition.

This would mean that no finite manifestation of religion could be universal. If it were not universal, then of course it could not be normative for all times and places. Rather, the universal element would apply only to the source of harmony from which all our finite sources spring—only God could be named as the universal source of redemption. To name the finite manifestations "universal" would be to border on assigning a divine quality to a finite condition. To treat the relative as if it were absolute leads to the idolatry of misplaced worship.

How can this be, given the reality of the incarnation? We have already discussed the conviction that God was in Christ, that in Christ God is revealed as with us and for us. Doesn't this make the relative—the finite person of Jesus—absolute? If God is at work for us in Jesus, doesn't this mean that God restricts the divine activity for redemption to that incarnation in Jesus? How can there be any other way whereby God works for the well-being of humanity? And if there is, doesn't this detract from the incarnation—make it less important, somehow, and faith less urgent?

The process understanding of reality provides one way to understand the ability of God to work many means for our good. Remember the analysis of Catherine, and the three irreducible elements of existence that emerged in the course of that analysis. "One," "many," and "creativity" are necessarily implicated in every existent reality. To have understood Catherine simply as "one" would have been insufficient, for that would have obscured the reality that who she is depends upon many others beyond herself. Alternatively, to understand her as a sort of multiplicity would not have been sufficient. She is, after all, but one person. The missing term, whereby this manyness and this oneness take on their proper perspective, is creativity. Catherine's integration of the influences upon her is a creative unification that results in her being herself. Finally, of course, each of the terms—one, many, and creativity—is dependent on the other two for the fullest understanding of its meaning. Each is like an empty shell without the others. One, many, and creativity are a triad of relational principles, each of which needs the others for its fullest meaning.

From any member of this triad, we can derive the other two. This follows from the essential implication each has for the others. "One" implies, as the conditions for its existence, the reality of "many" and "creativity." Likewise, of course, with the others: the many make no sense without one and creativity, and creativity is nothing if there is not something to be created. The very process of creation is the unification of the many into a new one. There is a balance, a harmony, between the three terms.

Notice, however, that the balance may be approached from three different directions. It may start with the one and arrive at the harmony, or with the many, or with creativity. However, the final harmony will reflect the starting point. To begin with the one will lead to seeing many and creativity primarily in relation to the original term. They could even be viewed as being for the sake of the one. But of course the same could be done with either manyness or creativity. If manyness is the route to ultimate balance, perhaps the complexity of the harmony will be valued. For instance, to understand Catherine in terms of manyness is to value the richness of diversity in her life, and the many relations that comprise her daily living. Contrarily, if the one is the basic route for understanding, her unity and uniqueness might be taken as the chief value. But if creativity is the entry to understanding her, then we might value her dynamism, that movement of her personality that combines the many into her own responsive uniqueness.

To generalize from this small illustration, couldn't it be possible that these three basic terms might be used by God as different routes to lead us into realization of harmony in our own existence? Each route is a valid, even an ultimate way toward harmony, but there would be three different ultimates. The three ways would not contradict each other—to the contrary, in a profound sense each would imply the other if one looked deeply enough into any of the routes.

What would the world look like if God used three basic modes to lead us toward reflections of the divine harmony? Wouldn't there be religions which, following the way of creativity, would see into the universal flux of things, of the rising, falling, coming-to-being nature of existence? Forms of harmony in such a religion might emphasize communities attuned to relationality, extending beyond the human community to the world of nature. "Given that, this arises," might be a maxim of the religion, and adherents would strive to live in harmony with the nature of this creative world of centerless centers, being and becoming, harmonious depths of ceaseless flow. Buddhism is something like that. There are many forms of Buddhism, of course, but a common quality—a universal quality?—is attention to creativity in the processes of existence.

There might be modes of well-being in the world that find an entry to harmony not through creativity per se, but rather through the manifold nature of the world around us. The concrete manyness of us all in the world might be seen as an ultimate reality, deserving an ultimate loyalty and commitment. Wouldn't it be possible to visualize the harmony of the many in the one world as a goal worthy of one's best faith and efforts? The "one" visualized might be seen as the complex one of a unified world—although of course there could be many interpretations of what would constitute the world as one! There are secular modes of living like that—Paul Tillich calls them "quasi-religions," since they place ultimacy not in the infinite God, but in the finite world. But perhaps God could lead people into such a mode of life, by emphasizing for them through the initial aim a route to harmony via "manyness." Perhaps secularism in at least some of its forms is not the great enemy of religion, but simply a different mode of religion, with its own rituals and holidays. Why is it not quite possible that God would lead some people toward meaning and well-being in relationships through this focus on "manyness"?

Christians, of all people, would recognize a route toward our well-being and toward finite modes of harmony through revelation of God as the "One" who is supreme. Judaism and Islam would vie with Christianity in this regard, for both also find their well-being in the One. In fact, adherents of these religions raise the question to Christians, suggesting that we have fallen from the purity of monotheism with our conviction that God is triune.

"One," "many," and "creativity"—each of these terms implies the others. However, only as we push past the surface to the depths of the one, or many, or creativity, would we begin to see the interdependence of mutual implication. The deeper we go into a religion, the nearer we get to the heart, not only of that religion, but to the heart of other religions as well. Buddhism, for instance, is a form of religion that emphasizes creativity. But in the history of that religion there have been telling variations on the theme of creativity. There are forms of what is called Pure Land Buddhism that stress that only by calling on the name of Amida Buddha in faith is there salvation, for this Buddha—the One—has accomplished redemption for the many. By no means is this an anomalous introduction of Christian principles into Buddhism. The fundamental insight is thoroughly Buddhist. But is the similarity to Christian insight entirely a coincidence? Could it be that at the heart of creativity, one might discover the pulse beat of the one? Alternatively, there are forms of Buddhism that place an extraordinary emphasis upon the acceptance of the dailiness of things around us, seeing in this the ultimate, and in the ultimate, just this. Haiku poetry frequently reveals this sensitivity. Does the heart of creativity also yield a pulse beat toward the many?

Christianity profoundly affirms the one: "There is one body and one Spirit, just as you were called to the one hope that belongs to your call, one Lord, one faith, one baptism, one God and Father of us all, who is above all and through all and in all" (Ephesians 4:4–6). But the very stress on creativity that is found not only in process forms of theology, but also in the whole mystical tradition of the church, gives witness to the impulse toward creativity that the route of the one can yield. Also, secularism is itself uniquely a child of Christian sensitivities. Could it be that our love for the world, inspired through our love for God, has generated the child of secularism? It would take a careful historian to answer these questions, but surely the evidence suggests that the depths of the "one" can be plumbed to give rise to the "many" and to "creativity."

The doctrine of the trinity likewise shows an interdependence of one, many, and creativity, for through this doctrine, the oneness of God requires a pluriform manifestation in creative relationship. Christianity has always dealt with a tension in the doctrine, for a strict emphasis on the unity of God challenges the pluriform expression of three "persons," while a focus on the "persons" threatens to break away from the oneness of God to a tritheism. The peculiar unifying qualities of the Holy Spirit can be viewed as the creative link that holds the threeness into a dominant unity. Given the doctrine of the trinity, it should be no surprise that Christianity, while primarily focusing upon the One, nonetheless generates forms of religiosity through manyness and creativity.

How would God bring about the many manifestations of harmony in the world? The dynamics, of course, would be the very same dynamics by which we understand God to be for us through Jesus Christ our Lord. God responds to the needs of the world, feeling the world as it is, transforming that world in the divine nature and feeling modes of harmony that fit the continuing particularities of the world as initial aims for the future. God bends to the condition of the world in order to fit the divine harmony to the world. In keeping with the divine feeling of the world, God can raise up a Moses, or incarnate in Jesus Christ. Can God not also raise up a Buddha, or a Confucius? Just as Christians unite themselves with Christ by faith, thus opening themselves to christly identities as God mediates the benefits of Christ to them, can't Buddhists likewise adhere to the teachings of the Buddha? And won't God then be able to work peculiarly Buddhist possibilities of well-being for them? Won't the Buddhist be informed and identified through the Buddha by the grace and power of God fully as much as the Christian is informed and identified in Christ by the grace of God?

A Buddhist, of course, might disagree, claiming instead that to speak of "the grace of God" is to introduce an inaccurate dualism into the sheer interdependence of things that is the Buddha nature. Christian objections often stem from a sense of threat if Christianity is not the sole salvific religion in the world. There is sometimes a feeling that the importance of God's incarnation in Christ is denigrated if God also works through other figures and other religions. And what of that verse thundering down from Acts 4:12, "And there is salvation in no one else, for there is no other name under heaven given among humankind by which we must be saved"?

Throughout the Christian ages, believers in God through Christ have been caught up in wonder at the magnitude of the incarnation. That God would be for us to the extent of taking on our condition, revealing the divine nature in all the lowliness of a poor Galilean—that God's love should reach to this extent makes us exclaim in joy, gratitude, and awe. But surely God would not do such a thing for but a few! Only if this great act has universal proportions does it make any sense to us—it must have saving significance not only for us Christians, but for the whole race of humanity, and indeed for the whole cosmos! Only in that cosmic context have we been able to make sense out of such cosmic love.

Long before we reach the pages of the gospels in our Bibles we can open to the book of Genesis, and see the love God can have even for a few. Abraham worried about the destruction of that wicked city, Sodom—as well he might, for his cousin Lot lived there. But in the story of Genesis 18, the Lord was going down into Sodom to see if there were any righteous ones for whose sake the city could be spared. Abraham fidgeted. The city was large, and its reputation was bad, but what of Lot? What if there were fifty righteous people, he asked. Would God spare the city for just fifty righteous? And the divine answer was yes. But Abraham was not convinced that the Lord would find fifty righteous people, and so he began to narrow the number. Forty-five, forty, thirty, twenty, and then, "Oh let not the Lord be angry, and I will speak again but this once. Suppose ten are found there." And again the divine answer: "For the sake of ten I will not destroy it." The story moved on to recount the wickedness of Sodom, where there were not even ten righteous people—only Lot and his family were saved.

Isn't it so that the history of revelation shows divine action not always on a great cosmic scale, but directed to the particularities of people in their histories? Even for ten the Lord will act thus and so—even for ten! The Lord will go into the city and experience its condition to determine its judgment, not because of universal conditions in the cosmos, but because of the dire realities in that one city. Likewise, if God goes through incarnation even for the benefit of ten, how does that make incarnation any less a wonder? Isn't it rather a greater wonder, that such a salvation should be wrought for even these few? Jesus reveals the boundless grace of God, but to say that the grace is boundless is to say that we cannot set up the limits of that grace. We do not *know* its boundaries!

Another aspect of claiming that God can save only through incarnation is that we absolutize the mode of God's action, rather than the God who acts. God bends to our condition, yes, but why does that mean that we then must universalize our condition? Further, if God acts in freedom, how can we limit God's freedom by saying that what God does once must be the only way that God can act? To the contrary, we seem to deny the message of Jesus if we limit God to one mode of salvation, for Jesus touched people with forgiveness and salvation in ways as various as their needs. Does God do less? Finally, what we know of God's action in the incarnation is what God has done *for us*. We cannot presume to universalize our own needs, binding God to only ourselves. Just as God bends to our condition out of the divine character of love, even so God might well bend to the condition of others in other ways.

But the scripture verse from Acts states that "there is no other name under heaven given among humankind by which we must be saved." Why can't we read that verse with the emphasis upon the "we," in keeping with the whole revelation that God bends to our condition, providing us with the redemptive mode of harmony to which *we* can respond? We in the church know that God has acted for us in Christ. By faith in Christ, we know that God's grace has accomplished our salvation. What God does with others is up to the divine good pleasure in the faithfulness of the divine character. That faithfulness has been manifested to us in the incarnation, which is greater, not less, by virtue of the wonder that God would go to such great lengths even for us, the "ten."

If God is understood to be the properly universal one, and if our own mode of salvation in Christianity is but one manifestation of God's aim toward humanity's well-being, what does this say about missionary activity? How does it affect the stance of Christianity toward other religions?

Even for the ten God would have saved Sodom. Even for us God goes to the extreme of incarnation. Should we do less? Human beings are a peculiar lot, and while groups of us do very well sharing characteristics and sensitivities that mark us as being twentieth-century Americans, or participants in a certain cultural matrix, there are always those who cannot fit the dominant mode. Not all of those in a western culture find Christianity a route to their own well-being; not all of those in an Asian country will experience well-being through Buddhism. Missionary experience, whether Christian or Buddhist, has shown that there are always a few in a culture who are not met by the religions of their own environment. Because these are few, should we feel no concern? Is missionary activity dependent upon numbers for its reward? Or is such activity rather for the sake of well-being, whether in the form of a different religious faith for the few, or for the sake of expanding the togetherness of diverse faiths in human community for the many?

Missionary activity is hardly abandoned in a church that places the universality of salvation in the nature of God. But it is undertaken in humility and love: humility, because one knows that salvation comes from God in many ways, and we are simply sharing the way that has been manifested to us; love, because while one might consider going into a work with rewards of great visibility, admired by all the world, only if one loves deeply will one go to do a small deed—to see to the well-being of the ten.

What of our relationship to those who find well-being in other religions? Humility and love—the marks, after all, of the incarnation—are also to be the marks of interfaith dialogue. Humility follows from the knowledge that we are only sharing ourselves and the message from God that has made us ourselves. But if we wish to share ourselves, then we must be receivers as well as sharers, that the others, too, might be sharers. We listen as well as speak. In humility we do not impose our own mode upon all others, nor declare it normative for all others. Rather, we listen for the grace of God in other ways and other harmonies.

Is there a hint of arrogance as we dare to name well-being through the mode of creativity as a response to the divine faithfulness? Do we inwardly smile and rejoice, rather liking the divine anonymity? How marvelous that God does not insist upon a name tag on every gift! How like the God we know in Christ to work so quietly in the depths of people's lives! But if we see a warm smile in the eyes of the other, we must recognize that the other might be nodding in inward glee to see the universal effectiveness of creativity, or manyness, even though we cloak it in the name of God! For both of us, we might next find the startled shock of a deeper recognition. While at first we might translate the other's experience to the categories familiar to ourselves, we might also find that deeper level, that truer insight, that our own most revered truths are implied near the heart of that once alien religion. One, manyness, and creativity mutually imply each other. If and when that happens, how would interfaith dialogue proceed? Here is where love might move from intention and concern to reality. The other remains the other, and we can affirm that difference, and be pleased by it. But there are links of likeness, routes to understanding from the depths, not just from the surface appearances of things. With this recognition and understanding, love grows.

But if love grows among the religions of the world—among the peoples of the religions of the world—so that we are no longer competitors and strangers and enemies to be feared, then we will be encountering a new possibility for harmony in the world. The many might become one in an entirely novel way. Couldn't we experience a world community of religions as a unity created through diversity by love? Won't love bind us into a gladness at the differences, and at the samenesses that are cradled within those differences? There would be a new mode of harmony in the world, a new mode of community, a new mode of well-being.

If universality is located in God rather than in our own particularities, then there is a basis for such a new community. There is a basis for genuinely hearing the other rather than trying to make the other like ourselves. God's aims are for the well-being of the world. God's aims take that mighty divine harmony and fit it a thousandfold to the situation in the world, so that all our harmonies might reflect that divine harmony till we be brought to the image of God. Love and justice, bursting the boundaries of outworn forms, take on deeper forms, all through the leading of God. In this newly small earth, where we are forced to know one another in love or die, could we be experiencing a new direction from God toward human community through the affirmation of many who remain many and yet are as one? If that were the case, and if we responded, we might know something of the reign of God on earth.

Part Five

POWER

The Reign of God:
A Process Eschatology

15

THE REIGN OF GOD

CHRISTIAN faith proclaims that we have a double destiny: to live deeply and richly in this life through personal and social structures of love, and to participate everlastingly in the life of God. Both destinies are social in nature: to live in love is to live a societal existence, mindful of the needs of all, creating communities of justice. To participate everlastingly in God is to know judgment and salvation in solidarity with all creation in the righteousness of God. The biblical texts use a symbol that denotes both forms of this destiny, "the reign of God." The symbol has been called the kingdom of God, kingdom of heaven, city of God, or simply the Greek term, *basileia*. No translation of this rich term is entirely adequate, for the symbol holds within itself all the nuances of a rich past and an anticipated future; it pulls eternity into time, and then flings it into history. Through the symbol of the reign of God there is an intuition or announcement that an everlasting destiny informs historical time, and that historical time itself will culminate in an everlasting destiny. Consideration of these things, sometimes called "the last things," comprises the Christian doctrine of eschatology.

For much of Christian history, eschatology was limited to a discussion of death and life beyond death, whether for the individual soul or for history as a whole. What happens to people when they die? Is there a "death" of history, or even of all creation? If so, what are the particular events that signal the death of creation? In response to these questions, great discussions developed around the notions of resurrection, Christ's second coming, a last judgment, and everlasting salvation and damnation. In these discussions God's reign was imaged often as "the city of God," and while there was indeed attention given to the life of the church in history, the dominant role of the image was to function as the denouement of history. The church is a pilgrim people, journeying toward that city not made with hands, eternal in the heavens, and some day the road will lead us toward that home. Augustine's great *The City of God*, and Paul Bunyon's *Pilgrim's Progress*, capture respectively the social and personal dimensions of the church's journey, but it is never in doubt that the journey *is* a journey precisely because of that eternal city toward which God calls all history. In that city we will all be judged and meet our eternal destiny.

In our own time, due in large part to biblical scholarship, there is a renewed emphasis upon the historical aspects of the reign of God. Whereas for most of Christian history our primary focus was on the birth, death, and resurrection of Jesus, biblical scholars have now shifted the focus to include the preaching of Jesus. With this shift, the centrality of the reign of God in the preaching of Jesus has become apparent, and with it, the fundamental question: What did Jesus mean by the reign of God? How we develop our notions of eschatology must now depend greatly upon how we answer this question.

In the time of Jesus, language about the reign of God was not an unusual thing—there was a long history to the symbol that Jesus presupposed and evoked. But precisely because of this long history, stretching over the whole Jewish past, many layers and varieties of meanings lay embedded in the term, along with a host of emotive associations.

The "reign of God" functioned in Jesus' day as a symbol with rich nuances within Jewish history, and the wonder is that the symbol is recoverable to us at all given the break in time between its living use in Jesus' day and our attempts at reappropriation within contemporary Christianity. If the traditional Christian use of "reign of God" relegated the symbol primarily to post-historical time, our reappropriation calls upon us to see as well its meaning for historical time. As we reappropriate the symbol, however, we cannot discount the 2,000 years of its Christian adaptation to a time beyond all history. Rather, we must weave the times together in a unified eschatology that once again conveys the richness of a tensive symbol.

So what did the symbol mean to Jesus and his hearers? The answers vary, and different scholars focus upon different aspects of the reign of God. Here we must simply lift up central themes. The primary meaning of the symbol was of a fullness to creation existing according to just relationships and in covenant with God. However, this fullness was not seen relative to any present time; rather, it related to a historical future. It was more a call to a certain kind of existence than a description of existing conditions. Thus an important qualification of the reign of God was that it must be achieved over against a brokenness in creation caused by injustice in human society. The reign of God held within it a judgment of the world as it is, and a call to what the world might be. The judgment was itself salvific, being the means of creation's healing.

Perhaps a key to understanding the positive aspects of the reign of God is to look more closely at the nature of the correction required in history to prepare the world for God's reign. Donald Gowan, in *Eschatology in the Old Testament* (Philadelphia: Fortress Press, 1986), sees this correction as involving a transformation of the human person through eschatological forgiveness, the transformation of human society through good government and peace, and a transformation of nature itself so that hunger is eliminated, and there is no destruction. God is the chief actor in all three modes of transformation, and yet not in such a way as to eliminate the responsibility for human participation. To the contrary, the demand of God's reign is precisely that humans shall know and therefore obey God, rejoicing and living in this knowledge, with the result that all shall participate in the good life of the community. Neither handicap nor illness nor age shall be an impediment, for the reign of God is well-being toward all and for all, in community with one another and in covenant with God.

Existence in the reign of God is thoroughly communal, so that even the forgiveness that transforms persons through freedom from the sins of their past had as its end joyful participation in the community. Forgiveness, ordinarily dependent upon repentance and therefore human initiative, was "eschatalogical" in that the initiative for forgiveness would come from God, thus enabling repentance and transformation. God's reign also entailed God's provision of a righteous king, who would transform social institutions so that they were justly ordered and therefore conducive to justice among the transformed people. Further, the reign of God was not limited to one nation, not even the chosen nation of Israel. Gowan points out that several Old Testament eschatological texts (notably

Isaiah 2:2–4 and Micah 4:1–4) contain a minor but most astounding reference to God's grace toward all the nations of earth, even though these texts are but few compared to the more usual texts that speak with triumphalism or hostility toward other nations. The intimation is that all peoples belong to God, and that there shall be a peaceful community of all nations, living together in the joyful and just reign of God. God's ultimate restorative work also involves the transformation of nature so that peace among the nations is echoed by a peace in nature itself. Isaiah 11 is a key passage, speaking of a time when there shall be no killing in all of nature; Isaiah 43 adds the image of animals praising God, and other passages speak of a glorious abundance of nature.

If we take these passages to refer to the reign of God, and to be the background against which Jesus proclaimed God's reign, then God's reign does indeed betoken a new heaven and a new earth in a recreation of the total order of things. But the focus is on history: it is in human time that this reign will come.

A summation of the nature of the reign of God as represented in the New Testament texts is given by theologian Hans Küng in *The Church* (Garden City: Image Books, 1967). He defines the reign as containing five aspects: first, it is the reign of *God*, and thus is brought about by a sovereign act of God alone. Second, it is the telos of history, the driving force that propels history toward God's reign as its final destiny. Third, the reign of God transcends all political and cultural boundaries; it is not limited as to place, but is relevant to every place, so that it is "a purely religious realm." Fourth, this reign is a liberating event for sinners, and therefore gives reason for rejoicing. The reign is good news for all, excluding none. Fifth and finally, the reign of God calls for radical human decision; we are called to open ourselves to God's reign.

Küng's summation shows New Testament continuities with the eschatological themes of the Hebrew scriptures: the divine initiative in eschatological forgiveness, the sense in which God's reign is inclusive of all nations, and the liberating, joyful nature of justice within God's reign. But by the time of Jesus, a note of radical discontinuity with history had entered the symbol. This is seen most clearly in Jesus' parables that speak of the coming of God's reign in very ordinary images drawn from everyday existence—a fig tree, leaven, a seed, and lost things found again. There is something familiar about the reign of God—and yet at the same time, something most unfamiliar, so that it jolts us with a shock of surprise. The surprise, however, is finding unexpected treasure—or growth, or fruition, or restoration—in the ordinary, so that there is joy. Accompanying the joy is a total reorientation to the ordinary, so that its previous everydayness is utterly overturned.

Indeed, the whole established world is overturned, for with the advent of God's reign there is a reversal of accustomed values. It is as if one receives the extraordinary through the ordinary, only to discover that in fact the ordinary is not so ordinary after all, but demands the total renewal and reorientation of the self in conformity to a new order. One sells all one has, or utterly reverses one's prejudicial opinions of another, or goes to a great banquet in rags. In short, the accustomed order is turned upside down as the advent of God's reign recreates the world. Thus the theme of the reversal of values enters the New Testament discussion of the reign of God.

The New Testament question, then, so debated by scholars, concerns the timing of God's reign. Is it still, as in the Hebrew texts, in the historical future? Is that future near or far? By the time of Jesus, the Jewish nation existed under the oppression of Rome, and rumors were rife that God would intervene in history, overturning the oppressive order and vindicating Israel in the universal establishment of God's reign. The righteous king would appear, inaugurating justice and obedience to God. Did Jesus consider himself that righteous king? Did he look for God's reign within his own lifetime? Or did he connect God's reign with eternity, as did his followers in the long centuries of Christian history? The emerging scholarly consensus seems to be that Jesus understood God's reign already to have begun in his own person, as is evident by his exercise of eschatological forgiveness, but that he also looked for the fullness of God's reign in a time yet to come.

What are we to make of such a reign in contemporary Christianity? Clearly, biblical scholarship concerning the reign of God in the preaching of Jesus no longer allows Christian eschatology to relegate the reign of God only to the end of all time. Rather, we are called to a "both/and" development. We must recognize its announcement in the preaching and in the person of Jesus, and therefore ask in what sense the church, as the extension of Christ in the world, must also proclaim the reign of God in its words and deeds. What kind of hope does the promised reign of God offer to human history and in human history? Second, we must ask what relation history has to the eventual and ultimate realization of God's reign. Can Christian hope reasonably speak of the fullness of God's reign beyond history? And if so, what is the connection between God's reign *in* history and God's reign *beyond* history?

Process theology addresses these questions through the dynamics describing the interaction between God and the world. God works with the world as it is to guide it toward what it might be. This means that God's own nature influences the world in every developing moment. Insofar as the world responds positively to this influence, the world will be living according to the reign of God in history. In this sense, process theology is most compatible with the biblical portrayal that Jesus is the realized presence of God's reign in history, for the process understanding of the incarnation is that Jesus responds positively to God's influence in each moment of his life. In Jesus, therefore, God's reign is already present.

But the process dynamics do not stop with the influence of God on the world; the world also has an effect upon God. This return dynamic relates history to God's own everlastingness, intimating that in God, beyond all histories, there is a fully actualized reign of God in which the world participates. But once again, the dynamics call for the return motion toward history. The world does indeed have an effect upon God, meeting its own judgment and transformation in God—this is precisely the event in God that God turns into a redemptive influence in ongoing history.[1]

From the Godward side of the dynamics, then, one would say that God receives the world in every moment of its completion. This moment-by-moment completion of the world is the result of what the world has done with God's providential influence. God, receiving this world within the divine life, judges and transforms the world according to God's good pleasure. This is the basis upon which God yet again offers providential influences to the world, guiding it toward its own finite reflection of God's infinite and everlasting reign.

1. Readers may find it helpful to refer to the diagram portraying the interaction between God and the world given in the Appendix, page 254.

From the worldward side of the dynamics, one would say that in every moment the world responds to many influences, the most important of which is the providential aim of God. Insofar as the world responds positively to that aim, the world will transcend whatever destructive influences it receives from its past, moving instead toward a form of redemption in history. This redemption will embody the justice of God in human society. This mode of justice worked out in time will once again be received by God in every moment, so that the world always moves toward its meeting with God in the everlasting reign. The world is called to anticipate that reign within its own history, move toward that reign beyond history, and receive from that reign in every new formation of its present.

To express a biblical eschatology within these process dynamics requires a threefold interpretation of the reign of God. The reign is already present in history through Jesus; it is also already present within God's own life; and it is present by way of anticipation in the life of the church as the church lives "between the times" of its participation in Christ in history and its participation in God in everlastingness.

The reign of God is present in Jesus through his free responsiveness to God in every moment of his life. But the Hebrew expectation could not limit God's reign simply to the personal—the reign of God, to be the reign of God, must be communal. And indeed, in Jesus' life of ministry his own freedom released others, creating a new community. Out of the fullness of his own freedom, he drew on God's initiative of forgiveness, pronouncing the eschatological forgiveness of sins. This is particularly evident in the account of Zaccheus, where Jesus' pronouncement of forgiveness empowered Zaccheus for repentance and new life; the order is the eschatological order of forgiveness already associated with God in the Hebrew scriptures.

But eschatological forgiveness is not for one's own sake alone; it is for the sake of the wider community. Forgiveness conveyed renewal of life, and all who received this forgiveness entered into a new community whose governance was just, facilitating the joyful knowledge of God. The creation of such a community is present in Jesus' own declaration of the reign of God, for he took those who were outside the structures of well-being and drew them in to a new community of God, existing through the reversal of his contemporary society's values of exclusion and marginalization. Jesus symbolized the Hebrew expectation of a gathering of the nations through his own crossing of political and cultural boundaries. Romans, Syrophoenicians, and Samaritans participated in the grace of his freedom. Even the abundance of nature is reflected in his ministry through the multiplication of loaves and fish, so that finally the question was raised, "Is this the King of the Jews?"

If a reversal of values was operative throughout Jesus' ministry and preaching, he himself most profoundly manifested that reversal of values by overturning the notion of kingship. Not the coercive power of might, but the relational power of love of God and neighbor marked his reign, even, as we noted in chapter nine, in crucifixion. "Behold the King of the Jews." This is the "already" aspect of the reign of God.

As to the "not yet" aspect of the reign, or the sense in which God fully establishes the divine reign by the resurrection and transformation of the world within the divine nature, this will be developed in the following chapter. The remainder of this chapter will look to the "between the times" aspect of the reign of God, or the sense in which the church is called to be an anticipatory sign of God's reign in human history. We live *from* the fullness of God's reign in Jesus, and *toward* the fullness of God's reign in God's own life. This "from" and "toward," or source and destiny, qualifies our communal life in history.

How, then, do we approximate the reign of God in history? And how, in a process context, do we appropriate the biblical imagery of God's reign? As we consider the first question, process philosophy tells us that God's influence upon us must be at the deepest layers of our being. Consciousness, in process thought, is a late development in the concrescent process of each moment. It is like the tip of the proverbial iceberg, held above an ocean containing supportive but subterranean depths. God's action upon us must be at that depth level, since God's action launches us upon our way of becoming—that is what God's aim is all about. But if God works in us at such depths, then in principle it is a rare thing for God to be part of our conscious awareness. God is present in the mode of hiddenness.

Further, God's aim is always oriented toward well-being in the world—there is a world-directedness in the aim. This means that by God's own design, we are pushed not so much toward an awareness of God as we are toward a deeper awareness of the world and its interrelationships. The content of God's aim is toward the finite reign of God. Once again, God's presence is in the mode of hiddenness. How, then, do we discern guidance from God from other desires and influences? The matter is complicated still further, since God's aim is not a pure reflection of the divine nature. How can it be, since it must be fitted to the world as it is, and the world as it is may exist in perversion of the will of God?

But we have a means of discernment in the scriptural account of God's reign. The reign of God is marked by the freedom of the forgiveness of sins, and a transformation of social and personal structures of existence. The reign of God looks toward a gracious inclusiveness toward all peoples and nations, and toward the abundance of the natural world. With these guidelines drawn from the revelation of God, we are called to discern the providential aim of God as God calls us toward forms of the reign that are appropriate to our times.

Just here, however, the notion of "reversal of values" comes again into play. The temptation is to think that the reversal of values was accomplished once and for all in Jesus, so that in our present time we have no need to expect such a reversal; we have only to perpetuate the values we have received. But in a process context, such an attitude overlooks the centrality of the notion of reversal, and the sense in which God fashions transformative possibilities of justice for the world in every moment. To live in anticipation of the reign of God is to be open to an unexpected mode of justice and love in society. The guidelines are that God will always lead toward freedom in community, and will always reach toward inclusiveness, and that there will be implications for the renewal of nature. But the call to God's reign can also shock us with unexpected demands for forgiveness, for community, for openness to well-being beyond our borders. The reign of God continuously calls us to a new future in history, and even if this future is actualized, God will transcend it once again with yet another call to anticipate God's reign in new ways. Continuity rests with the guidelines, but discontinuity rests with their ever new application in time. The church, living as the sign of God's reign in history, is called to no easy nor comfortable task—but it is called to the adventure of a faith that dares to risk the

future. It is *God's* reign; therefore the church is freed for a future
that transcends its past.

How, then, do we actualize the reign of God on earth? We do so
by trusting God and looking towards the needs of the world in light
of the divinely revealed criteria of justice, renewal of nature, and
inclusiveness of well-being among all peoples and nations. We
must, in this trust, dare to see unexpected needs and unexpected
applications. Our natural tendency is to draw back from new ways
of actualizing justice, for we would rather hold to the security of the
past. But the reign of God does not allow us that luxury. Our trust
must not be placed in our past ways, not even when those ways
were enacted in response to concrete divine guidance. This would
be akin to a person at age forty claiming that seven-year-old behavior was still appropriate, since once it had been in response to
God's guidance. Our trust must be placed in God, who leads us in
faithfulness into the future, and hence toward continued creative
response to God's reign.

Can we perceive God's guidance today? Can we tell the shape of
the contemporary call to the reign of God? If we take the biblical
criteria seriously, then we can identify several forces at work within
Christianity today that seem to be pushing toward new manifestations of the reign of God. Each carries within itself the power of
transformation through an eschatological forgiveness of sins, and a
form of the reversal of values characteristic of God's reign.

The first is the contemporary movements toward liberation, most
assuredly among the most awesome events of the twentieth century.
These have been experienced as political movements away
from colonialism and economic oppression, and as movements
against the marginalizations of people, whether because of race,
class, gender, sexual orientation, or physical condition. These
movements are congruent with the reign of God, since each
one exhibits continuity with Jesus' own identification with the
poor and the outcast. In the cries against racism, there is a
similarity to Jesus' refusal to accept the racial barriers dividing
Jews from Samaritans; in the cries against sexism, there is
continuity with Jesus' radical reversal of woman's role within his own society. In the call to eliminate classism we re-
call Jesus identification with the poor in the great passage
from Matthew 25, and in the matter of oppression oriented

around one's sexuality, there is Jesus' own refusal to condemn persons who were spurned for sexual reasons. Issues of our relations with persons who are differently abled most assuredly ring with reminders of Jesus' own connections with persons who were lame, blind, or deaf. And the tragedy of AIDS, heightened by social ostracization of those living with AIDS, is in direct parallel with the dread disease of leprosy in Jesus' own day. He met the agonized cry of "unclean!" with a touch of healing presence. Thus each of the contemporary calls for liberation and an inclusive society of mutual well-being for all peoples can easily be read as a contemporary call to the reign of God.

But eschatological forgiveness and the reversal of values also are signs of God's reign. How are these manifest in the call to liberation? In a sense these two qualities frame the spiritual depths of the inclusiveness to which we are now called. The harsh problem attending to each mode of oppression is the degradation of original sin. In chapter two we outlined a process understanding of sin, beginning with the sin of the demonic, or original sin. We are born into structures that already shape our existence, molding our identity. We absorb these structures into our normal way of perceiving things, so that we are not only shaped by the structures, but we perpetuate them. Insofar as the structures incorporate oppression of peoples, we perpetuate that structure, and therefore participate in the guilt. The problem is not simply the random actions of persons acting in oppressive ways, but the invidious permeation of the whole social structure with the normalcy of oppression, catching all persons within the society in the web of original sin.

One of the peculiar phenomena of liberation movements is that in their early days, each clearly saw the oppressive structure of the mainstream of society, but did not see their own participation in original sin. There was a tendency to locate the fault "out there," in those who were not like oneself, and who were therefore responsible for the ills of oppression. But the coming-of-age of the liberation movements has shown the pervasiveness of original sin, particularly as each oppressed group becomes aware that it itself participates in the oppression of others (e.g., the womanist theologians have unveiled the racism of feminist theologians and the sexism of their black brothers; as their own movement likewise comes of age they may discover to their sorrow that they, too, are caught in and perpetuate original sin). Original sin captivates the psyche, distorting perceptions, even in the effort to be free.

It is not enough, therefore, simply to call for liberation in the name of the reign of God. Oddly enough, the true power of liberation is received by naming the demons, not simply "out there," but in here, within one's own psyche and kind. This is no "blaming the victim," for the point is that there is no more ground for the myth of presumed innocence. There is indeed a solidarity in sin, original sin, and naming this becomes a release of energy for the work of liberation. Eschatological forgiveness is God's initiative in breaking through our inabilities, whether they be inabilities to confess our participation in oppressive structures, or inabilities to repent of such participation, or inabilities to break the habits of our structured past.

How does eschatological forgiveness break through the forbidding structures? Forgiveness follows from the divine initiative in receiving us and transforming us within the divine nature. God already knows who we are, in all our demonically good intentions. God deals with our evil every moment within the divine life, and *still* returns to us an aim toward our transformative good. This aim toward our good is our release from the binding past, and our hope for a new future where the values of the past can yet be reversed. It is the gift of eschatological forgiveness, making possible the transformed community. To name our need and accept our hope is to move into empowerment for the liberation of all social structures for which we yearn.

Such forgiveness breaks the grip of original sin, but not so that it disappears, for it is ingrained too much in our psyches; its power is broken rather than eliminated. Thus if we are open to the reign of God we cannot rest on a forgiveness in a distant past; rather, we are called to live daily from the forgiveness of sins and toward transformation. "Give us this day, our daily bread, and forgive us our sins, as we forgive those who sin against us" is an eschatological prayer relating to our dailiness.

If eschatological forgiveness is the foundation for liberation for the reign of God, the reversal of values is the fruit. Insofar as we are freed from the structures of oppression, freedom is primarily a recognition *that* the structures are oppressive, together with an energy toward transformation. After all, eschatological forgiveness is for the sake of the community of justice, and the community of justice is a radical reversal of the structures of oppression. The reversal is not chaos, but a new order in which there are no longer boundaries drawn around well-being, restricting it to a few. Rather, the vision of God's reign is a vision of deep inclusiveness, of openness to diverse peoples. It is not easy—how much safer it is to stay with one's own kind, with settled expectations!—but it is better, more akin to God's own reality. In God, the resurrected creation is woven into a transformed togetherness. In history, God calls the church to mirror this reign through deeper and broader modes of inclusiveness.

The biblical reign of God had implications for the renewal of nature; surely in our own day we face an ecological crisis that threatens the goodness of the created order. In this process universe we live in ever-enlarging circles of interdependence. Everything and everyone affects all else to some degree. There is an intense responsibility to exercise our freedom in responsible community, not simply among human beings, but as participants in the community of the earth. Today we must hear anew such biblical texts as Romans 8, declaring that all creation groans in travail as it awaits its redemption. Suddenly, in a century when we face the bewilderment of increasing pollution of the environment, and when we worry about the loss of layers of atmosphere that are essential for the protection of life, and about the decimation of the very sources of the oxygen we breathe, we finally hear in earnest our responsibility to nature. We realize that we, too, are nature, and that our caring cannot be restricted to sisters and brothers in the human community, but must extend toward "brother sun and sister moon," and all the earth and sky.

God's reign calls for justice extending beyond the human community, uniting with the sustaining community of nature. We are "shepherds of being," those through whom the world is given voice, and speaks. Therefore, we must exercise our responsibility by bringing nature into our caring and into our meaning. This is no longer a luxurious option, but a means to our very survival. Justice, says an old Rabbinic tale, is the foundation of the universe. It is not so strange, then, that the lack of justice toward nature results in a shaking of the foundations. The renewal of nature that takes place everlastingly in the recreated world in God has its own earthly analog as we incorporate responsible care for the earth into our anticipation of God's reign.

Again, as in the liberation movements, the renewal of earth as a sign of God's reign must be surrounded by the themes of eschatological forgiveness and the reversal of values. We must name our own lack of concern that has brought us to this brink of concern and anxiety, drawing on God's forgiveness for the strength of transformation. And we must look to the reversal of values, moving from profligacy and violation of the earth toward care and respect. The reversal of values again is no easy thing, for whether in the first world or the third world, it places demands upon lifestyles. Only by living from the grace of eschatological forgiveness can one dare the reversal of values now associated with the demand of God's reign upon our histories.

If the contemporary call of the reign of God challenges us with liberation movements and with ecological responsibility, there is yet a further challenge that bears affinities with the scriptural criteria. In both the Hebrew texts and in Jesus' own living, God's reign broke through political and cultural boundaries. In our own day, might it not also break through religious boundaries? There is precedent for this, for in the book of Micah the prophet gives an eschatological picture of God's reign. The nations, while each is depicted as walking "each in the name of his god," nonetheless come to Zion to learn of God's justice (chapter 4). There is a diversity of religious beliefs, but a unity of justice. Is God calling us today, in this small world of relatively few major religions, to seek a community of communities, struggling together with the great issues of justice, even while we remain diverse communities? And if the religions of the world work together on issues of justice, will they not also work on issues of peace?

If the church is called to be an anticipatory sign of the reign of God, mirroring God's nature in its own life, then perhaps it follows that the church must learn to rejoice in diverse modes of mirroring the justice of God, even when those modes take place in other forms of religion. Surely such a call would require a reversal of values, for most of Christian history has been built on an intolerance of other religious ways. From the pogroms we have mounted against Jews, to the holocaust we supported through condoned anti-semitism, to participation in religious wars both among ourselves and against "the heathen," we have not been noted for our openness to other modes of being religious. We have hardly been able to handle the diversity within Christianity—witness the centuries old tensions between Roman Catholics, Orthodox, and Protestants, or the contemporary tensions between "evangelical" and "mainline" Christians—let alone the diversity outside it! To be open to other religions in a cooperative mode, seeking to befriend one another and to learn justice together, calls upon us for a great reversal of values. But in order to answer such a call, it again behooves us to name our past, and to open ourselves up to God's transforming power through the grace of God's forgiveness. Who can say what treasure might be found in the field of interreligious dialogue?

It may be a treasure we would rather reject, for becoming open to others brings about the risk of change in ourselves. The risk involved in openness to another is that one's welfare then depends to a high degree upon that other. The interdependence that is always operational in a process world is highlighted and strengthened in its intensity. In a sense, the other gains power over one, for the sorrows of the other become sorrowful to oneself, and the joys of the other become joyful to oneself. Further, there is the risk that apart from this openness, one determines one's own future and one's own path as much as possible, but with openness toward the other there is a joint working out of the path.

Can we trust God's wisdom to guide our response to such a situation? Can God guide us in our becoming Christianity, even though we risk becoming a community among communities, subject to changes in our perceptions and in our self-understanding through our dialogical openness with others? The preaching of the reign of God consistently calls for that kind of trust—it is God who lures us to this good. Insofar as the church is true to its called nature, it will take the risk.

We can discern the directions of God's call into the future today by being open to eschatological forgiveness and God's reversal of values. We must test the present challenges by the themes of transformation of persons and society in accordance with God's justice, and inclusiveness of the nations, and renewal of creation. We can, as the church, evaluate the opportunities, and explore the future set before us. The details of following through are more than theology can delineate, for the movement into God's future is the task of the whole church, using its great diversity of gifts and grace to discern the way.

The caution that must ever be sounded, however, is that the shape of the reign of God can never be finalized. The source of the reign is God, leading the church toward forms of community in justice and love. There is no stopping point, no time when a temporal reign is complete. No sooner do we achieve one form of God's reign than we must critique the achievement, and look again for God's leading, for the reign moves on. We participate in present forms of God's reign in faithfulness to our particular task, sharing in benefits with the whole community. Individually and collectively, we as the church anticipate the reign of God—only to find that doing so involves us in continually looking to God and to the needs of the world, seeing how our various instantiations of God's reign may yet be surpassed. We do indeed make our journey toward that City of God in a provisional sort of way. The surety of our journeying is the presence of God's reign already given in Jesus, and the assurance that in God's own everlastingness, the ultimate form of God's reign exists, luring us into our future.

16

THE REIGN IN GOD: EVERLASTING LIFE

"WE look forward to the resurrection of the body, and the life of the world to come. Amen." So concludes the confession of the Nicene creed. These two brief clauses indicate the Christian hope of God's final victory over evil on the basis of the resurrection of Jesus. The Christian tradition proclaimed that there is an ultimate reign of God, to be inaugurated by a general resurrection that will bring about the fruition of God's redemptive work. The partiality of God's reign in history will meet the fullness of God's reign in the life of the world to come.

What is "the life of the world to come"? Based upon biblical imagery, this life is a resurrection that leads to judgment and justice. But, as was evident in our brief study of the biblical notion of the reign of God, the justice of God's reign was not conceived as a blind balancing of virtues and vices, but as the concrete caring for the well-being of persons within society. It had a particular view to disadvantaged persons, or what is often called "a preferential option for the poor," so that their welfare was the litmus test of whether or not the society was just. Were there homeless people wandering on the streets of the city, with neither shelter, nor the means of care? Were the sick and the maimed left to fend for themselves? Were orphans and widows left destitute? To the degree that such things marked the society, by the ancient criterion, the society was unjust. The biblical image of an ultimate judgment is in continuity with this social image of justice, as is evident in the Matthew 25 depiction of a final judgment. There the criterion of judgment is based upon Jesus' own identification with the oppressed; our actions toward the disadvantaged are our actions toward God's own self, and we are judged. Thus "the life of the world to come" bespeaks a future life where there is an ultimate judgment according to justice, with the intimation that at last there shall be a restoration of all things.

Notice how much hinges upon resurrection and judgment if God's justice is finally to be vindicated. In historical life there simply is no fullness of justice. Even when there is a redress of injustice through new modes that establish justice within a society, those who have fallen victim to the earlier modes do not participate in the new order. Where is the vindication of justice for them? If the fullest understanding of justice involves redress of evil and restoration of well-being, it is all too clear that a temporal world marked by the passage of time and death cannot sustain the reality of such justice. Is the dream of justice simply a chimera, then, with no hope of fulfillment except in the bits and pieces world of fragmentary lives?

Consider one example of an injustice that history cannot correct. One particular woman was burned at the stake as a witch in medieval Europe. Injustice came upon her as a maelstrom, crumbling her world of meaning and well-being into a welter of panic, pain, and ashes. Five million women living in a world of justice and mutuality make no difference to that one woman's experience of fire, agony, and death. She feels no affirmation of her existence and no redress of the crime, no matter how fervently women five centuries later decry patriarchy and its evil of witch burning. Justice for the many is good, but it does not answer the requirement of justice for her. Without "the life of the world to come," her unredeemed experience stands as a finality of injustice, mocking the power even of God's justice. Without resurrection, there is no fullness of justice.

Without judgment there is no justice. As we wrote about the life of Jesus, we called attention to the way in which his desire toward the well-being of Simon required him to judge those things in Simon's attitude that were against justice. Simon's false presumptions were that the woman at Jesus' feet should be excluded and condemned. His failure to care about her well-being meant that he cut himself off from relationality and justice. His true good involved him in loving care for the woman and her condition. Jesus judged his smallness, revealing to him his true state and his true welfare.

Like Simon, we also—whether through ignorance or intention—limit the notion of well-being to ourselves or those just like ourselves. Like him, we too act against our own well-being. What good is resurrection if in resurrection we persist in the same evils? Only as resurrection leads to judgment is there any clear avenue toward the justice that is proclaimed in Ephesians as "the reconciliation of all things." The issue of "the life of the world to come" that is affirmed by the church involves far, far more than the simple popular theme of rewards and punishments. It involves the full establishment of God's justice.

But how do we express such things? The apostle Paul, in his first letter to the Corinthians, referred to that which is beyond what any eye has seen, or ear has heard, or heart has conceived. The apostle John could only express his own vision in terms of metaphors of majesty, terror, and beauty. Precisely because of the inexpressible nature of that which is envisioned in "the life of the world to come," we seem to fall into several problems. Some simply discredit notions of a resurrection as wishful thinking or fantasy, unfit for a twentieth-century world view. Such Christians frequently fail to see the tremendous issue of justice that stands or falls on the reality of the resurrection. Some others will affirm resurrection, but with a vision too small, making "the life of the world to come" but an extension of earthly existence without frustration or pain. The depths of biblical justice receive scant due by such limitation, for well-being means more than contentment for just a few. There are also those who loudly affirm the resurrection, but concentrate almost wholly upon reducing the book of Revelation to a code book that they alone can decipher. The symbolic depths of the book are ignored, replaced by identifying various contemporary nations or persons as evil powers who will be consumed in an apocalyptic catastrophe that is just around the corner. The decipherers of this history, of course, are never among the unfortunate consumed. Self-righteousness and revenge are odd entryways into the reign of God.

Perhaps because of the inadequacy of the above views, there has been a lessening of the full vision of the reign of God in contemporary Christianity. If the vision is important for our efforts in establishing finite forms of justice, and if our work in the world ultimately has an everlasting effect in God, then we cannot afford the luxury of dismissing or belittling the Christian affirmation of resurrection, judgment, and justice. But how do we understand the resurrection of the dead?

The New Testament imagery refers to resurrection always in the context of a transformation of things—there is a new heaven and a new earth. Whatever else such statements mean, surely they indicate that resurrection cannot be understood as the extension of the present order. We must use imagery from the present order—as does John in Revelation—but that imagery pushes ordinary understanding to its very limits, straining at the edges of vision. For example, John speaks of a river, and a tree—but the river is as crystal, and it flows from a throne! And the tree bears twelve different kinds of fruit, one kind for each month! Imagery is stretched to its limit in order to become a symbol to convey that which no eye has seen, nor ear heard, nor heart conceived. To be faithful to the imagery is to let it break out of its confinement in temporal existence to point to that vision beyond sight.

To use process language to express resurrection is likewise visionary, and presses beyond itself. The metaphor of the actual entity that is used to describe finite existence carries within it a congruence with our own experience—we can affirm a model that speaks of the internal nature of relationships; the model speaks cogently to the very sense of identity that marks our days. When we interpret the model relative to everyday existence, or even with reference to the world of physics, there is a certain recognition from our own experience that carries over into the extension of the model to other aspects of finite existence. We are anchored in a familiar harbor. However, to use the model to express not ordinary existence, but extraordinary existence in the fullness of the reign of God is to leave the moorings and to explore the open seas, with nothing but the model as the tiny boat that takes us so far. The model then presses beyond the familiar, linking us fragilely to a world that might be.

The process model of God as an actual entity pushes us to say that God is heaven, and heaven is God. We must express resurrection as taking place in the life of God and through the power of God. To do so is strangely consonant with some of the oldest expressions of Christian faith, for in the biblical texts we are told that we will be made partakers of the divine nature, and that immortality belongs only to God. Early church theologians expressed the resurrection as a promotion into God and as a participation in God. Process theology must reiterate these sensitivities, and suggest that resurrection is a rebirth of ourselves in God through the fullness of God's feeling, or "prehension," of us into the divine life. We are made partakers of God's life through a movement from the edges of God to the everlasting depths of God, from God's consequent nature to integration with God's primordial nature. This is a process that moves from resurrection through judgment into transformation; the process is governed by God, and is the ultimate reign of God.

How can these things be? The process term, "prehension," gives the means to discuss resurrection—and immortality—in God. In the model, prehensions refer to those feelings with which every occasion of existence begins. A prehension is a feeling of that which is other than the self. This other is also composed of feelings that have been unified into a unique subjectivity. To feel the other is to be in touch with the other's feelings of itself. For this reason, Whitehead spoke of prehension as a "flow of feeling" from one subject into another. The connectedness that exists between one subject and another is the transition of what was felt "there," now re-enacted "here." It is as if everything exists in and for itself, and yet finds itself at home in otherness. That which is for itself is also for others; what is created "here" comes to rest "there" through the vehicle of prehension.

However, no finite subject can feel the totality of another subject's feelings. This is because every subject feels not simply one other, but many others; there is a multiplicity of feelings vying for inclusion in every subject. These many feelings must be unified within the new self through a process of selecting, comparing, contrasting, and unifying the past in terms of that which the new subject chooses to become. This selectivity necessarily eliminates some portion of every other's total subjectivity; no finite entity can be incorporated in its entirety within another. Therefore, even though there is a flow of feeling, this is never a flow of the total subjectivity of one entity into another. The mystery of otherness is that in principle, the other can never be fully known.

There is an illustration of this issue in our experience of relating to friends. Each friend calls forth a different aspect of ourselves, so that each friendship is unique. One friend might bring forth feelings for a particular kind of music, so that there is a frequent enjoyment of each other's company while listening to this music. Another friend might share childhood memories, so that the special quality of being with that friend is the warmth of having shared a similar history. The two friends do not know each other, so that while in the presence of one, the qualities that are usually evoked in the presence of the other are dormant. Imagine that both friends unexpectedly visit at the same time. Won't there be a peculiar tension in the meeting? Since neither knows the other, nor that aspect that the other evokes, there is a conflict concerning which interests and which bond shall form the core of the meeting. If the relationship to the musical friend proceeds as usual, the childhood friend will be left out; conversely, to speak about common memories with the childhood friend excludes the musical friend. The almost unconscious selectivity that operates in each friendship alone is now painfully apparent, and some wider basis of shared experience must become the content of conversation. Unfortunately, the immediately obvious shared fact is that one friend is shared in common by the other two. Relating on that basis dilutes the fullness of each friendship on its own, and there will be a measure of discomfort and stiltedness among the three until deeper commonalities emerge, rendering the three persons friends together. The triadic friendship, however, will have a quality of its own not found in either of the two single friendships. Selectivity and unification always utilize some but not all elements from the past, so that while there is a flow of feeling from one subject to another, the full subjectivity of the other can be neither exhausted nor retained by the prehending subject.

This does not hold true with regard to God's feelings of the world because of the reversed polar structure that is necessary in God. That is, whereas every finite subject begins from the multiplicity of feelings of the past, and modifies these feelings into a single new unity, God "begins" with a primordial unity of all possibilities. This is a conceptual "beginning" that then moves toward the physical feelings of the world. But since the great unity of God already includes all possibilities, there is no actuality in principle that cannot be introduced into the unity of God. Therefore, there is no categorical reason why God cannot prehend the whole of another's feelings. The primordial nature of God is the common ground by which diverse subjects in their full subjectivity can be felt, contrasted, compared, and unified. In our finite illustration, the common ground uniting the three persons into friendship had to be discovered through selectivity, sifting out those factors that were alien to the interests of each and finding those mutual interests that could unite the three as friends. For God, the primordial nature is the basis of unity. God, and only God, can feel the entirety of the other. Thus the flow of feeling that takes place as God prehends the other is a flow of the full subjectivity of the other into the full subjectivity of God. This is subjective immortality for the world within the life of God.

Is this resurrection? In the imagery of 1 Corinthians 15, resurrection is a transformation brought about by the power of God wherein our dead physical bodies become spiritual bodies. Our mortal nature becomes immortal; sin and death shall be no more. "We shall all be changed," said the apostle. Through the nearly two thousand years of the church, Christians have been attempting to express this vision, knowing finally that we can only fall back upon the beginning words of 1 Corinthians that confess that the fullness of the vision is beyond our comprehension. In this process expression of resurrection, we simply use the metaphysics as a metaphor to express a mighty transition from a finite subjectivity that is alone with itself to that same subjectivity within the presence of God.

This understanding of resurrection requires that one reaffirm the creedal statement, "I believe in the resurrection of the body." Resurrection cannot be limited simply to a world of souls—God feels the entirety of the world, in all its manifold forms. In a process universe, subjectivity is not limited to human beings, nor even to all sentient beings: subjectivity is the essential reality of every actual occasion, regardless of whether it forms part of the reality of a human being or of a drop of rain. God feels *all* subjectivities in the process vision. Transformation is not restricted to humanity, but must be extended to the whole universe. There will be a new heaven and a new earth, but the locus of both is God's own being through God's power of resurrection.

This resurrection is spiritual, not material. The world is not simply transposed to God, so that it exists in a sort of parallel state. The world is *transformed* in God. This is why resurrection, which connotes transformation, is a more precise term than immortality, which could imply simple continuance. In a process framework, one can push toward an understanding of a spiritual resurrection by remembering the earlier discussion of God as pure spirit. The physical pole was defined as the means of relating to others; God relates to all others in their entirety, and hence if spirituality is understood as a depth of relatedness, God is pure spirit. A spiritual resurrection must be understood along the same lines. If a subject experiences itself as subject in God, then the new context of subjectivity is the pure relatedness of God. In God, as will shortly be developed, there is a new fullness of relatedness to all others. The finite development of subjectivity required selectivity and a clear demarcation of boundaries. The results of that demarcation remain, but the circumstances are changed. Whereas in finite existence the parameters of existence might have been the societal togetherness of many actual occasions so that a material existence developed, in God the parameters of existence are simply God. *All* relatedness, not *some* relatedness, is found in the environment of God. Therefore, the subjectivities that are resurrected in God are no longer definable in terms of material togetherness. Materiality falls away, since the conditions for materiality do not exist in the single reality of God. Resurrection is to a spiritual body.

How can this subject resurrected in God continue to experience anything at all? The basic objection being raised here relates primarily to an important qualification in process philosophy, for it is axiomatic that the "satisfaction" of a subject (or completion of a subject) can sustain no addition. If there is an addition to the subject, then the subject is no longer the same subject, but another. If a subject experiences transformation in God, how is it the same subject? But if a subject does not experience transformation in God, how is there judgment and justice? Resurrection alone is not sufficient to establish the reign of God.

In order to address the problem we must summarize again the movement of process. Every occasion begins with prehensions, or feelings of the multiple entities of the past. Concrescence is the subjective comparison and contrast of these prehensions in light of one's subjective aim, or immediate feeling for what one can become. Satisfaction is the conclusion of the process, the determinacy of all the data into just this subjectivity. The whole process is highly unitary—if any one part of these dynamics is not present, there is no subject. It is not even that the subject is stillborn; it is more radical than that. The subject *is* the entirety of the process, indivisibly. Only upon its completion (or satisfaction), may the subject be felt by another. In one sense, satisfaction is a Janus-type of creativity, for it is a bridge between the concrescent creativity of the subject's own process, and the transitional creativity that evokes the prehensions of a subject yet to be. It is a dynamic holding together of the results of concrescence, retaining the subjectivity of the occasion, but giving it up through transitional creativity to the prehensions of others. When the other is a finite successor to the occasion, the subjectivity will be objectified through the very selectivity by which it is felt. But when the other is God, the subjectivity will not be objectified; it will be felt in its entirety.

God prehends the completed subject's satisfaction. Since God feels the totality of this satisfaction, God feels as well the subjectivity of that satisfaction, prehending—and, therefore, resurrecting—it into the divine life. If, during its temporal existence, the satisfaction was grounded in the brief process of its own concrescence, in the divine life that same satisfaction is grounded in the everlastingness of God's concrescence. Thus while the satisfaction in temporality is born to a flickering moment of life, in God it is born again into everlasting life.

But what happens to it there? If it stays itself forever, isolated into its own achievement, everlastingness could be a most dreadful evil. At least in history time sometimes heals—but if every moment of existence is retained everlastingly, doesn't that mean that every moment of pain as well as every moment of joy becomes unendurably enduring? Redemption is not answered at all by resurrection; only if there is participation in a justice more full than that of finitude is there an answer to evil. In order to posit such a fullness of redemption for resurrected occasions of experience in God we must inquire into the dynamics of a reversed concrescence in God.

Remember that in God the reversed polar structure means that God's ordering of all possibilities into an infinite mode of harmony is the presupposition of every prehension. For God, satisfaction is the ground of concrescence rather than the conclusion of concrescence, and the subjective aim of God's concrescence flows from this primordial satisfaction. Prehensions—or resurrections—must then be compared and contrasted with one another in light of the aim flowing from the divine satisfaction. Furthermore, since the divine satisfaction has been the source of the initial aim (or providence, or prevenient grace) that launched the occasion into its finite becoming, the contrasting with God's own subjective aim will also be a contrast between what the occasion could have been and what it actually became. This comparing and contrasting that marks the successive genetic phases of God's concrescence is in fact a process of judgment and transformation for the resurrected subjects in God.

But how does the occasion itself participate in this? After all, it has been resurrected as a particular subjectivity in God, no longer concrescing, but simply holding together in the dynamics of its own satisfaction the immediacy that it became, along with its appetition towards its successors. This subjectivity is no longer either prehending or concrescing; it cannot add new experiences to itself—for such activity belonged to its incomplete mode of being during concrescence, not to the fullness of its satisfaction. To talk about the subject continuing to experience in God, in such a way that the judgment of God is an experienced judgment, would seem to pose an enigma. By definition, the immediacy contained in the finite satisfaction cannot be increased or decreased. It is one thing to talk of God's experience of the subject within God's concrescence, and quite another to talk of the subject's experiential participation in this. How, then, can this resurrected immediacy go beyond its own experience, as it must, if it is to participate in the judgment of God's concrescence and justice of God's satisfaction?

The answer to be explored is based on the fullness of the divine consciousness, and the sense in which the finite satisfaction includes appetition for that which is beyond itself. Consciousness pervades God; it is a subjective form qualifying the divine satisfaction and therefore pervading the entirety of God's concrescing being. It is not as if God's consciousness is interrupted by each finite consciousness. Rather, God's consciousness must be more complex than that which is given to human experience, including a multiplicity of viewpoints within its complex unity. God's consciousness holds within it the consciousness of each resurrected subject as coexperienced by God. The resurrected subjects, in turn, share in the fuller consciousness of God in whom they participate. In a sense, by virtue of God's concrescence, they have entered a double identity—themselves and God, and the process of their own transformation consists in the movement wherein their primal point of view, while retaining its origin, becomes the point of view of the whole, which is God.

There is a role in this dual identity that is played by the appetition belonging to each finite satisfaction. Remember, the satisfaction is a dynamic holding together of the results of concrescence, together with an appetition that generates transition to the future. In God, couldn't these appetitions become the linkage whereby the consciousnesses of the resurrected subjects share in the full consciousness of God? Could the many appetitions from the occasions of one's full life now, in their final unity in God, yield a subjective form that, empowered by God and conjoined with God, becomes the self's transformation? Perhaps the composite self in God yields a new unification, a new "I" that, taking place through God's concrescence, is the most intimate conjoining of self and God for the purpose of the self's ultimate transformation. There would be a dual and yet unified consciousness in such a situation, being the composite consciousness of the self, known through the deeper and sustaining consciousness of God.

Words crack and strain when trying, from the limited viewpoint of the flickering in-and-out consciousness of our historical existence, to imagine what the deeper consciousness of God might be like. We look for metaphors— perhaps a symphony, in which all the notes are intensely alive. Each note in this symphony of fantasy would feel itself in relation to all the others, feeling its place in the whole and the whole as well. The life that sustains the lives of the notes would be the symphony as a whole, with its own overriding purpose and sense of beauty. Posit a deeper locus of awareness than the aliveness of the notes, in the symphony itself. Think of it as a living symphony, sparkling with awareness of its own beauty both from the perspective of the whole and from the multiplied perspective of each part—the single beauty is intensified through the multiple awarenesses merged into the unified awareness of the whole. This is a fantasy, obviously, and if it is hard to imagine what such a symphony would be like in its own nature, it is still harder to imagine how one outside the symphony could be attuned appreciatively to such a complex beauty. Imagine that every listener becomes a participant in the symphony, adding a new note, and that the symphony is everlasting, ever deepening, ever intensifying, as one infinitely complex, inexhaustible beauty. Whether we try to speak of God after the metaphor of a living symphony or after the metaphor of an actual entity, we struggle to say that which in the end must finally yield to the recognition that "it must be much more than this."

God is the overcomer of evil. The intuition is that in the concrescence of God, the resurrected self would always retain its own sense of "I," and yet by the concrescent power of God would *at the same time* experience God's experience of itself in the totality of the divine life. This abstract and metaphorical description needs to be supplemented with a more concrete illustration in order to see how the vision might answer the intuition that there is an ultimate justice that redresses all evil. What would happen, in this speculative vision, to the woman we mentioned at the beginning of this chapter who had been burned at the stake for witchcraft? Can we apply the dynamics of resurrection life to her?

In this process understanding, resurrection takes place not upon the death of the whole person, but throughout life, as God continuously feels the occasions of the world. God continuously coexperienced each moment of that woman's existence. God coexperienced her childhood, her teen years, and every moment of her adult life. God coexperienced her fright just as she felt it when she heard the frenzy in the voices of her neighbors discussing witchcraft; God felt her own terror as she realized the accusations were directed against herself. God felt the paralysis with which she endured the humiliation of examination and "trial," and God felt the agony as the fire began its searing work. God felt her death. Because God felt with her every moment, there is resurrection in God. This is the point where it becomes essential to realize that an occasion is not raised to immortality locked into its finite experiences; hell indeed would be eternal if her fiery death were untransformed in everlastingness. The center of the resurrected subjectivity must be able to flow from its finite creation into the wider experience of God. The woman must feel herself in God through God's own consciousness.

If the woman-in-God experiences herself through the divine consciousness, then the first phase of her "more than herself" movement into God is a phase of personal judgment. She knows herself as God knows her; she knows herself as she could have been, and as she is. The first phase of judgment is the knowledge of ourselves from the divine perspective. "We shall know as we are known," says the apostle Paul in 1 Corinthians 13.

The second phase of judgment in God would have to take place due to the subjective unity of God, wherein all prehensions are felt relative to each other. This is called "mutuality of subjective form." If we posit that the consciousness of the resurrected occasion participates in the consciousness of God, then through God, the occasion will feel all others, and therefore will experience itself from the perspective of those others. "We shall know as we are known."

Consider the ways the woman might experience this second phase of judgment. A distinction must be made between the totality of her life experience in the unity of her personality, and the myriad actual occasions that successively formed her person, each of which was felt by and therefore resurrected by God into the divine life. The "mutual sensitivity of subjective form" would first relate each particular moment of the woman's resurrected self with all previous moments; there would be a "regathering" of her selfhood in God. Consequently, she would experience not only the momentary judgment of a particular instant, but also a composite judgment concerning her total being, all through the comparative feelings of God whereby her many moments, or occasions, are unified in God.

This would mean that there is a togetherness of one's total personality in the resurrection body. In our finite existence, we exist in a "stretched out" manner, one event following another, one year replacing another, inexorably moving in one direction from birth to death. The continuity is provided by the flow of feeling from one moment to the next, but always in a context of progression and loss. But in God, there is no loss, for nothing is ever past. It can't be, if God is a single entity. And God has felt every single occasion in that movement of our lives, and still feels them all. There is a composite gathering of the personality in God, and the totality is known for what it was and for what it could have been.

This is both a positive and negative form of judgment. In God, every moment is always itself and yet more than itself. This means, in our illustration, that the seven-year-old child feels the thirty-seven-year-old woman burning at the stake—but it also means that the thirty-seven-year old woman feels again with a simultaneity the delights of other moments of her life. The regathered personality in God in the resurrection body is all ages and no age, transcending every moment of existence in the reunion of all moments of existence. This phase of judgment is the suprapersonal totality of the self, feeling one's whole existence as copresent in God and with God, and as felt by God.

But one person is hardly the sum total of God's feelings—God feels the world! Thus the mutual sensitivity of subjective form that allows a knowledge of the composite self in God only begins the judgment process. In our finite existence, it would be foolishness to think we stopped with the edges of our skin. We are relational beings, and we are completed in and through our many relationships with others. In God, those with whom one has come in contact are also resurrected, and the relationality that bound us with those others on earth is felt as well in heaven.

In the resurrected life, self-knowledge will extend to an awareness of the way one was experienced by others. Through the power of the divine sensitivity, each is mediated to the other, knowing oneself through the heart of the other. Joys that were given will be experienced; alternatively, the same dynamics mean that pains that were inflicted will also be experienced. In the faithfulness of this experience of the self through the other, there is continued judgment.

This dynamic can be illustrated by considering not simply the woman of our earlier example, but the judge who was most responsible for her accusation and conviction. He, too, experiences resurrection in God; he, too, experiences the totality of himself; he, too, experiences his effects upon others. In God his knowledge of himself will be completed through his knowledge of how he affected the woman. He shall know as he is known. But he will know her pain along with God's judgment of what might have been, so that while she might experience God's feeling of her as the compassion of shared pain, he will experience God's feeling of her as a judgment of wrath against himself for what might have been had he only responded positively toward God's aims for himself for an alternative mode of action and being.

Furthermore, his experience of the woman's pain will also connect him with God's wrath against the social constructs that led to and allowed such injustice in human society. The judge will feel his complicity not only with regard to the woman, but with regard to the system that caught her in its web. He will experience his "might have been" in his systemic responsibility of participating in and so perpetuating structures of injustice; this, too, involves him in God's wrath.

There are now three phases of judgment: first, the judgment with regard to the individual moment of experience; second, the judgment following from the totality of a life; third, the judgment following from the totality of our personal and social relationships. This is a process of movement into the fullness of God's subjectivity. From the point of view of the resurrected self, it is a movement into deeper and deeper levels of self-knowledge, with an attendant sense of judgment. From the point of view of God, it is a movement into integration, whereby the many feelings in the consequent nature are brought into increasing modes of harmony. The many feelings are being pulled toward the vortex of God in the primordial vision, where the many are together as the expression of that vision in unfathomable depths of unity and justice.

There are several things to be noted about this process. Notice that it is a movement toward unity according to the divine purpose. It takes place according to God's will, for freedom belongs only to God in the divine concrescence. The resurrected self *must* experience judgment; there is no option. Insofar as the finite self has been conformed to God in its own finite self-creation, the finite self will feel this movement toward unity as a wonderful degree of freedom. The movement would feel like a freedom long dreamed of but frustratingly difficult to achieve in the conflicts of finite existence. Here at last, in God, there is a movement beyond the self in a feeling with others; here at last in God there is a fully realized empathy; here at last in God is the elusive fullness of self-knowledge. But to those whose finite choices had set them against the good of others, the freedom of God will be as unfreedom. That which to the one is heaven, to the other is hell. The judge *must* feel the woman's agony, not only as she felt it but in the full knowledge of the pain and impoverishment inflicted upon society in the days and generations to come through his act. To know as he is known is pain for him in regard to this action. The inexorable movement whereby God pulls his subjectivity into increasing self-knowledge is experienced by him not as freedom, but as that which goes against his own freedom. And indeed it does. The divine freedom governs the divine concrescence; insofar as one's own use of freedom was in conformity with the nature of God, one will experience God as heaven; insofar as one's freedom was against the nature of God, one will experience God as hell.

How is there redress? How is the woman requited for her agony? And is the judge to feel the movement of God as a hell forever? The same movement by which there is judgment is the movement by which there is ultimate redemption, and therefore ultimate justice. Notice that by the will of God, the resurrected self must move beyond the confines of any one aspect of personal ego. In the first place, there is a composite ego, or "I," and in the second place, the ego is continuously growing through the increase in self-knowledge. This means that the "I," by the power of God, can no longer remain locked within its narrow structure. The finite subjectivities are being held in existence by that infinite subjectivity, God. The mutuality with which God feels each subjectivity in relation to all others pulls each subjectivity into that coexperiencing that we have described as judgment. But hell, to remain hell, must have the reinforcement of a narrow ego. What is happening in the very process of judgment is that the ego is being opened up to that which is more than itself. The participation in the other through the power of God is not only judgment, it is the route to the transformation of justice. Consider the woman and the judge. She is aware of him experiencing her pain within the divine nature. But her own movement is beyond that pain into transformation. The judge is not locked into her pain, any more than she is; the judge, too, experiences her transformation in God, and therefore participates in that transformation. She contributes to his redemption.

The further aspect of this follows from what it means to be completed through the other. This very completion through others is a breaking down of the limitations of the finite ego, which tends to see others as competitors or contributors to the self. In the context of divine transformation, that boundary of the ego into self-as-opposed-to-other breaks down. With its breakdown, the self becomes wider and wider. There is no longer imprisonment in the ego. The breakdown of the ego becomes the breakthrough to God. Judgment issues into transformation. In this transformation, there is an increasing identity of the self with the whole—but the whole is now God, governed by God's aim toward harmony, pulling all the multiplicities of the consequent nature into the single beauty of the primordial nature.

If one has been initially completed by one's effects upon others, this route of "beyondness" never ends in God. Those elements that have been highly valued by God insofar as they are near, not distant, to the goodness of God gain an increasing importance, and are felt by those in the process of transformation as supplementing their own reality. The judge moves from a knowledge of himself— mediated by God—to a knowledge of himself in God, which moves yet deeper into a knowledge of God. This movement is one wherein multiplicity moves deeper and deeper into unity: the judge moves from alienation from the others toward supplementation by the others toward completion through and contribution to others in the full integration of God. Just as the redemption of the woman he harmed contributes to his redemption, even so, his increasing redemption contributes to her deepening joy. For the ultimate transformation and unity in God is love, pervasive, deep, everlasting.

Thus judgment moves into justice. The increasing integration of the resurrected subjects in God pulls them deeper into unity with each other in God's primordial satisfaction. In mutual completion, each experiences the other's joys, gratitude, wonder, and love. These qualities are intensified since they mirror the divine ability to hold the many together in unity. The edges of God are tragedy through the feelings of pain in the universe, but they are the edges only. The mighty center toward which we move in judgment is the overcoming of evil through its transformation by the power of God. In the center of God, the many are one everlastingly.

The vision of justice in God is simply the primordial satisfaction in its everlasting expression. The reality of the world is transformed in judgment into conformity with the nature of God. The consequent nature of God is one where multiplicity moves to deeper forms of unity; this is the concrescence of God, pulling the prehended world into the unity of the divine nature. But the dynamic depth of God is still a diverse unity, with composite harmonies, all held together in the intense unity of the overarching whole. God's primordial and inexhaustibly expressed vision of the togetherness of all things is a harmony of harmonies.

Earlier, in our discussion of the incarnation of God in Christ, we noted that since Christ is the manifestation of the divine nature in finite circumstances, there is little transformation needed of Christ in God. Indeed, the whole transfiguration account given in the gospel of Matthew suggests that to eyes that could see, Jesus was already shimmering with the glory of God in his embodiment of God's reign. Therefore, when we speak of the depths of God as being the actualization of the harmony of the primordial vision, sparkling in the brightness of God's glory, we must speak of Christ in God, transfigured rather than transformed. Further, Christ in the primordial nature is everlastingly being completed through God's reception and transformation of the church. God completes the church through its union with Christ in the primordial nature, even as the church completes Christ.

But if Christ and those who have been led to conformity with God through him have a place in the brightness of that actualized primordial vision, it is also so that every distinctive route toward the realization of well-being in conformity with the harmony of God has a place in that divine center. Each route is like a constellation in the whole sky of God, retaining its uniqueness even in the wider sense of unity. Each constellation that has manifested the transformation into God through a particular route retains the diversity and particularity of that route, like a flow forever entering into God by the will and grace of God. But still deeper than the diversities is the unity: the mutual sensitivity that begins the process of judgment and transformation continues in the depths of God, forever manifesting in intricate combinations made possible by the transformed world the beauty, holiness, and love of the divine nature. Here the beauty that is Christliness is felt and feels itself in harmony with the beauty that is Buddhistic, and Judaic, and every other constellation realized through the far-flung universe and now completed through its transformation in God.

There is a home in God, a home for the whole universe. In that home, multiplicity finally achieves unity, and fragmentation is embraced in wholeness. The unity and wholeness receiving and transforming each part is more than the sum of them all, for the unity is the ever-living God, drawing upon the divine resources of infinite possibility to blend all reality into the giving and receiving of the whole. Differentiation remains in the primordial depths of God, but it is a differentiation that is divinely sustained as the most fitting actuality of unity, beauty, and holiness: the reign of God which is the reign *in* God, which is God.

17

"THY KINGDOM COME"

WE are empowered by a vision of hope that justice is, in fact, the fundamental reality of the universe, achieved everlastingly in the joy of God. Such a vision encourages work for justice despite the odds of history; from it we draw strength for transforming history towards justice. And yet for all of this, the call to God's reign is so great: economic justice, liberation, renewal of the earth, openness to the nations of the world for the peace of the world, and openness to other religions in mutual dialogue. How can we as individuals possibly answer the magnitude of the call? We can only be involved in a portion of the world and one aspect of the work, and our effectiveness seems terribly small. Do we simply concentrate on our own task, and hope others will take responsibilities elsewhere? In bits and pieces, will the kingdom come?

We are called to reflect the reign of God in human society: that which is contained in the beauty and justice of the divine nature is to be mirrored in our own circumstances. In God, the many are one everlastingly, each contributing to the others and receiving from the others in the unity of God. If this image is to be mirrored within human society, then the fragmentation of each doing a task in isolation from the others is antithetical to the reign. It is not enough to confine oneself to one's own task—we must contribute to others and receive from others throughout the breadth of the work. But how can this be?

Prayer is vital to the coming of God's reign. Through prayer, we enlarge the effectiveness and scope of our work in the entire task. Also through prayer we bring to conscious realization the unity that belongs to all Christians by virtue of our identity in Christ. Finally, it is primarily through prayer that the reign of God finds an avenue for its finite mode of actualization in history. Is there a reign of justice within God's own self, awaiting us as our destiny? And does God adapt this justice to our own historical circumstances in every moment, calling us into a future that will to some degree reflect God's own justice? As we respond to that call, our future affects our present reality. The call comes through the providential aim of God, and prayer can heighten our attunement to that aim, and aid us in its actualization. Thus prayer is a channel of union between the reign of God that is in God, and the reign as it is reflected in history.

How do we enlarge the effectiveness and scope of our work through prayer? Every moment of our existence begins with the touch of God through God's provision of an aim toward our good. The aim is directive, guiding us toward a best mode of action in our given circumstances. This gracious touch of God is at the deepest levels of who we are, below the layers of consciousness, and therefore, it is only indirectly accessible to our conscious selves. As has been noted, the orientation of the aim is toward the world around us, and the distractions and needs of the world serve to reinforce the hiddenness of God's aim. That the directive force in our lives comes from God is more a matter of faith than sight.

Frequently through meditative forms of prayer we can quiet ourselves, screening out the distractions of our surroundings, centering in toward the depths of who we are. We can direct our consciousness inward toward the place where God touches us. The Christian tradition of prayer has often cited the paradoxical claim that the way "outward" to God is the way "inward" to ourselves. Meditation is an inward focusing in order to break through the self, first to God, and then to immediate service in and to the world. Prayer is that inward step, seeking the strength of the guidance of God as it is given through the initial aim. God is faithful; the aim is ever given, and it is a grace-laden gift. The direction of God is based upon our fullest realities, and therefore is a direction that is really possible for us. God's will *can* be done; else, how could we pray "thy will be done"? As we allow ourselves to become more open to God's aim in the quietness of prayer, that specific guidance from God will become more apparent to us.

Prayer is the road to renewed confidence in the guidance of God as we work toward the reflected image of God in our lives and in the world. The confidence that comes from prayer is strengthened also by the conformity between what we perceive as God's guidance for us, and the criteria of the reign of God that we see in the scriptures. Can we see the personal guidance received in prayer as enhancing modes of liberation, or tending toward the renewal of earth, or communities of peace and justice? Does it enable us to break down barriers erected between peoples or nations? The faithfulness of God means that there is a consistency to divine action, so that personal guidance is always congruent with the wider purposes of God. While the actions of any individual will seldom embrace all of these great themes, there will be a resonance with the redemptive spirit of God's reign. The inward guidance of prayer and the outward guidance of scripture converge, and our confidence is strengthened.

This confidence is the means, gained through prayer, whereby we enlarge the effectiveness and scope of our task. Without such confidence, we might grow discouraged by the weakness of our singular work. With it, we know that God's guidance for us fits in with the larger task of the whole community. Our weakness is supplemented by divine strength, and our singularity is complemented by the many others who are also colaborers with God in God's reign. And since no action is without effects, that small task that is before us will have repercussions that can be useful for the wider work. God can weave those effects into the total fabric of God's reign. The confidence gained through prayer increases our vision and hope; consequently, we act with more zest. Our effectiveness increases.

Through prayer we participate in each other's work, thus actualizing the unity that belongs to the church through identity with Christ. In addition to the mode of prayer that centers us inward in order to focus upon God's guidance in the initial aim, there is also intercessory prayer, through which we participate in God's aims for others in a direct way.

Consider an example of this. Michael lives in a small town in Pennsylvania; he feels a responsibility to work for alleviation of severe health risks that endanger the workers in a factory in his community. His background in industrial hygiene fits him for this work, and his sense of God's guidance in the direction of justice leads him toward this action. But there are many factors involved in the complexity of the dangerous working conditions, and much resistance to the kinds of changes he thinks must be made. Michael is just one individual—what can he do against the status quo of these long established practices?

Garth lives in Dallas, and his own work is in quite a different field. But Michael is his friend and cousin, and he feels Michael's sense of helplessness. In fact, he feels it himself, for apparently he is powerless in this situation. How can he help? His only resource seems to be prayer. Is it a weak resource? What happens as he prays for Michael?

Remember that God works with the world, for the world. The initial aims God gives to Michael are woven from the realities in his situation, together with what is now possible given those realities. Imagine that the realities in Michael's world include a sense of hopelessness on the part of the workers themselves: It has always been this way, and it always will be—my parents worked in these conditions, and so will my children. Hopelessness goes hand-in-hand with complacency, since it reinforces the nonnecessity of change. God must reckon with these attitudes in fashioning the really-possible aim for Michael. The odds *are* great. And Garth prays. All that this means is simply that against the negative realities in the world, suddenly a positive reality vis-à-vis this particular situation is introduced. There is not only Michael, who is a potential agent for change, but there is also Garth, who in the action of prayer molds his own concerns to Michael's situation. God can work with the material of Garth's praying, for in fact his praying changes the world. He is a part of the world, and as he directs himself through God to Michael's concerns, he becomes a part of Michael's particular situation. Therefore, the situation is qualitatively different than it would be if he neither cared nor prayed. By prayer, he adds to the material world with which God works in providing redemptive aims. Hope supplements hopelessness, and a desire for change supplements complacency. Because Garth prays, Michael can receive possibilities through initial aims that will be stronger than they could have been if Garth did not pray. Thus Garth participates in Michael's work through prayer.

Prayer changes the world. The statement is not metaphorical but literal. In a process universe, everything that happens in the world matters. God works with what is, in order to lead the world toward what can be. To pray is to change the way the world is by adding that prayer to the reality of the world. Because prayer is added to the world, the reality of what-can-be changes. Redemptive possibilities that might have been irrelevant, and therefore inaccessible to the world without prayer, can be released by the power of prayer.

By no means is this because God begrudges those redemptive possibilities to the world. God does not need to be persuaded in order to release them. Far to the contrary, God yearns for our redemption, and cares passionately for our well-being, and in fact prompts us to pray. As we pray, we change the world by changing ourselves in our deepest orientation. And with that change, we alter the total situation with which God works. Prayer releases the power of God to lead the world toward the reign of God.

Notice the implications of the fact that through prayer we change the world first of all through a change in ourselves. Garth prays for Michael. At first his general sense of helplessness may form the content of the prayer; he knows of no specific direction to pray, simply that his deepest concern is to be for his cousin through God in prayer. It is enough that divine wisdom will utilize his prayers for Michael's good. This can be simply through God's leading Garth toward more specificity as he is open to such leading in prayer. Also, Garth's openness to God and to Michael's welfare in prayer creates a readiness in him for further action. There will be a quiet prompting in his life directing him to this or to that activity with regard to Michael's situation. Prayer is a form of action that yields still further forms, and these further forms are an extension of the prayer. God will use Garth's prayers not only in direct reference to the kinds of initial aims that can be offered to Michael and those others involved in that whole situation, but God will use Garth's prayers to extend his own involvement in other areas of his life.

This means that Garth participates in Michael's work, even though he is hundreds of miles distant. Michael works for his community, not only for the sake of those in need, not only for his love and responsiveness to God, but for Garth as well. Michael is Garth's representative in the work. When Michael, in turn, prays for Garth, he is his representative in his own form of work. The underlying unity that they both share in Christ is actualized through prayer, and their bondedness with each other is a participation in each other's work.

Apply this principle on a wider scale. One Christian is called to be an ordained minister, another is called to work in a mill. Through prayer, each participates in the other's work: the millworker represents the minister, and the minister represents the millworker. When the unity of all Christians is manifested in prayer for one another, we can understand that each works for all, and all for each. Both forms of work are vocations responsive to God's call. The unity underlying the diversity is the mark of the reign of God, and all alike share in that reign.

Jesus gave a parable illustrating this reality. In Matthew 20, the reign of God is likened to a householder who hired laborers for the vineyard. Some were hired early in the morning, with the promise of a specific fee. Every three hours during the day the householder hired more laborers, each time with the promise of the same payment. When evening came, to the surprise and dismay of the earlier workers, everyone received the same payment. "Do you begrudge me my generosity?" asked the householder. In our own application, we tend to ascribe a high value to some work for God, and a low value to others. But if through prayer each participates in the work of all, then we are what we are for each other. Finally, there is but one value, the value of the whole of God's reign. From this value, by the grace of God and through the power of prayer, we all receive.

How is it that in prayer the future reign of God can find realization in the present? Perhaps the best illustration comes from the Lord's prayer. The prayer is for the coming of God's reign, "Thy kingdom come." This is immediately followed by the petitions for bread and for forgiveness. Both petitions have reference not only to the immediacies of the present, but to the future as well. The petitions are not separate from the prayer for the coming of God's reign, but are in fact avenues for that coming.

The gospel understanding of the final coming of God's reign was communicated through the imagery of an eschatological banquet. There was to be a meal at which we would sit with the Lord and rejoice in the abundance of salvation. This meal-to-come was foretold in the feeding of the five thousand; it was also foretold in every humble meal that Jesus shared with the disciples. Daily bread was an image for the bread of life. The one was temporal, the other eternal. In no sense was the daily bread considered simply a poor substitute for that final spiritual banquet. Rather, physical needs and spiritual needs were integral to one another, so that the daily food was an apt portrayal of that everlasting sustenance of life in the world to come.

"Give us this day our daily bread," says the gospel petition. Some see in this wording a request today for that which is ours not only today, but everlastingly. Not only today's supply, but tomorrow's and tomorrow's. However, if tomorrow's supply comes today, the future is made present. The reign of God comes as that reality in our future affects our present action. The results of this action will be well-being for the wholeness that is ourselves, body and soul in human society, living in the light of that everlasting reign that takes place in God's own self.

The next petition likewise pulls the future into the present through the asking for forgiveness. "And forgive us our debts, as we also have forgiven our debtors." In the Aramaic language in which Jesus gave this prayer, the word for debt was also the word for sin, so that the petition is for the forgiveness of sins. But why should God's forgiveness of us appear to be contingent upon our own forgiveness toward others? What can this mean? For we know that God acts toward us from grace.

The well-being of one has an effect upon the well-being of the others. God works with what is, to bring about what can be. When we retain attitudes of hostility or resentment in unforgiveness toward another, that attitude has a real effect upon the other. We refuse to allow ourselves to become part of the redemptive reality of the other, wishing instead that the other shall experience ill. But God feels the world in every moment of its completion. In our last chapter, we drew a vision in which we will each know ourselves as the other knew us. This mutual participation in each other forms the basis for our own judgment and transformation. In the final unity of divine justice, the redemption of one is felt by the other, so that God is the reality of reconciliation. Within that final reign of God, we will move toward acceptance of each other.

When we block that acceptance on earth, we act against the eschatological reality. Further, our own lack of forgiveness puts us in the position of needing forgiveness ourselves. The petition of the Lord's prayer reflects that circular interaction between what is in God and what might be on earth. In recognition of that divine reality of forgiveness we ask for and act from the forgiveness of sins.

The prayer for forgiveness invokes that which will be in the eschatological reality of God into the present order of our existence.
The future is made present through prayer.

All prayer is finally a variation on the theme of the Lord's prayer.
Through prayer we open ourselves to the divine will, so that the
guidance fashioned for us in heaven might be felt and effected on
earth. We change the world by molding the world toward the divine
concern for well-being in justice, renewal of nature, and openness
and peace among all peoples. As these changes are effected through
prayer, always the note of gratitude must sound. It is from God this
glory comes, and through God this power is released, and by God's
faithfulness that these modes of redemption are made possible.

Through prayer, we risk being open to the coming of the reign of
God. The conformity with the purposes of God that is sought in
prayer brings upon us the startling possibility of revaluing our
ability to work in a significant way for God's reign. Prayer is a means
whereby we open ourselves for conformity to God's purposes for
the well-being of the world, for the reflection of the image of God in
human society. Prayer is a catapulting activity, pushing us to appropriate action in the world. Prayer is a unitive activity, through which
our fears of fragmentation are put to flight in the deep reality of the
togetherness within God's final reign.

The reign of God places before us two destinies, blending into
unity. On the ultimate level, there is the reign which is God, our
everliving and everlasting destiny. It does not now appear what we
shall be, but we shall nevertheless be transformed, reconciled with
all creation in the depths of God in a justice that is inexorable love.
This destiny undergirds and empowers our efforts for the second,
which is the reign of God as it is anticipated in history. Time echoes
everlastingness, reflecting divine justice in whatever way is appropriate to the goods and evils of each age. Prayer is the union of the
two modes of God's reign, the avenue whereby we open ourselves
to the power of God for the world. And the whole church is called
to be the embodiment of the ultimate prayer, "Thy kingdom come."

CONCLUSION

18

GOD FOR US: TRINITY

WE have spoken of God as presence, seeing this presence exemplified supremely in Jesus of Nazareth; as wisdom, understanding this wisdom as the providence of God experienced by Christians in the history of the church; and as power, interpreting this as the triumph of God over evil, ultimately in the divine nature and persuasively in the world. Presence, wisdom, and power: are there grounds for extending the discussion of these three divine attributes into an understanding of the trinity? To follow this route is to develop a doctrine of the trinity that is based on the human experience of God. It is in the gospels that we know of God's presence in Jesus, in the history of our church that we know of God's providential wisdom, and in our hope that we dare to speak of divine power. We are in the position of saying that the actions of God for us indicate the very internal nature of God. What God is for us, God is in the depths of the divine being. If God is presence, wisdom, and power for us in our human experience, then God is presence, wisdom, and power internally and everlastingly. But if the ground for saying God is presence, wisdom, and power rests in our human experience, then we are understanding God's inner nature through our own experience.

The legitimacy in this procedure is in the assumption that God cannot be less than that which God can do. The cause must be sufficient for the effects. The actions of God bespeak the nature of God. If God's actions are experienced as presence, wisdom, and power, and if each always seems to point back to an initial unity responsible for the separate expressions, then the unity that acts so powerfully must be triune in nature.

On the other hand, a caution must immediately be introduced. We experience each other as being present to us, as influencing us, and as having both internal and external power. In fact, we have given a philosophical analysis that attributes such qualities to every existent reality whatsoever. We do not, however, call every existent reality triune. The most that can be said is that we experience these qualities in varying degrees of intensity, naming the most intense—the human world—as personal. Could it be that the argument for God as trinity, when based on the experience of intensity involved in God as presence, wisdom, and power is reducible to an argument for God as personal? Such would seem to be the logical result of an argument that God cannot be less than the effects that result from divine action.

However, there are philosophical reasons for maintaining that God is not only personal, but also triune. This follows from the qualitative difference between God and finite actuality because of the reversed concrescence of God. To exist is to be in relation, and internal relations presuppose external relations. The many become one, and are increased by one. Relationships signify strength of being. God is the ultimately related one, because of the reversed concresence. God and only God relates positively to every single element in the entire universe; only God has such power. Furthermore, this relation to every element in the universe involves the gift of resurrection for all the world in God. God's subjectivity contains and transforms every other subjectivity that has ever existed. God is many and one in a way totally different from anything in our experience.

How shall we name such a unique reality? "One" is accurate, for it is the single unity of God that encompasses all things with redemption. God's is the beauty, God's is the adventure, God's is the joy. God is one, but infinitely complex. The unity of God is of a complexity far transcending that which we can experience, pushing us to the edges of our imagination to fathom what it must be like. This awesome complexity of God is preserved for us through the notion of trinity, for otherwise we might fall into the arrogance of thinking that God is but humanity writ large upon some cosmic screen. The degree to which God surpasses our own experience creates a qualitative difference in kind, for the leap between God and ourselves in intensity of experience is vast.

God incorporates the world into the divine life; the world becomes the complexity of God in an apotheosis that is participation in the divine life. The embracing reality of the divine life is an ever-increasing divine complexity in unity. God as trinity becomes a symbol to indicate the sense in which the unity of God embraces a complexity of a magnitude greater than which none can exist.

If we thus retain the term trinity to indicate the infinite complexity in unity of the divine nature, we push the word far beyond its traditional meaning of threeness. It is so, of course, that in the process doctrine of God we must speak of God in the threefold way of primordial nature, consequent nature, and what Whitehead called the superjective nature, by which he simply meant God's provision of initial aims for the world. The reason against naming these "natures" trinity is because the terms are abstractions for our understanding, ways of describing the reality that is God. If we wish trinity to name the subjective reality of God's own experience, we cannot use abstractions. We must instead look for an expression signifying the infinite richness of the divine life. God is the subjectivity of subjectivities, the many who are nevertheless one in living unity, without loss of individuality nor qualification of the integrity of the whole. God is the supremely complex One. If trinity can be expanded beyond its traditional use to indicate this mighty complexity in unity, then it retains a symbolic appropriateness in its designation of the inner nature of God.

"Trinity" denotes the magnitude of the divine power that accomplishes the vision of the divine wisdom, all within the everlasting unity of presence. Presence, wisdom, and power: those qualities we perceive in our own experience of God for us can be understood in reference to the divine nature itself when that nature is expressed as complexity in unity, trinity., Thus "trinity" is a symbol that faces in two directions. There is the God-ward signification, in which the symbol expresses our sense of the divine subjectivity, and there is the world-ward direction, in which the symbol speaks of our own experience of God.

Traditionally, that which we are developing as presence, wisdom, and power has been expressed through the names of Father, Son, and Holy Spirit. There are strong consistencies between the traditional formulation and that developed here. Our christology was developed under the rubric of God's presence for us in history through the revelation of Jesus Christ. Ecclesiology developed from an understanding of God's providential wisdom in creating, guiding, and sustaining the church, and of course this is the traditional interpretation of the work of the Holy Spirit. Eschatology rests upon an interpretation of divine power, centered in the depths of God; does this not bear analogy to the doctrine of God as Father? While the trinitarian names of Father, Son, and Holy Spirit have not been used, the trinitarian work of God usually described through Father, Son, and Spirit has been pervasively present in this process theology. Far from eliminating any understanding of the trinity, the development has been profoundly affected by an understanding of the trinity. God is trinity in presence, wisdom, and power in the dimensions of human experience. The deepest way to express this is to say that God is for us. "God for us" thus expresses the trinity and the gospel simultaneously.

That the trinity and the gospel are both indications of "God for us" is seen most clearly in the fourth gospel. The third chapter recounts a discourse between Jesus and Nicodemus. Background to this chapter is the contrast presented in chapter two between the believing disciples at Cana who receive the sign of the wedding miracle, and the unbelieving crowd in Jerusalem, to whom no sign is given. Nicodemus comes to Jesus from the crowd, neither believing nor disbelieving, but wavering in the dilemma of doubt. He identifies himself with the crowd, but comes out from the crowd, as would a disciple. Haltingly, he begins to question Jesus, asking who he is, and what he is saying. The evangelist presents Jesus' answers as revealing the nature of God in terms that we have come to call the trinity, and the gospel. Jesus first speaks of God as Spirit, bringing us to birth. He then speaks of the passion of the Son, lifted up and drawing all humanity to God. Finally, in the culmination of the passage, he speaks of the transcending, sending Father: "God so loved the world that he sent his only Son, that whoever believes on him should not perish, but have everlasting life." In this text, the gospel writer concludes the triune presentation of God with what will become identified as the most concise expression of the gospel. God as triune is God for us, and God for us is the good news of the gospel.

The fact that God is revealed as Spirit, Son, and Father in the context of being "God for us" has tremendous implications for our understanding of the trinity. It means that God as Spirit, Son, and Father refers to the world-ward direction of trinity. As world-oriented, the words are inexorably reflective of the distinctiveness of the time and place in which the words were given. To take the words out of the historical context and push them to the trans-historical description of God carries certain dangers.

To speak of these terms as historically relative is in no sense to speak of them as false. It is simply to recognize that the naming is conditioned by particularities that are not always shared by all peoples. The terms have a particular and not a universal meaning, and therefore must be constantly translated for changing places and times if one is to be faithful to the intent of the original meaning. God fashions aims for the world that must take account of the particular past and the real possibilities relative to the world there and then. In no sense are aims somehow false because they are not universal. On the contrary, their truth is dependent upon their absolute relativity, their conditioned and therefore appropriate nature. Likewise with revelation. That which God reveals and manifests for us is conditioned as much by us as it is by the divine nature. The inexorable implication of this is that a revelation of God as trinity in its world-ward orientation will always be suited to the conditions in the world, taking its coloration from those conditions. This means that the world-ward expression of God as triune is not exempt from historical relativity, and in fact that it *must* partake of historical relativity if it is to be a true manifestation of God for us. Precisely because this is so, we cannot take the designation of trinity as Father, Son, and Spirit in an absolute sense.

If God as Father, Son, and Holy Spirit is a specific way to speak of God's power, presence, and wisdom toward us, for us, and with us, then there are serious considerations for moving today toward emphasizing this trinity as power, wisdom, and presence rather than as Father, Son, and Spirit. The consideration is simply in the historical relativity of the terms. They no longer convey that which was implicit in the words in their initial use.

For instance, the term "Father" for God comes to us from Jesus, and we assume that what we mean by father today is precisely what he meant by father, for does not father mean first and foremost the relationship of physical generation? Yet Joachim Jeremias tells us that the meaning of the word "Abba, Father," as used by Jesus fundamentally signified the transmission of wisdom. A father in Judea taught his son the secrets of his trade, training him to carry on his own work. For Jesus to call God Father connoted first and foremost the intense intimacy whereby Jesus knew God's work and did God's work. Given the fact that what God does is in deep consistency with who God is in the divine character, for Jesus to do God's work was to reveal God's nature. Today, however, we no longer consider "father" in the sense of a transmission of knowledge. Rather, we tend to think of the term in the sense of male progeneration. Maleness rather than work or character tends to define the word for us, and we attribute our own meaning to the intent of Jesus. We only confuse the issue further when we take that historical meaning and push it to the ontological understanding of the inner nature of God.

Likewise with the word, "Son." Through sonship, Jesus draws us to God. How can we understand this all-important sonship? And what does it say about the nature of God? How was Jesus "Son" to God? Incarnation is historical, fitted to a particular time and place, depending upon a moment by moment actualization of the character of God. Incarnation is dependent upon the whole of Jesus' life, and not simply upon the moment of his conception. Thus Jesus' relationship to God is created far more through his life than through his birth. What, then, is the significance of the virgin birth narratives relative to Jesus as Son?

Nelle Morton relates the virgin birth to the hierarchical social structure that marked the Jewish society into which Jesus was born. All humankind was divided in terms of social value, from king to slave. Men had precedence over women, and women over children. Legitimate sons, who would carry on the patrimony of Israel, were valued next, followed by legitimate daughters. Below the legitimate daughters in ranking were the illegitimate daughters, and lowest of all were the illegitimate sons. The daughters could receive a name in Israel through marriage, but of course the sons could not. Unable to carry on the patrimony, illegitimate sons were lowest on the social scale.

Whatever else the doctrine of virgin birth means, it surely indicates the social status of Jesus of Nazareth. If Joseph was not his father, then Jesus' social ranking was that of the illegitimate son. Further, the ministry of this son in his adult life continued the theme of lowliness, for he called himself a servant and washed the feet of the disciples, which is the work of women and slaves. The hymn of Philippians 2 carries on the theme, attributing the form of a slave to Jesus, and throughout its history the church has associated Jesus with the suffering servant of Isaiah 53. Illegitimate Son and Servant, all within the context of incarnation—what can these things mean? What other meaning can be read into the situation than that the incarnation embraces the whole of humanity, rendering our caste systems meaningless? Incarnation is one more great reversal theme in the Christian story, for the highest becomes lowest.

But surely this annuls our whole value system! The lines that divide humanity into "higher" and "lower" are no longer valid. If they are broken down by God in incarnation, how can we still raise them up in the name of incarnation? Had incarnation—the revelation of the nature of God for us—taken place through a woman, the incarnation would not have embraced the lowest dregs of our human attributions of value, and the lowest of the low would have been left out of incarnation and the revelation of God for us. As it is, however, we have the amazing inclusion in the gospels of an emphasis upon virgin birth, and of the servant function of the Son. When we take the virgin birth narratives into consideration, the deepest meaning of God as Son is not at all the maleness of Jesus, or even the Sonship of God, but the inclusiveness of God who reverses all our social values. Today, however, when we hear the designation of the trinity as including "Son," we tend to overlook the radical implications of inclusiveness, and turn it instead into a reason for attributing the restrictions of maleness once more to God. By doing so, we violate the fullness of the revelation of God for us given through God in Christ. We make the revelation small. Through our foolishness we build up again the partitions that God broke down, and dare to say that the prejudices are ultimately affirmed by the inward nature of God! We use God as Son to deny the work revealed through God as illegitimate son and slave in the history of humanity.

"Spirit" does not fare much better in our contemporary milieu. Even here, there has been an evolution of the word toward an unbiblical emphasis upon maleness. Originally, the word conveyed the wisdom of God in the ordering of the church. Such precision is lost to our contemporary world, for our use of the word lists where it will, blowing with every contemporary wind of preference. Spirit can become a means of declaring degrees of holiness within the church, such that "higher" and "lower" again become divisive marks of prejudice and value. Alternatively, Spirit has been taken in an anarchial sense defying modes of order. Given this option, there is some irony in the fact that a still further perversion of Spirit appeals to God as Spirit in a legalistic sense to declare a preferred way of doing things as God-endorsed and therefore unchangeable. How do such interpretations of God as Spirit indicate the all-embracing grace of God, empowering and guiding our redemptive living in the world? How do these interpretations of the trinity convey to us the deep richness of the gospel?

The further theological difficulties with such distortions of the trinity through our failure to look at the words Father, Son, and Spirit as historically relative expressions of God for us is that we push the distortions back into the nature of God. With regard to maleness, we encounter the difficulty of saying on the one hand that God is not anthropomorphic, that God transcends sexuality, or mere maleness and femaleness, and yet on the other hand we insist that God is indeed a male, and that only another male can properly represent "him." We reinforce this confusion by insisting that all our language concerning God must be portrayed through masculinity. We deify the language and representatives of God, rather than God's own self.

The problem, it must be emphasized, is not in the initial revelation of God through use of the words Father, Son, and Spirit, but in the fact that the historical relativity of the words is lost to view. The initial context of the revelation is lost to our contemporary sensitivity, so that we are in the topsy-turvy position of using the same words equivocally, conveying a meaning far removed from the revelation in Christ of God for us.

We advocate, then, that the triune nature of God be expressed directly through the understanding of God's presence with us and for us through Jesus of Nazareth, through the wisdom of God whereby God brings the church to birth in each generation, guiding it through divine providence in its manifestation of apostolicity, unity, and holiness, and through the power of God, bringing the world to justice within the transformation of the divine nature and guiding the finite world toward societal forms of justice. This is "God for us" in the world-ward orientation of the trinity. This is continuous with the God-ward orientation of the word, for it is the reality of God who is present for us in Jesus; it is God's integrative wisdom that produces aims of divine providence, and it is in God's own self that the fullness of justice and love in an everlasting dynamism of beauty is finally achieved. The complex unity that is the God-ward designation of trinity issues into our experience of God as presence, wisdom, and power. We know God as trinity by knowing God for us.

One further implication of the trinity as God for us is that the phrase itself contains transcendent, immanent, and relational elements. "God" transcends the world in divine power, working with the world according to the divine will and purpose. Yet this God is "for" the world, relating infinitely to the world through receiving and guiding the world, curing the world and caring for the world. The very word "for" conveys the intensity of divine love. God is "for" the world in relationality and covenant. "Us": the world is not abstract, not universal, not some generalized reality, but the world is as concrete and as particular and as peculiar as "us." Through the relative provision of initial aims, the transcendent God is immanent in the world for us and for our good. In the everlasting reciprocity of the process, the immanence of God returns again to the transcendence of God, as God receives the world. Receiving the world, God fashions for it an aim that will lure it toward its good in its next moment of becoming. "God for us" conveys the trinity; "God for us" conveys the gospel; trinity and gospel are finally just this mystery: that God is for us.

If the traditional formulation of the world-ward direction of the trinity was historically conditioned and therefore relative to time and place, it is certainly true that the present development partakes of the same relativity. A theology developed through process thought must underscore the relativity of its perception. It is finally not at all a photograph of the way things are between God and the world in Christian experience. Theology presents but a vision of reality, a way of expressing from a particular perspective in time and place how we may interpret our experience of God through Christ and the church. The purpose in stating the vision is simply that our vision of reality matters. In itself it becomes a part of our redemptive experience. How we think about reality enters into our attitudes toward others, toward God, toward ourselves. When the vision of God as seen though the divine presence in Christ is such that it inspires our love, then that lovingness opens us more deeply to the influence of God and hence orients us as well toward God's caring purposes in the world. When the vision of God bespeaks the wisdom of God, given in faithfulness through divine guidance in every moment, then through the vision God evokes our trust. In trust, we dare to move into a future that takes us beyond that which we thought could be achieved on the basis of the past alone. And when the vision of God expresses the divine triumph of justice, then it elicits a catalytic hope with regard to the achievement of justice in forms of our earthly society. If God cannot overcome evil, how can we? But if God's overcoming of evil in the depths of the divine nature is in fact a call to our own efforts to overcome evil in our finite sphere, then there is every reason to work for social justice, every reason to open ourselves to conversion from personal forms of evil, every reason to live in the joyfulness of a community dedicated to holiness. How we think about reality matters; our expressions of a vision of reality are part and parcel of that life that we call redemptive and Christian.

That the vision is relative is essential to the openness of the vision and to the redemptiveness of the vision. Because it is relative, one can hear the different expressions of others in openness rather than fear, learning from the richness of another how better to perceive reality from one's own perspective. Because it is relative, there is freedom in the expression—the tight burden of being able to say what is so absolutely from a perspective where we see only relatively is lifted, and one can play with the vision, measuring it always with that vision that is a beauty just beyond sight, yet felt. Finally, perhaps the expression of a vision of reality that is relative to our time and place is simply a mode in finitude of what might finally be an everlasting dialogue, each sharing with another a vision of beauty from a particular perspective, yet keenly and gratefully and joyfully feeling the depths of beauty from which all our visions spring.

APPENDIX

A: The Process Model

THERE is a museum in Gettysburg, Pennsylvania, where artifacts from the battle of long ago are displayed. Prominently featured is a greatly blown-up newspaper photograph that depicts a soldier. From the doorway of the room, looking at the photograph, one clearly sees the soldier, but the closer one gets, the more the picture changes from the outlines of the figure to a mass of dots that make up the image. Individually, each dot is simply that—but together, they recreate the figure once captured by a camera, and transposed to print.

In a similar way, the process model developed by Whitehead has its primary reference not to the large figures of our everyday world, but to the myriad dots of energy that in fact make up this larger world. Some of these "dots" are concentrations of matter, made up of smaller dots, and existing—as do the dots in the photograph—in the midst of apparently empty space. But all of space, whether between galaxies or between atoms in a solid, is permeated with radiant energy that is made up of a series of many units. In concentrated configurations, these units become particles of matter; in increasingly larger groupings of these particles, they become the items familiar to human experience. Whitehead would have it that each unit, whether in "empty space" or in a table or in a person, is the reception, unification, and transmission of energy. Each unit constitutes and is constituted by relation.

What happens in this primal giving and receiving, receiving and giving? Whitehead's model for the internal dynamics of one such unit addresses the question. Each unit of reality presupposes the existence of all units in its past. In chapter one, we illustrated the influence of the past on the present through Catherine. Catherine, as she sat in the library, presupposed studying, students, family, and environment. Even so, each unit of energy presupposes a multiplicity of influences transmitted from its past. The unification of these influences constitutes the present. However, as we explore this more deeply we must leave the illustration of Catherine, since personal reality masks the microscopic nature we need. That is, "students" cannot really be understood as merely one influence, since "students" is but a group name for many, many influences, simplified for convenience into the category, "students." In order to understand the very process of simplification wherein the many become one, it is necessary to go beneath the level of personal existence to the microscopic existence of the most fundamental droplet of reality.

Whitehead's model posits that energy is itself particles, quanta, all characterized by the rhythm between internal and external relationships. Each quantum is called an *actual occasion*.[1] By the term "actual," he designates something concrete and real. By "occasion," he means that this reality is a "happening," an "event." Each unit of existence is an actual occasion, something for itself as well as something for the larger group of which it is a part.

The process of becoming an actual occasion might be illustrated through a series of increasingly complex diagrams. The first simply designates three occasions.

The diagram may be taken further through recognition that each unit is a complex unification of the many influences in its past, each of which experienced the process we are about to describe. Therefore, the components that make up the units of A, B, and C are internal relations to the items of their past.

Each component represents some influence that has been incorporated into the final unification of the entity. If, however, each of

---

1. Technical terms used in this chapter are italicized and explained as they are introduced. They are also defined in the glossary. Whitehead's basic work, is *Process and Reality*, edited by David Ray Griffin and Donald Sherbourne (New York: Free Press. 1978).

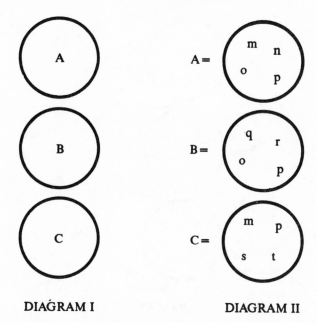

DIAGRAM I   DIAGRAM II

these three units of energy is completed, each also now has an influence beyond itself. At the simplest levels of existence, this influence is integrally related in content to that which the unit became, which is to say that A pushes for a repetition of precisely its own achievement of m-n-o-p. The creative energy, first utilized in self-becoming, is now transitionally effective, pushing toward the becoming of another, as in Diagram III.

According to Whitehead, every unit of energy has a vector effect; he calls this the *superjective nature* of the actual occasion. By this he simply means the manner in which the occasion pushes beyond itself, indicated by the arrow. The occasion is both "subject" and "superject." While the occasion's own subjective reception of the influences of its past was internal to the occasion, creating internal relatedness to its predecessors, its superjective transmission of energy toward a future is external to itself. Thus its relatedness to its past is internal and subjective, but its relatedness to its future is external and objective. The completed occasion is no longer capable of unifying further influences—it has become an influence for others which are beyond itself in a future made possible in part by the influence of this occasion. Thus the occasion moves from being

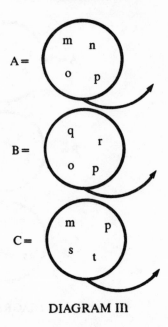

DIAGRAM IIl

a subject with internal relations to becoming an object with external relations.

One of the difficulties with trying to diagram an essentially dynamic process is that while the diagram hopefully clarifies, it also distorts. For example, the superjective nature indicated by the arrow is not simply "tacked on" to the unit: it *is* the unit, in process of transmission. That which the actual occasion is in itself, it becomes for others. Its subjectivity is offered to the world, along with the many subjectivities of its contemporaries, simplified here to the occasions of A, B, and C. The combining of A, B, and C begins the production of a new subject.

But A, B, and C are not necessarily amenable to combination. That is, each unit is precisely itself. If A is a creative unification of m-n-o-p, then its influence on the future is going to be for that same unification. Its transitional impulse of energy calls for some kind of repetition of itself. The same is true for B, and for C, each calling for repetitions of their own reality. The power of the past, at its most basic level, is a call for conformity—but conformity, in the very nature of the case, is impossible. How can the new occasion repeat everything represented by A if in fact it must also take account of B and C? Even if it chooses to reenact A's achievement, it will nevertheless be different by virtue of the fact that, unlike A, it has had to negate B and C in the process. Since negation of B and C is not a component of A's actual achievement, the new occasion might choose to become similar to A, but it cannot be identical with A.

This principle can be illustrated by moving to the level of human experience. Consider the power of habit, as seen for instance in the smoking of a cigarette. The act of smoking may not appear to be different between the first cigarette and the thousandth cigarette. In both cases, one picks up the cigarette, puts it in the mouth, lights the cigarette, and puffs. Yet for all the appearance of similarity, the two acts are not the same. The first cigarette will be smoked with the sensation of novelty, while the thousandth may be smoked almost automatically, attention being given not to the cigarette, but perhaps to a conversation, or to the reading of a newspaper. Intervening between the two occasions are 998 repetitions of the act, each repetition making the power of influence, and in this case, addiction, that much greater. Each repetition adds something that the previous instance could not have. Despite the similarity between the 999th cigarette and the thousandth, the bare fact remains that the thousandth time must take account of the 999th time, whereas the 999th only had to take account of the 998 preceding it. The past calls for repetition; insofar as it succeeds, its power is reinforced. This power, however, is always qualified by an element of novelty, however slight, that must be introduced. The novelty is, in part, in the changed circumstances. This novelty provided by constant change is the wedge through which the power of the past may be broken. Habit need not endure. No element of the past may be repeated in its entirety. Every element of the past must be modified.

To return to the model, the beginning of the new occasion is a feeling of the total past. Whitehead terms this beginning a *physical pole*, constitutive of each instant of becoming. Note that "physical" in this instance means a feeling of otherness. Physical does not here mean materiality or bodiness. Whitehead further breaks this physical pole down into the multiplicity of feelings of otherness that must be present, given the multiplicity of the past. Each feeling of otherness is called a *prehension* of the other, a taking into account of the other. The new occasion begins therefore at this physical pole, with feelings, prehensions, of A, B, and C.

If, however, A must be modified in terms of B and C, and likewise with B and C, each being modified in terms of the others, then a certain amount of contrasting must take place. The components of the past must be sifted in respect to each other; the comparabilities within them must be drawn out in order that unification may happen. Unification, after all, is a harmonization of the many into one. Harmony, or *satisfaction*, cannot occur apart from some basic level of compatibility. The compatibility may be felt through some common element each possesses, or through the introduction of some new element that renders the past harmonious. In either case, selectivity occurs. This selectivity is the inner process of creativity essential to the unit's becoming.

Consider the selectivity first in its simpler form, which would be the sifting of the past. Picking up from Diagram III, the further process might look something like this.

The quality "p" is selected from the past, due to its high level of

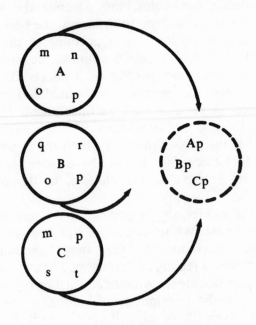

DIAGRAM IV

compatibility. In a sense, "p" is almost an appeasement of the demand of the past, for if all three units call for repetition, and "p" is an element of all three, then "p," selected for reenactment in the new occasion, is a way to harmonize the demands of A, B, and C.

However, it is not quite so simple, for the quality "p" in the becoming occasion cannot be quite the same as its occurrence in either of the three past units. Imagine the reasons for this by thinking of the color red existing in a group that includes orange and yellow. Take the same color red and put it now in a group including only red, blue, and violet. While the individual color red may be precisely the same shade in both groups, its effect is changed by its companions. If red be combined with orange, yellow, green, blue, and violet, the effect is yet again different. The selfsame red is different, depending upon its setting. Even so, the quality "p" must be somewhat different in A than in B and C. It will be yet again different in the new occasion. Selectivity, even in terms of harmonization, involves a movement into difference, into novelty.

The dynamics of relational existence will therefore always include novelty, or a movement beyond the sheer past. The past can never be simply repeated. This is seen not only in the fact that the context qualifies the repeated elements of the past, but in the fact that the very process of harmonization eliminates portions of the past. A is repeated in the new occasion insofar as the quality "p" is repeated, but what of the other qualities? They are negated in the very process of sifting out the past in terms of compatibility. These *negative prehensions*, as Whitehead calls them, are not without effect. Part of the effect that takes place in the reenactment of "p" without m-n-o is the loss of a former milieu, the death of a former unit.

Negative prehensions can have positive or negative effects. Positively, they allow a sharpness of contrast and discrimination such as is necessary to consciousness. But negatively, too great a use of the power to block much of reality from feeling results in triviality. "Negative prehensions bear the scars of their birth," says Whitehead, indicating that whether used for value or for triviality, the negation of data from feeling nonetheless qualifies the actual occasion's satisfaction with some intimation of that which was omitted. Prehensions in our model must therefore be understood as selective, with the selectivity involving positive and negative feelings of the past. In positive feelings, a component of a past actual occasion is selected for repetition; through negative feelings, the rest of that occasion is relegated to nonbeing relative to the present.

An analogy may be drawn through human history. Those elements that a historian lifts into the thread of human consciousness are woven into the total story of a segment of humanity. But there is more to what happened than those elements of emphasis noted by the historian. History writing involves a selection from the past, not a sheer repetition of the past. Those things that never enter the historians' works are, in effect, lost in the limbo of untold tales. Yet even so, stories that are told are haunted at their edges by the intimations of those elements left out. A sensitivity to the tales omitted can lead one to look for the traces, the "scars of their birth," and begin to write a fuller history. But even that fuller history will involve yet again a selectivity. Selection is inevitably involved in the movement of all stories from past to present. The present must always be purchased at the price of vast portions of the past. *Perpetual perishing* is the tale of a moving, relational existence.

If perpetual perishing describes reality, so does immortality. If it is true that much of the units A, B, and C are consigned to the lost past, it is also true that a portion of each lives on in the present. This vectoral factor of existence is termed *objective immortality* by Whitehead. It is immortality, since it is the real living on in the new occasion of a quality earlier felt as part of A, B, and C. It is objective, because the subjectivity of A lay in the unique copresence of "p" with m-n-o. When that unity is broken, so is the holistic reality of A. In unbroken unity, A is a subject for itself. In selectivity, A is an object for the new subjectivity of the present. While A offers its subjectivity to the world, the necessity of selection is such that A's subjectivity is broken and objectified by the new present. There is only objective immortality in the finite world.

We mentioned that unification of the past may take place through the introduction of a totally new quality that has the merit of rendering many components of the past compatible. Again, the metaphor of color might convey some sense of this. An artist, looking in dissatisfaction at her painting, feels a sense of disharmony, missing the result she strove to produce. Suddenly she reaches for a new oil, and adds it precisely so to the canvas. The effect of the new shade is to give a different center of harmony, a different tonality, to every other portion of the canvas. The added element has created the harmony that the previous elements alone could not achieve. Similarly, the components selected from the past may achieve their unique mode of harmony in the new unit of existence by the introduction of a harmonizing factor never before combined with this particular past. In such a case, the novelty created in the present becomes a qualitative leap into that which was beyond the power of the past in and of itself. Yet continuity is nevertheless achieved, since the new quality is used in conjunction with the objectively immortal retention of the past.

The process of becoming thus far described is a model that begins with a physical pole, or feelings of the past, proceeding by a movement called *concrescence* by Whitehead. Concrescence is simply the harmonious unification of feelings. It is the "making concrete" of the actual occasion. Notice, however, that another dimension to existence is being implied in this process of concrescence. That from which the occasion derives its initial power is the actuality of the past, but there is another power at work. If the physical pole accounts for the effect of the past as it influences the new occasion's becoming, there must be another pole accounting for the effect of the future. The very fact that the occasion, given numerous unifying possibilities, selects one rather than another possibility for unification indicates that there is a power of selectivity at work. This selectivity indicates a drive toward a particular becoming, a *subjective aim* toward harmony. But this aim is toward a very immediate future, with some at least primitive grasp of what that future might be. Since that future is not yet in existence, it is not actual, but simply possible. Something that is only possible is ideational, existing simply as idea. Ordinarily, we associate ideas with mentality: one grasps ideas through thought. But if every actual occasion is involved in the dynamics of reaching toward a possible harmony, then every occasion whatsoever must have some form of that capacity we call mentality. Not thought, not consciousness, but something much more rudimentary must exist throughout reality—the power to grasp a sense of what one might become through unification of the past. The physical pole must be complemented by a *mental pole* in order for existence to be unified.

The mental pole is understood as the grasp of possibility, as the feeling for what might be the case. This feeling then affects the way the actual occasion sifts the feelings of the past. This feeling for what might be is the aim toward individual becoming, the subjective aim, the unifying, creative force toward harmony. Through the force of this aim, the components of the past are relegated to their respective places. Harmony is achieved with the completion of the process.

Whitehead refers to this final harmony as the satisfaction of the process, the completion of its creative moment. The *concrescent creativity* of the occasion culminates in the satisfaction, which then generates *transitional creativity*.[2] This mode of creativity enters the universe as one more impulse of energy, calling for repetition of the process. The many have become one—but in doing so, the many have been increased by one. A new multiplicity exists, calling for creative unification into a new one. And so the universal dance continues, with the rhythm passing from the many to the one to the many again. In the process, relational existence continually comes into being.

The model now becomes far more difficult to diagram, for the motion of becoming is hard to portray in the static limitation of lines. Imagination now suggests not a circle, but a spiral, formed through many converging lines. These lines are like the physical pole, drawing closer together in the process of contrasting as the mental pole does its unifying work. All lines converge in the vortex of the center, whereupon the spiral is a complete unity, one thing, unified through all its parts. With this internal creativity completed, the spiral bursts into external effectiveness. It forces a new future into existence, for which it itself is now the given past. And the rhythm of the universe is in the mystery of the dance between past, present, and future.

B: The Model and God

The model of relational existence also pushes toward development of a doctrine of God, for the model as thus far given is

2. I argue in *The End of Evil: Process Eschatology in Historical Context* (New York: SUNY Press, 1988) that "satisfaction" is also a mode of creativity, intermediate between concrescent creativity and transitional creativity. Simply that Whitehead goes on to discuss the sense in which relationality turns into the togetherness of things so evident to us in our world, nor even that Whitehead describes the rise of consciousness through complexity and intensity. These things belong to an application of the model in the world. What is further needed is an explanation of the power of the future.

incomplete. It is not simply that Whitehead goes on to discuss the sense in which relationality turns into the togetherness of things so evident to us in our world, nor even that Whitehead decries the rise of consciousness through complexity and intensity. These things belong to an application of the model in the world. What is further needed is an explanation of the power of the future.

The difficulty comes at the point of Whitehead's major principle that where there is power, there is actuality. Power does not materialize out of nothingness—if it does, incoherence is introduced into an otherwise carefully developed model. Power rests in actuality. The future, however, "exists" as possibility, and possibilities by very definition are not actual. How, then, can that which is not actual have such power? The problem is further complicated by the infinity of possibilities that affect actual occasions. If Whitehead wishes to find a source in actuality for the power of the future, he must find a source not simply for one future, nor even for the future that materializes in each instant of becoming, but for all possible futures whatsoever. Whitehead needs a source for possibilities per se. Only an existing entity, an *actual entity*,[3] can provide such a source.

Actual entities, however, have been so defined that each must eliminate possibilities in the process of becoming its determinant self. The welter of data received through the physical pole is simplified and unified through an aim toward a single possible form of existence. If the very process of becoming involves elimination of possibilities, how can an actual entity *ground* possibilities? Furthermore, the possibilities associated with each actual entity are limited to that occasion's standpoint. How can a single actual entity ground possibilities for all reality? The dilemma, then, is this:

1. Possibilities exert power in affecting the actions of actualities.
2. But all power must be located in actuality.
3. If possibilities exert power, they must do so through the agency of an actuality that is their origin.

3. Whitehead used two terms to describe actuality: "actual occasion" and "actual entity." Whereas "actual entity" could apply both to God and to finite reality, "actual occasion" was always used only in reference to finite reality. The dynamics of existence for God and finitude are seen to be the same, but there is a necessary distinction in how they apply, with implications for spatio/temporal location for one, but not the other. In order to preserve this distinction, Whitehead never used the term "actual occasion" for God. We will follow his usage here.

4. But no finite actual entity thus far described can perform this function.

The problem rests in the finite nature of the actual occasions and in their movement from the multiplicity of the physical pole to the integration of existence through the mental pole. What if the order of concrescence were reversed? Would the same limitations hold? The mental pole per se is not limited in terms of possibilities. To the contrary, a mental pole not bound by the prior restrictions of the physical pole could conceivably be infinite in possibilities. If a unique entity "began" in the mental pole and was "completed" by the physical pole, perhaps a source for possibilities could be named. This entity, of course, would have to conform to the characteristics of existence for the metaphysics to retain coherence. Relationality must occur through feelings of others and effects upon others within the dynamics of a physical pole, mental pole, subjective aim, concrescence, and satisfaction. But the entity must be a mirror image of all the others in order to account for the power of possibilities.

The situation is somewhat analogous to putting a puzzle together, having it almost done, and then finding the last piece missing. The place is ready, the outline of the final piece is clearly shown. However, the final piece that completes the puzzle must be the reverse of those surrounding pieces. Where the puzzle loops in, the last piece must loop out. Otherwise, it will not fit, and the puzzle will remain incomplete. Completion of the puzzle depends upon an exact reversal of the shape. Such a reversal does not render the puzzle incoherent. It completes it, fully in keeping with the principles of puzzle-making. Even so, the reversal of the dynamics of reality for one actuality in order to account for the power of possibility does not violate the model, it completes it.

How would it work, this reversal of dynamics? An actuality beginning in the physical pole moves toward unity; an actuality beginning in the mental pole moves from unity. But note that an actuality beginning in the mental pole cannot properly "begin" at all. If an entity contains all possibility, then that entity can no more begin than possibilities begin. Possibilities are time-related only in reference to actuality; in their own nature, they are nontemporal.

Relationality to time takes place purely in the context of the successiveness of actualities. If possibilities are nontemporal, existing eternally, then an entity containing all possibilities must likewise be eternal. When Whitehead says, then, that God "begins" in the mental pole, he is not talking about a time when God did not exist. Quite the contrary, he is talking about the sense in which God's eternal nature is the basis for all divine activity. This activity proceeds from the mental pole. To keep this eternal quality of the mental pole in view, Whitehead always refers to it in God as the *primordial nature*.

What does it mean for God to "begin" primordially through the mental pole? It must mean, in terms of the model, that God's primordial beginning is a "satisfaction" in which all possibilities are everlastingly unified in terms of value. There is much meaning condensed into that statement; it should be unpacked first by noting the sense in which possibilities are given value.

Possibilities in and of themselves are vague with regard to value. For instance, someone might mention to Catherine, our historian in chapter i, that she should become a medical technician. Is that a good possibility or a bad possibility? "To become a medical technician" is neither a good nor bad possibility in and of itself. In order to value it, we need some reference to actuality. We would ask Catherine about her inclinations, talents, and background, asking if she preferred and/or was more suited to work in medical technology. At the same time, we might ask about the value of medical technology in the society as a whole. It might be that an answer to the latter question would give a very high value to the profession, but answers to the questions addressed to Catherine would indicate that medical technology as a profession for her was of low value. One can value the sheer possibility of "becoming a medical technician" only in reference to concrete situations.

What does it mean, then, that God unifies all possibilities, giving them value? It means more than that one or another possibility is assigned a value by God. It must mean that God is the actuality in reference to which all possibilities receive value. Because God unifies the possibilities, they achieve the value of concrete unity. Because God holds all the possibilities together within the unity of the divine nature, they are harmonized. Because possibilities are harmonized within the divine nature, they are given beauty. If God is the locus of all possibilities, the very fact that it is a single reality that gives a home to possibilities means that the possibilities are clothed in the value of unity, harmony, and beauty. God *is* the valuation of all possibilities. This is the primordial satisfaction of God, and the primordial definition and exercise of the divine character.

In the reversal of the dynamics of existence, satisfaction must issue into the subjective aim of God. For finite reality, the subjective aim is first for itself (toward the achievement of harmony), and secondly for others (toward affecting the world beyond itself). Every finite reality, becoming itself, hurls its effects upon the newly becoming world, calling for repetition and possibly transformation of its own achievement. God, "beginning" with eternal satisfaction, must reverse the dynamics of the subjective aim. First, God's aim is for others, which can now only be all finite reality. Second, God's aim serves to direct the divine concrescence through the physical pole. Both concrescence and the physical pole must be as applicable to God as satisfaction and the mental pole if the model is to hold.

If God "begins" in the primordial nature, then the physical pole will be consequent upon that primordial "beginning." For this reason, Whitehead calls the physical pole in God the *consequent nature*. What must this physical pole, or consequent nature, be like? Remember that a physical pole is simply the feeling of realities other than the subject. Hence in this definition, to consider God as having a physical pole does not at all contradict the spirituality of God. On the contrary, the physical pole might give us the most adequate understanding of God as spirit. We ordinarily term persons spiritual when their concerns go beyond themselves, when their sensitivities relate them to a range wider than ordinarily accomplished. For example, the spirituality of a Mother Teresa is created/manifested in the great breadth of her care for others. Such spirituality is in part a wide attunement to the physical pole. Hence, to associate a physical pole with God is by no means to deny God's spiritual nature. It is in fact a way to define God's nature as pure spirit. Finite spirituality is always partial, given the selectivity involved in our feelings of others. Further, few of the relations affecting us are raised to the level of conscious relationality. Most, by far, remain at subliminal levels of awareness. But God's physical pole is unlimited by any need for selectivity, given the already achieved unity of all possibilities in the primordial vision. God can feel every actuality in the universe in its entirety. God's physical pole, therefore, unlike ours, is all-encompassing. God is the supremely related one, with a fullness not possible to finite occasions. Consequently, if ordinary usage be followed, God is the most spiritual of all beings. God is pure spirit.

To return now to the matter of divine concrescence, God's eternal satisfaction generates a subjective aim that directs the concrescence of God. In keeping with the dynamics of reversal, the aim moves toward the world and then through the world in prehension to direct the concrescence of God. In the everlasting process, the consequent nature is integrated with the primordial nature in unity.

In moving toward the world, the aim flows from the divine satisfaction. God's aim is that the harmony of possibilities shall issue into a harmony of actualities. How this aim is fitted to the world will soon be suggested. For the present, however, simply note that at this stage the fulfillment of God's aim depends upon the becoming realities of the world. From the perspective of God, the aim given to the world is God's own *subjective/superjective* aim that the world actualize a harmony as conformable as possible to the divine nature; from the perspective of the world, the aim is the *initial aim*, giving initial guidance to the occasion. The occasion's prehension of that aim appropriates it, more or less, as the occasion's own subjective aim. The aim given to the world depends upon God; what the world does with that aim depends upon the world as it actualizes its freedom. The second stage of God's subjective aim is consequent upon the first, and now depends entirely on God, since it relates to the free concrescence of God. The actualities of the world are felt by God through the consequent nature, and integrated into the harmony of God, the primordial nature. Thus the harmony of possibility within the primordial vision is ever more deeply intensified through God's feeling of reality according to the subjective aim of harmony.

To expand further upon this integration of the consequent and primordial natures, consider that just as a finite occasion feels its physical prehensions of others in terms of its own subjective aim, God also feels the world in terms of the divine aim toward an actualization of harmony. Just as the finite reality unites the physical with the mental, thus achieving harmony, even so God unites the feelings of the world with the primordial vision, intensifying the harmony already achieved in the vision of possibility. What must happen in this divine intensification of harmony is that a merely possible component of harmony becomes actual through the feeling of the world integrated with the vision. God, as well as finite reality, is a unification, a becoming. Whereas the world's becoming simplifies, God's becoming "complexifies." The divine satisfaction is everlastingly intensifying—if that satisfaction is one of harmony, the harmony moves into deeper and deeper intensities. God's eternal satisfaction, based upon the primordial vision, has an everlasting dimension based upon God's feelings of the world everlastingly transformed into integration within that satisfaction. The character of God, primordially existing in the unification of all possibilities, moves from intensity to intensity in an ever-shifting wonder of beauty. *That* the character of God is freely chosen and exercised in the primordial vision remains constant; *how* God manifests that character through everlasting concrescence is dynamic. The primordial nature is the ground of God as love; the consequent nature is the ground of God as faithful, steadfast, and sure; the satisfaction of God is the union of love and faithfulness in ever-changing beauty.

By coming full circle back to the satisfaction, we can now indicate more specifically how this satisfaction affects the world, and how God accounts for the power of possibilities. God integrates the feelings, or prehensions, of the world into the primordial harmony. This integration is God's concrescence, directed by God's subjective aim toward the continuous actualization of the divine harmony. This means that as God prehends the world in each of its completed moments, God draws that world deeply into the divine nature in a transformative process, conforming the world to God's harmony. Each prehended occasion of the world is felt relative to all others within the divine nature, and in light of that comparison, is qualified with divinely chosen possibilities for transformation and ultimate unification. But remember that what the becoming world most needs in its own process of dealing with its multitude of prehensions from the past is a sense of how that past can be unified, and therefore transformed, in its own becoming. God's initial integration of the world within the divine nature not only indicates the mode of divine transformation and unification, it also implies a finite counterpart for each occasion's finite successors. God's feeling of this implication, drawn from the divine satisfaction, become the initial aims for the many standpoints in the world. God and the past actual world evoke the new occasion into being, but the directive element in that creative power is from God through the initial aim, drawn from God's moving satisfaction. Our final diagram illustrates the process.

The newly becoming occasion feels God's initial aim as its own possibility for dealing with its situation. The energy received from God is freely turned by the occasion from God's initial aim into its own subjective aim, directing the occasion's concrescence toward satisfaction. Upon completion of the occasion in satisfaction, the occasion then transmits its creativity to its future in God and the world. God is the source and destiny of the world: source, through provision of the initial aim; destiny, through prehension and transformation in God.

To summarize the model, existence is through and through relational, with every actuality, whether a subatomic particle or God, demonstrating relational dynamics. In turn, relationality constitutes reality as becoming, as change. Relations occur on the finite level as feelings from the past evoke new unifications of that past. The past is unified through a selective comparison of feelings in terms of a single possibility of becoming. This possibility becomes actualized in the unification of the new actuality. Upon completion of this process, the creative energy that accomplished this unification is turned to transitional energy, or the relational thrust into the future. Relationality occurs on the divine level through God's feelings of the world, integrated with God's vision of harmonized possibilities. God's vision is the source of possibility for the world. God's integration of feelings of the world with the primordial vision results in one possibility rather than another becoming relevant to the world. God's harmony is shaped to the situation of the world, and made available to the world as a real possibility for its future.

If the dynamics of God and the world are to be understood as a mirror image of reversal, the same is not so with regard to divinely willed harmony. The harmony of God is not begrudged the world. Rather, the harmony of God holds the world together, fitting the possibilities for each single occasion into a harmony that blends with the possibilities for other occasions. The world is to be an

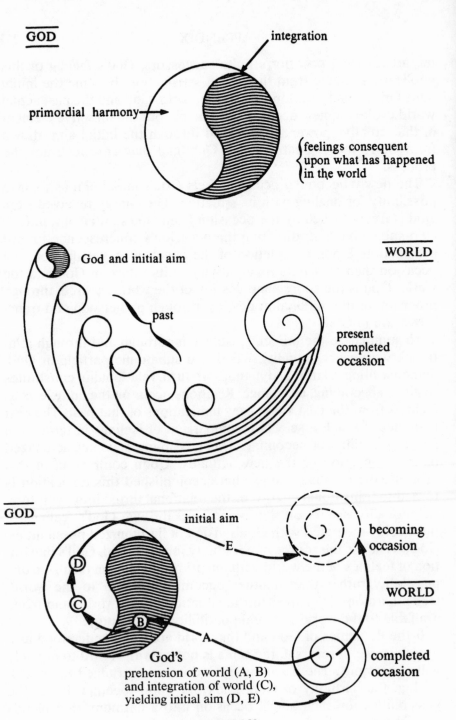

DIAGRAM V

The completed finite actuality is felt internally by God through prehen-
sion, indicated by line "A." (A difficulty with the diagram is that it
suggests distance between God and the world—the lines are drawn simply
to indicate the direction and sequence of prehension, and not to indicate
spatial distance or externality for prehension.) God, feeling the world
("B"), integrates it within the primordial vision ("C"). This integration
with harmonized possibilities has the effect of suggesting a new mode of
harmony ("D") which is now relevant to the becoming world. "E" then
represents both God's superjective nature relative to the world, and the
world's prehension of God. The occasion's prehension of God, as with all
prehensions, is felt internally by the occasion.

echo, not a reversal, of God. Whether or not these possibilities for harmony are achieved depends upon the decisions of the world. Each occasion, in the solitude of its own concrescence, decides its orientation toward God and the world.

This completes our sketch of the process model of reality used in theological reflection throughout this book. The model is drawn from Whitehead's *Process and Reality*, particularly Part I as a concise statement of the basic categories of dynamic existence, and Part V as an extension of these categories in relation to the reversal of the poles in God. The model is a tool, a language for expressing the way of things. Like all language, it participates in the ambiguity of being shaped by the reality it seeks to express, and also of shaping our perceptions of reality. It will draw out the relational and communal aspects of Christianity, and at the same time affect our continuing expression of Christian faith. Organic images of community will be highlighted, with a vision of the earth as an interdependent community of communities becoming increasingly compelling. But no model alone is sufficient to turn such a vision into reality. It finally depends upon God and the world.

GLOSSARY
OF
PROCESS TERMS

Actual Entity. Each unit of process is called an actual entity; it is a drop of experience that comes into existence through the creative process of concrescence. Actual entities are the "final real things of which the world is made up." They are the building blocks that, through an essential interconnectedness, make up the composite world of rocks, trees, and people.

Actual Occasion. This phrase is almost a synonym for actual entity, with the one distinction that it applies only to finite entities, not to God. "Actual occasion" implies a locus in the spatio-temporal extensiveness of the universe. Since God is understood to be nontemporal in respect to the primordial nature, God is always referred to as an actual entity, and never as an actual occasion.

Concrescence. This refers to the activity of becoming; it is the unification of many feelings into the single actual entity or occasion. In concrescence, feelings are contrasted and evaluated until they are integrated into a final unity, called the "satisfaction." The activity of concrescence is the self-production of the subject.

Consequent Nature. Whitehead refers to the physical pole in God as God's consequent nature. This is God's feelings of the world. It is "consequent" in a twofold sense. First, it follows from the primordial nature in God, and second, it follows from the actual happenings in the world.

Creativity. "Creativity," "many," and "one" belong to what Whitehead calls the "category of the ultimate." Every actuality is an instantiation of creativity, or the process whereby many feelings are unified into one determinate subject. In Whitehead, creativity proceeds in two forms. Concrescent creativity is the process of becoming, and transitional creativity is the process of influencing another's becoming. It is possible that there is yet a third form of creativity, relating to the satisfaction as a dynamic unity. This would account for the generation of transitional creativity from the satisfaction of the occasion.

Eternal Objects. These are potentialities for becoming, or forms of definiteness that exist only as possibilities. Their locus is the primordial nature of God. In this book, the world "possibilities" is used as a synonym for eternal objects.

Immediacy. Often called "subjective immediacy," this refers to the entity's own experience of itself in the concrescent process.

Initial Aim. This inaugurates the becoming of the new occasion. The aim originates in God. From the point of view of God, God's knowledge of the becoming occasion's entire past is integrated with God's own purposes. This yields a particular possibility for what the new occasion might become. Through God's transitional creativity, this possibility is given to the occasion as its initial aim. It provides the occasion with an optimum way of unifying the many influences the occasion receives from its past.

Mental Pole. Every actuality has both a mental and a physical pole. The mental pole is the grasp of possibilities relative to the subject's own becoming. This grasp of possibilities guides the entity's integration of feelings from the physical pole into subjective unity.

Negative Prehensions. Every item in the universe is felt. These feelings are called "prehensions." A negative feeling is one in which the particular item felt is excluded from positive integration within the concrescent process.

Objective Immortality. Every actual occasion affects every successor. The effect is the transmission of its own value to another by way of transitional creativity. There can be both repetitive and transformative elements in objective immortality. All entities demand a measure of conformity to themselves, or an accounting of their own particular value in the universe. The more complex entities, however, can also anticipate their own participation in some wider scheme of things, and hence become a force for transformation through objective immortality. The process is objective, since no finite occasion can prehend another in its entirety. The other is felt as object. This process is termed immortality, since it perpetuates one's continuing effect throughout the universe.

Physical Pole. This is the means by which a becoming occasion prehends the transitional creativity of the past. Actual occasions originate in the physical pole, whereas God originates in the mental pole.

Prehension. The feeling of others is called "prehension." It is the process of transforming transitional creativity into concrescent creativity. What is "there" is felt "here" through prehension. Positive prehensions are often called "feelings."

Primordial Nature. This is the equivalent of the mental pole in God. The primordial nature is God's grasp of all possibilities. This grasp involves an ordering evaluation of possibilities into a harmony that is called the primordial vision, or primordial envisagement.

Satisfaction. This constitutes the achievement of unity whereby a subject is itself. It is the goal of concrescence, and completes the occasion. Because of the reversal of poles in God, satisfaction in God relates to the primordial vision, and therefore is everlasting in God.

Subjective Aim. This is the self-selected purpose that governs what an actual entity shall become. An actual occasion adapts the initial aim to its own becoming, making that aim its subjective aim.

Subjective Form. Every prehension is felt with a certain positive or negative value from the point of view of the feeling subject. This constitutes "how" the other is felt. The term "mutuality of subjective form" refers to the way in which each feeling conditions all others as the becoming entity contrasts and compares data in the process of unification.

Superject. To be something for oneself necessarily entails being something for others. "Superject" refers to the sense in which an occasion has an effect beyond itself. This is not optional; it is simply a matter of fact. Whitehead underscores this frequently by calling an actual entity a "subject/superject."

INDEX